The Glossy Years

By Nicholas Coleridge

NON-FICTION

Tunnel Vision

Around the World in 78 Days

The Fashion Conspiracy

Paper Tigers

FICTION

Shooting Stars

How I Met My Wife and Other Stories

With Friends Like These

Streetsmart

Godchildren

A Much Married Man

Deadly Sins

The Adventuress

The Glossy Years

Magazines, Museums and Selective Memoirs

NICHOLAS COLERIDGE

FIG TREE
an imprint of
PENGUIN BOOKS

FIG TREE

UK | USA | Canada | Ireland | Australia
India | New Zealand | South Africa

Fig Tree is part of the Penguin Random House group of companies
whose addresses can be found at global.penguinrandomhouse.com.

First published 2019
001

Copyright © Nicholas Coleridge, 2019

The moral right of the author has been asserted

Set in 12.5/15.5 pt Bembo Book MT Std
Typeset by Jouve (UK), Milton Keynes
Printed and bound in Great Britain by Clays Ltd, Elcograf S.p.A.

A CIP catalogue record for this book is available from the British Library

ISBN: 978–0–241–34287–9

www.greenpenguin.co.uk

MIX
Paper from
responsible sources
FSC® C018179

Penguin Random House is committed to a
sustainable future for our business, our readers
and our planet. This book is made from Forest
Stewardship Council® certified paper.

Foreword

For my sixtieth birthday, I invited 330 friends to dinner at the Victoria and Albert Museum. There were people from every part of my life: magazine friends, newspaper friends, museum friends, school friends and London friends, Worcestershire friends, political and heritage friends, fashion friends, Indian, Russian, American and German friends. Family, of course. Some celebrity friends to sharpen us up, but mostly very old friends. What they had in common was that all had made some decisive contribution to my life.

I am biased, but I think the Raphael Gallery at the V&A looked particularly glamorous that night, with its three long tables, its funky black-and-white striped tablecloths and five thousand multicoloured tulips. The Raphael Cartoons, loaned to the museum by the Queen, glistened in candlelight. I had known the guests for an average of twenty-five years each, many far longer. If you totted it up, it was eight thousand years of friendship.

My wife, Georgia, made a sweet speech, and each of our four children did too. It was unexpectedly moving. Our daughter, Sophie, burst into tears.

As I scanned the tables, I felt grateful for the number of people who had made me laugh, and taken part in one escapade or another. But I was struck too by how much my world has transformed and mutated over six decades, by the rise and rise and then fevered reinvention of the media business, by the evolution of manners and values, by social and technological disruption, by the wholesale re-evaluation of almost everything considered normal in the first third of my life, now swept away.

My prep school, where I boarded from the age of eight, belonging to an entirely different, almost Edwardian era, and no single thing I learnt there, other than survival, is of much relevance to the world I now inhabit. The university life I experienced hardly now exists. The London in which I first worked, before the magazine and fashion industries went global and digital, was another country. And nobody predicted the transformation of the museum world – the shiny new galleries and wings, the spin-off museums across Britain and the world.

These are my selective memoirs. Selective because I include only episodes which interest and amuse me, and remain vivid in my mind. I have tried to exclude the dull stuff. Consequently, the impression is of many more deaths, suicides, jailings, celebrities, ambitions and rivalries than was ever the case day to day. My best friends feature less often than they ought, by virtue of their virtue, despite providing the context and a large part of the pleasure.

I dedicate this memoir to my much-loved Georgia, Alexander, Freddie, Sophie and Tommy Coleridge, who have lived through large sections of it, and brought such happiness, and put up with a lot. And to my excellent parents, David and Susan Coleridge, without whom . . .

I was born in London on 4 March 1957 at Queen Charlotte's Hospital, Hammersmith, at ten past ten p.m. – inexplicably late at night for the morning person I turned out to be.

My parents, David and Susan, had met at a London drinks party in Hamilton Terrace when my mother was sixteen and my father had recently left Eton. My mother was alert, pretty and had led a largely cloistered life at my grandparents' London house, No. 2 Egerton Place. She was supervised by a sharp-tongued governess, named Miss Lynch, who taught my Aunt Deirdre. My father was considered handsome and, in those days, was broom-stick thin. He had been a conspicuously successful Eton school-boy with a razor-sharp mind, which he concealed very effectively all his life underneath a carapace of charm and warmth.

He was intended to go into the Green Jackets, but at the eleventh hour he was discovered at his army medical to have flat feet, which was then a bar to a commission. He tried instead for a last-minute scholarship to read History at Christ Church, and was driven over to Oxford by his Eton tutor, Giles St Aubyn, to sit the entrance exam. They stopped for lunch in a pub on the way, somewhere outside Maidenhead, lost track of time, and arrived when the exam was already three-quarters over. No place was offered. Instead he joined Lloyd's of London as a junior insur-ance underwriter, straight from school, and courted my mother. They married at St Margaret's, Westminster, two years later.

I appeared two years after that, followed by my younger brother, Timothy. We lived in a noisy end-of-terrace house,

32 Chelsea Park Gardens, on the corner of Beaufort Street, with a strip of communal garden in front and a small paved yard behind. When the newly-weds bought the house, my maternal grandmother (who lived scarcely a mile away in Knightsbridge) declared, 'Well, I cannot prevent you from buying it. But you must not expect anyone to come and see you there, it is much too far out of London.'

Photographs of the Coleridge boys from this period show a conspicuously well-dressed pair, borderline effeminate, in matching shorts or tweed coats and caps from a shop named Rowes of Bond Street. By today's standards, we might be identified as disgracefully privileged or even 'entitled', as we were wheeled about the better London parks in a double-ended navy pram by our nanny, Dorothy Little. Nanny Little had looked after my father as a child in Bombay and been lured back from retirement from her thatched cottage in Hethe, Oxfordshire.

She was rather deaf (or 'hard of hearing', as she preferred). At night, when we should have been asleep, Timmy and I would creep into the nursery where she sat in front of a blaring television eating supper on a tray, and watch *The Black and White Minstrel Show* over her shoulder, undetected. With its cavorting blacked-up singers and dancers wearing straw hats, this was Nanny Little's favourite show; it was still regarded in those days as a cheerful piece of end-of-the-pier vaudeville, and not yet identified as an insulting travesty of cultural appropriation.

Our early childhood was a near-perfect exemplar of happy routine, with young and involved parents, and structured, repetitive days. We went to gym classes with Mr Sturges, dancing classes at Madame Vacani, and a delightful Chelsea nursery school named Mrs Russell's in The Vale. On Saturdays, we walked up the King's Road to Mr Lafferty's toy shop. For holidays, we were taken to Frinton and Westgate-on-Sea.

I had a complete set of four grandparents, all of whom (I can now see) had some impact upon my development and character. They were very different. My paternal grandfather, Guy Coleridge, had signed up for the First World War aged seventeen, and lost the use of the lower part of his left leg on the second day of the Battle of the Somme; he consequently wore a wooden splint which was removed at night and had to be strapped back on again each morning, a complicated procedure undertaken by his elderly maid, Lottie Kersey, who arrived at dawn at their mansion flat in Welbeck Street.

'Lottie! Lottie! Bring me my splint!' he would bellow down the corridor after breakfast.

'Coming, Mr Coleridge. I'm coming, sir,' she would meekly reply, entering with the wood-and-metal contraption, which was then laboriously buckled onto my grandfather's wounded leg.

Six feet four inches tall with a bristly moustache, he walked at speed with the aid of two mahogany walking sticks, and he made light of his injury, for which he had been awarded a Military Cross as the first man out of the trench. He had worked on the Cotton Exchange in Bombay, owned racehorses, and later became a partner in Knight Frank & Rutley, the estate agents (back then also auctioneers). His favourite museum was The Wallace Collection, round the corner in Manchester Square, and he would take me there on visits, powering down Welbeck Street on his sticks and urging me to admire Sèvres porcelain fruit bowls and Fragonard's *The Swing*, which I then considered ugly.

My grandmother, Cicely, was his second wife (his first wife having run off one afternoon in India with Jack Meyer, the man who was later to found Millfield School). Guy and Cicely lived in a large, gloomy, high-ceilinged flat in the heart of the dentist district near Harley Street, filled with brown furniture and Dutch paintings.

Granny Coleridge, to whom I was devoted, was the kindest of people, and adventurous. She had been one of the first pupils at Cheltenham Ladies' College and a leading light of the Indian Girl Guide movement, founding new packs across Maharashtra, and taking hundreds of Indian schoolgirls camping.

When the family moved back to England, she became a senior commissioner at the Girl Guide headquarters in Buckingham Palace Road, and regularly took me camping – just her and me in a small green tent – at the Girl Guide centre in the New Forest. It was Granny Coleridge who introduced me to butterfly collecting, the great passion of my schooldays; she was with me in a bracken-ringed oak glade when I snagged a Purple Emperor in my net, one of the last ever caught in the New Forest. I still have this endangered specimen pinned in my display cabinet, the purple powder of its wings now faded and translucent.

One of my proudest moments was standing alongside Granny Coleridge on a dais in Eaton Square, when she took the salute from a parade of teenage London Guides, badges gleaming on their blue uniforms. As pack after pack marched past – from Camden, from Putney, from Stockwell – swinging their arms and singing Girl Guide songs, Cicely stood to attention in permanent salute, jacket pinned two-deep with decorations, her grey hair neatly concealed beneath a blue Commissioner's hat.

My maternal grandmother, the Hon Norah Senior, could not have been a greater contrast to Granny Coleridge, but I came to have great affection for her and enjoyed visiting her. Impeccably well dressed by John Cavanagh, Christian Dior and Hardy Amies, she was pin-thin, and unbendingly correct. Her world largely consisted of lunching at Claridge's, attending certain fashionable race meetings, and spending the month of August at the Cipriani in Venice.

She had been brought up at Ford Castle, near Etal, in

Northumberland, eldest child of the 2nd Lord Joicey, one of several prominent coal-owning families of the North-East. Ford is a dramatic mongrel of a castle, with views across the battlefield at Flodden; the keep dates from 1278, but there are extensive, castellated additions and stable blocks in the faux-Norman style of the 1860s. My grandmother had grown up at Ford and my mother spent the war there, but today it is leased to Northumberland County Council as a 'young person's residential centre'. According to family legend, our ancestors, the Joiceys, had been fortunate to strike deep seams of coal on a distant part of their estate, and this piece of luck made them unfeasibly rich. It was almost sixty years before I realized that this version of events was almost entirely untrue.

Norah's younger brother, James, a subaltern in the 14th/20th King's Hussars, was thrown from his horse, Fancy Laureate, and broke his neck and died shortly after his twenty-first birthday, in 1929, while point-to-pointing at Folkestone. This tragedy led to the Ford and Etal estate passing to cousins; and consigned my grandmother to a life of dressmakers and hairdressing appointments in London, and a taste for everything that was congenial and correct. As I grew older, and visited my grandparents at their flat at 110 Eaton Square, to which they had eventually downsized, and later at 36 Sloane Court West, to which they downsized further, I learnt that nothing pleased Norah more than references to any smartish person I might recently have met or stayed with, or news of an upcoming dance. As a strategy for bringing pleasure to my grandmother, it could not be bettered.

Norah's husband, Ronnie Senior DSO, my other grandfather, was also rather correct, but had a sense of humour which Norah mostly did not. By the time I remember him, he was a striking, grey-haired, undeniably good-looking man in a suit — very often a tweed one, since he was a keen owner of racehorses. He was

Chairman of a shipping company, Port Line, and later Deputy
Chairman of Cunard, but his chief loves were racing, golf and
unconditional support of the Conservative Party. He spent
much time drinking pink gins at the Carlton Club in St James's
and it was here that, from time to time, family dinners would
take place. We would all assemble in the lobby, in our suits and
ties, and then would follow the ceremony of 'going upstairs'.
Female visitors, in those days, were not allowed to walk up the
sweeping club staircase, but had to use a lift. So my grandmother,
mother, aunt and so on would be ushered into a coffin-sized elevator, while the men strode up the staircase, under the portraits
of former Tory Prime Ministers, to meet the lift at the top of the
staircase. This 'no ladies on the stairs' rule persisted until Margaret Thatcher became leader of the party, and thus an honorary
member of the Carlton Club. At this point, it was quietly
dropped, since no one dared explain it to her.

My grandfather was an enthusiastic Chairman of the Swinley
Forest Golf Club, sited in the rhododendron belt between Ascot
and Sunningdale. The principal duty of the club committee was
to ensure no new members be allowed to join unless they were
identical, in every opinion and nuance, to the existing members. However, by special decree (and my grandfather was proud
of this early gesture to inclusiveness), on Wednesday evenings
certain non-members from the local community were permitted to play a round. These were referred to as 'the artisans'.
Sometimes when I caddied for my grandfather, he would point
out a golfing four on a distant green, and confide, 'Those are
artisans. Very decent chaps too, many of them. We are delighted
to allow them a round on Wednesday evenings, when the light
is going and it is less popular with the members.'

The Coleridge family of Chelsea Park Gardens was, in short,
a not untypical upper-middle-class family of the late fifties:

conventional, tribally Tory, unflashy. The only famous Coleridge ancestor was the opium-smoking Samuel Taylor Coleridge, whose poem *Kubla Khan* I was destined to learn by heart at every school I ever attended.

Hill House on Hans Place, the school at which I was enrolled aged five, is chiefly known for its brown corduroy uniform, and crocodiles of pupils on perpetual route-marches along London pavements. We marched from Sloane Street to play football at the Duke of York's (now the Saatchi Gallery), we marched to church for singing, to Hyde Park for games, and to various satellite classrooms. One of my five-year-old friends was named Charlie Tennant and he remarked one day, as we pounded the pavements, 'My father owns an island in the West Indies.'

I asked, 'Does it have cannibals?'

'I expect so. Though it is mostly deserted.' He added, 'He is giving part of it to the Queen's sister anyway.'

I can surely only remember this alluring exchange because I was impressed by it. The island turned out to be Mustique, and Charlie's father Lord Glenconner.

My own parents, less glamorously, had taken the lease on a farm cottage in West Sussex, on one of the Cowdray family estates at Iping. The cottage, named Crouch House Farm, was a half-timbered black and white, set on the edge of a wheat field, in that part of the country where the old drovers' lanes are sunk deep into the ground, their steep banks swathed with fern and gorse. The villages between Midhurst and the South Downs still felt untouched and unencroached upon, with belts of ancient woodland and acres of common land thick with bracken and the haunts of adders' nests.

Our cottage was surrounded by outhouses and hay barns, and in these my brother Timmy and I would devise fairs and village fêtes, with hoopla stalls and smash-the-crockery-with-a-tennis-ball attractions, and prizes of Fry's Turkish Delight and sherbet fountains; to these, my parents (the sole visitors) would dutifully turn up, expressing delight at the stalls and competing enthusiastically to win the confectionary that they had earlier paid for in the village shop.

My brother, by now aged six, was a keen horseman, which I was not, having been bucked by a pony named Sabrina into a clump of stinging nettles, after which I lost my mojo for riding. Timmy, however, was a leading light of the Midhurst Pony Club circuit, virtually the only boy in every class, his bedroom walls festooned with rosettes from the Graffham and Trotton gymkhanas. We attended endless gymkhanas in those days.

My role during these eight-hour marathons of 'bending' races and ponies jumping over cavalettis, surrounded on all sides by scary horsey mothers and their pigtailed daughters, was to sit grumpily inside the car, impatient to be home with my butterfly collection.

In my memory, the wheat fields behind the cottage, and the buddleia bushes against the lath-and-plaster walls, were perpetually alive with dancing butterflies – Red Admirals, Small Tortoiseshells, Painted Ladies from North Africa – and in adjacent woodland, explosions of jagged-winged Commas and Silver-Washed Fritillaries. The reader can picture me armed with a fine-gauze net and chloroform killing bottle, able in those days to identify every butterfly in the Collins' *Complete Guide to Butterflies and Moths*, determined to catch and pin every species in Britain. It was the first of many collections of this and that, all pursued with single-minded vigour.

If you consider my childhood up to this point a little bit too idyllic, or harbour feelings of compassion for the butterflies whose populations I was so intent upon reducing, you can take solace in the fact that I would shortly depart to an English prep school, where this carefree existence would come to an abrupt halt.

2

It had been suggested to my parents that the kindest way to deliver their eight-year-old son to boarding school for the first time was by train, where several carriages were reserved at Victoria Station to ferry pupils to the school near East Grinstead. The idea was that, during the train journey, I would bond with my fellow new boys and thus arrive at Ashdown House with a circle of firm friends.

So we said our farewells on the platform, and I clambered aboard in my grey corduroy shorts, grey shirt and snake belt, clutching a pencil case in which an array of new pencils, rubbers, protractors and compasses nestled in their plastic pouch. I remember my waving parents as the train pulled away from the platform, past the sooty shunting sheds surrounding the station, then the miles of suburban houses lining the tracks, and eventually out into open countryside beyond Croydon and Lingfield, and on to East Sussex.

I wish I could report that, as the train rattled along, I was soon the locus of a gregarious circle of welcoming schoolmates, but I was too shy to catch anyone's eye, and sat as still and inconspicuously as possible, hoping to evade notice. Meanwhile, hordes of rampaging older boys – they must have been twelve or thirteen, their shorts faded to light grey from constant washing – ran amok between the carriages, conducting trials of strength by hanging from luggage racks, and flicking each other with ties like bullwhips.

Eventually the train arrived at East Grinstead, we transferred into coaches and arrived at the school, at the end of a long rhododendron-lined drive. Ashdown House, near Forest Row, was considered an A-grade prep school at the time, with a good record of getting scholarships to Eton, for which it was a feeder school. The main building was an imposing Georgian mansion by the architect Benjamin Latrobe (who later designed the front portico of the White House in Washington DC), with sweeping grounds down to the River Medway. If you wanted to make a film, set at a picture-perfect English prep school, you might easily choose Ashdown, with its Lutyens-style cricket pavilion, grassy ha-ha, copses of Scots pine and an ancient spreading beech tree, the branches of which gave shade to a perfect lawn.

Behind the school lay several acres of wild scrubland known as 'the jungle', with winding paths and thickets of bamboo and brambles providing hiding places and secret camps. In the middle of the jungle was a concrete outdoor swimming pool, unheated and algae-green, in which school swimming galas shared the water with colonies of frogs, newts and sometimes grass snakes, which slipped in for an icy dip from an adjacent compost tip.

Presiding over the school and its random, ramshackle teaching staff of incompetents, bullies, recovering prisoners of war and borderline paedos, was the headmaster, Billie Williamson MA, a terrifying, caustic Classicist, upon whose rages and mood swings the tone of the establishment turned. His sheer physical bulk, his ability to speak fluently in Latin, his weekly sermons delivered from the pulpit of the school chapel in which he raged against Socialism, the Beatles ('Despicable, talentless baboons') and the hippy movement ('Layabouts'), left me cowed, and I did my best to avoid him at all times. Unmonitored and unrestrained by any higher power, his word was law, and his sudden spontaneous furies developed in me both a fear and an intense dislike of irrational explosions of anger, and perhaps an exaggerated respect and appeasement towards authority, which took years to loosen its grip.

Billie's wife, Mrs Williamson, privately known to the boys as 'Bicker', was a confused, genteel lady in pearls, herself much bullied, I suspect, by her husband; she hovered ineffectually around the margins of the school, preparing finger sandwiches and mini-eclairs for prospective parents. Billie had the power to charm and, when in a benign mood, made jokes in his daily spiel at the end of lunch, at which everyone knew to laugh compliantly. He was particularly adept at charming parents, and this ability drew ever-more prominent pupils to the place. Princess Margaret and Tony Snowdon sent David Linley, who wisely bailed out before the end. Boris* and Rachel Johnson† and the actor Benedict Cumberbatch‡ are always evoked as prominent old Ashdownians, though not contemporaries of mine.

It is only with hindsight I can begin to comprehend the peculiar roster of masters corralled to teach us: Mr Ebden, clinically obese, reputed to have once been a chess Grand Master (a rumour he encouraged) who taught nine-year-olds maths; Mr Keane, Irish Jesuit, whose tiny bedsit was imprudently sited directly between boys' dormitories, and whose wandering hands were so busy that they barely raised eyebrows; Mr Tidmarsh, Latin and chapel organist, rumoured to be in recovery from some unnamed trauma of the First World War; Mr Gabain, French, who may or may not have once been a member of the French Resistance, who drove me to his home in Forest Row to collect

---

* Editor, *The Spectator* (1999–2005). Mayor of London (2008–16). Secretary of State, Foreign & Commonwealth Office (2016–18), PM hotshot (2019).

† First female pupil at Ashdown House. Author, columnist. Editor, *The Lady* (2009–12). *Celebrity Big Brother* participant (2018).

‡ Film and TV actor: *The Imitation Game* (2014), *Sherlock* (2010–17), *Patrick Melrose* (2018).

a toboggan from an attic and, while holding me up to retrieve it from the overhead trapdoor, nonchalantly slipped his fingers inside my gym shorts and explored away.

In numerous respects, the staff of Ashdown House during that period recalled the cast of the seventies TV sitcom *Are You Being Served?*, only more sinister, with their line-up of army retirees and befuddled duffers. One master, Mr Sheridan, who taught me history for a year, I found inspiring, though his days were numbered owing to a beatnik cascade of shoulder-length hair. His career at the school came to an abrupt end on Sports Day when he slipped into a lavatory marked 'VIP – Strictly Private', reserved for the personal use of Princess Margaret. Billie Williamson ushered the Princess to her special restroom, and was perplexed to find it already occupied. After much knocking, there was the sound of a cistern flushing, a bolt being drawn, and there stood Mr Sheridan, with a disagreeable pong wafting behind him. He disappeared soon afterwards.

The daily routine at Ashdown in no way resembled the lovey-dovey, four-choices-of-main-course lunches, Superman-duvets, strawberry yoghurt, salad bar prep schools that my own children would encounter forty years later. Before breakfast, we marched and did stride jumps in an exercise yard; dormitories were wilfully spartan, with metal beds and balding candlewick counterpanes; underpants and socks were changed once a week; food consisted largely of mince and tinned sweetcorn, or slices of corned beef encased in a sleeve of deep-fried batter. Bad table manners were punished with a spell on the Pigs' Table, at which boys ate in silence for a week. A running list of candidates for the Pigs' Table – the 'Mensa Porcorum' – was kept on the dining-room mantelpiece, illustrated by a cartoon of a pink porker holding a knife and fork, greedily stuffing its face with food. Once twelve names were on the list, a 'Mensa Porcorum' was convened.

For a school with such a tip-top academic record (scarcely a year passed without top scholarships to Eton or Winchester), it was a shame that I benefited so little from it. Having arrived at Ashdown towards the top of the class, I quickly plunged down the charts, and then fell further, until firmly categorized as 'thick'. Several different masters struggled impatiently to teach me Latin, but I never got the hang of it, nor Maths, nor French, nor Science. Like Bertie Wooster, Scripture was my one redeeming suit, and the termly Scripture Prize was mine by right.

Scripture at Ashdown was taught as an entirely non-theological, non-spiritual discipline, and consisted of learning long shopping lists of synoptic trivia.

Q: 'What were the six things the Prodigal Son's father gave him when he returned?'

A: 'A robe, sandals, fatted calf, music, dancing and (trick answer here) a kiss.'

Q: 'Name seventeen living things that visited the infant Jesus in the stable at Bethlehem?'

A: 'Three Kings, three Shepherds, an Angel of the Lord, six sheep, four cattle.'

To this day, I am rather fond of numerical quizzes of this sort. On long car journeys, I challenge our children: 'Name ten houses belonging to the British Royal Family'; 'Name ten albums by David Bowie.' Useful, life-enhancing knowledge.

But, notwithstanding my biblical knowledge, I was soon firmly embedded in the dimwits' stream, along with barely-English-fluent sons of South American ambassadors and a pair of bedwetting twins. It is tempting to pin my dismal academic progress firmly upon the school. But perhaps I was simply entering a seven-year period of extreme dimness which would not lift, like early-morning Moroccan mist, until later in the day.

It should not be supposed I had no friends or fun at Ashdown. In fact, I had plenty of both. Hopeless at team games, and grown accustomed to being amongst the last boys picked for any sport, I was a fervent stamp collector, destined to become Deputy Secretary of the Ashdown House Philatelic Society. The Secretary of the club was Andrew Mitchell, later MP for Sutton Coldfield and unfortunate star of the 'Plebgate' episode outside Downing Street. I was greatly in awe of Mitchell and his extensive collection of First Day Covers, and still recall the joy when he reviewed my own collection of British and Commonwealth specimens (1919–1968) and commended my meticulous stamp hinge technique.

It became my habit on sunny afternoons to slip away into the shallow ha-ha which marked the boundary between lawn and cricket fields, and conceal myself in a particular spot in the ditch, where a wooden footbridge and thicket of long grass provided almost complete cover, and read the historical novels of Ronald Welch; the sensation of blazing sunshine overhead, the smell of mown grass, of refuge from an alarming world, held an appeal which has never entirely left me.

A journalist named Tom Stacey came and gave a lecture to the boys (itself a surprising occurrence, journalists normally being placed in the same reviled category as hippies and the Beatles) and he mesmerized me with stories about life as a foreign correspondent. From that day on, journalism loomed as a possible career. I started a school newspaper, the *Ashdown News*, which ran for two issues. The first issue was headlined 'Exclusive: Princess Margaret to visit Ashdown?'; and the second 'Princess Margaret visit a success, says Headmaster.'

On Saturday evenings, films were projected in the school

playroom. Although suitable movies were generally rented for the occasion, the school actually owned one film itself, the 1958 *Carve Her Name with Pride* starring Virginia McKenna; it was about a heroic British spy parachuted into France to disrupt Nazi occupation, who eventually gets caught, is tortured and dies in a concentration camp. This film, being free, was projected frequently, and after each showing Billie Williamson would address the school, on the brink of tears, urging us to show similar patriotism and fortitude when the occasion arose. After that, we sang the National Anthem.

One sunny Sports Day, I must have been nine or ten, my parents broke it to me on the picnic rug that my adored Granny Coleridge, the Girl Guide leader, had died of cancer aged sixty-one. To this day, I remember the sensation of abject misery and grief I felt at that moment, ham sandwich in one hand, can of Coke in the other. My grandmother had been quietly dying for a year, riddled with the disease, but didn't want the grandchildren to be aware of it. So strong was my reaction, I was sent home from school on compassionate leave for the weekend, and excused from participating in the 'patrol relay race', which cannot have been a great loss for the Elephants' Patrol (my school league).

As the years passed, and the Common Entrance for Eton loomed larger, it was increasingly signalled that passing the exam might not be quite the walkover that was part of Ashdown House's promise. My encyclopaedic knowledge of New Testament parables and miracles would not, of itself, secure entry, and in all other subjects, including all the important ones, I was definitely borderline.

Billie Williamson, his personal esteem tied up with getting pupils into Eton, began to fret. I was encouraged to take school books home for the holidays to revise, but somehow textbooks looked out of context at home, their dingy front covers and graffitied marginalia at odds with the smartness of my mother's interior decoration, so I scarcely opened them.

I sat the exam and, to no one's great surprise, failed it: the first Ashdown boy to do so in living memory. Billie Williamson took to his bed in dismay, and was not glimpsed for seventy-two hours. It was said he was gripped by depression, and by feelings of humiliation at having a pupil fail Common Entrance for Eton, and was only coping by bingeing on claret and whisky.

Fortunately, my father's old tutor, Giles St Aubyn, for whose Eton house I had been registered since birth, saved the day. Perhaps still feeling guilty over the Oxford scholarship debacle, when the overlong pub lunch had led to my father missing the Christ Church entrance exam, Giles offered to keep a room empty for a term, thus enabling me to have a second crack at Common Entrance.

This time I scraped in. My essay on the parable of the Prodigal Son hit the bullseye, and days later we were congregating at an Eton tailor, Tom Brown, where I was measured up for a tailcoat.

At my final prize-giving at Ashdown, I was presented with something called 'The Time and Talent Award' – an annual booby prize presented to a pupil who had served the time but with no discernible talent.

To this day, I remain profoundly ambivalent about Ashdown House. I was seldom happy there, and it made me watchful. Decades later, I was invited to give the speech at Sports Day, a task always undertaken in my time by war heroes from the Battle of Britain, but latterly fulfilled by Boris Johnson and celebrity film actors. As I drove down the drive for my first visit since 1969, I was struck by how every bend in the road, every Scots pine and rhododendron bush, was still deeply engraved upon my memory, and I felt myself overwhelmed by a regressive wave of nausea, which only with effort did I manage to conceal.

Whenever I run into fellow Ashdown alumni, I cannot feel altogether untroubled, as though complicit in some conspiracy of omertà. Then again, I have a theory that early tribulations are a spur to happiness and enterprise later on, and certainly heighten appreciation for life outside.

3

At the Eton new boys' tea party I eyed up my fellow new boys with suspicion. Parents and their sons milled around a table of sandwiches and cakes on the 'private side' of Baldwin's Bec, the Eton boarding house at which I was freshly enrolled. The house had a view of Windsor Castle on one side, and a graveyard on the other.

There was a wiry boy with a Ringo Starr pudding-bowl haircut named Craig Brown, with a pleasingly anarchic air about him; a good-looking sporty boy named Lord John Montagu Douglas Scott; and a beaky blond in glasses, Trelawny Williams, whom I had met once before as fellow pageboys at my uncle Anthony Coleridge's first wedding. There were other new arrivals too, but it was Craig, John and Trelawny who stood out.

That first evening, getting ready for bed in an alien environment, I went to brush my teeth in a large bathroom lined with basins. Two sixteen-year-olds entered the bathroom. They ignored me, of course, and spoke only to each other.

One asked, 'Did you have a good holiday, Alex?'

'Yah,' replied the other. 'My father said it was okay to go to the pub, now I'm sixteen. So I did that every night. Actually, it was a bit of a problem. My father said I shouldn't drink in any of the pubs on our estate, because it wouldn't be fair on our men, when they're trying to relax . . . so I had to drive six miles each way to leave the estate.'

'Yah, I get that,' replied the other boy. 'It wouldn't be fair on one's tenants either, to drink in one of one's own pubs.'

I remember thinking: this is a very smart school I've arrived at. My own parents, disappointingly, didn't own any pubs at all.

Having scraped into Eton by the skin of my teeth, it was no surprise to find myself in the bottom stream – F14 – a sort of holding pen for the academically challenged, presided over by an exacting midget, Mr Martin Shortland-Jones ('Shortie Jones'), a former Fives Olympian.

Many of my fellow F14ers seemed to live in Norfolk or Leicestershire, notoriously dozy counties, and are now Lord Lieutenants and High Sheriffs of their various patches. Other inmates, such as Benjie Mancroft and Percy Weatherall, went on to champion the Countryside Alliance in the House of Lords and to become Tai-pan of Jardine Matheson in Hong Kong, respectively. But, in September 1970, our highest aspiration was to make it through Trials, the end-of-term exams, and thus be allowed to stay on for a further term.

The Eton I encountered in the early seventies had hardly changed in many respects since the Eton of my father, thirty years earlier, with fagging and 'capping'; the latter a weird ritual whereby you raised your right index finger towards your forelock as though doffing an invisible top hat, whenever you passed a 'beak' (master) in the street. There was a full lexicon of school slang, now almost all swept away: 'socking in the street' (eating alfresco, forbidden), 'Which Tutor's are you in?' (Which house?), 'Who are you up to?' (Who is your form master?) For the first year, my fagging duties involved making the bed each morning for George Ramsden, now an antiquarian bookseller in North Yorkshire, though fortunately his expectations were low. He was very decent.

But it was also a school in transition. The corridors of Baldwin's Bec vibrated to the muffled beat of Led Zeppelin and the Grateful Dead, and the musky smell of marijuana. Boys clad their bedroom walls with rolls of kitchen tin foil, or Indian drapes and posters from the Isle of Wight rock festival. My friend Craig Brown subscribed to *Oz* and *It* magazines, and became an important and subversive influence on my world view. Each day, I 'messed' (had tea) with Craig, John and Trelawny in one of our rooms, where we ate toast spread thickly with Nutella, and bowls of cereal drowned in chocolate Nesquik. In those days, boys with country estates brought braces of pheasant, woodcock and partridge back to the school, which were left to hang outside their windows, creating a macabre spectacle as you strolled down Keates Lane or Common Lane, like the cold room at a game butcher's. These birds were eventually taken to Rowlands, the school tuck shop, where Mr Wells plucked and roasted them, and delivered them for tea with sides of Brussels sprouts and bread sauce. The rest of us ordered Brown Cows (a pint glass of Coca-Cola with two scoops of Wall's ice cream bobbing about in a vanilla scum) and plates of chips with a dipping bowl of ketchup. Or we hung out in a squalid back room in Tudor Stores, a rival tuck shop where the genteel Spellar family presided over a deep-fat fryer serving shrivelled bacon and fried eggs, with complimentary 'trash mags' (war comics) available to read at a special Formica-topped chef's table.

Thus my early years at Eton passed. At the end of each term the 250 boys of my year assembled in the Farrer Theatre for 'reading over', when your precise exam position in Trials was revealed by the Lower Master in reverse order, starting at the bottom. You sat in nonchalant suspense, hoping your name wouldn't be called out too early – certainly not in the first twenty – and then, as the occasion wore on, you eventually heard the names of the King's Scholars and brainboxes jostling for top position.

I had one lucky advantage. In those days, there was much

learning of poetry by heart in the Eton curriculum. It was called a 'Saying Lesson' and you were set a poem a week to memorize, which you declaimed in turn. I found myself being set the same poem over and over again.

An English master would say, 'Seeing as we have a Coleridge in the division [slang for class], I suggest we all learn *Kubla Khan* by Samuel Taylor Coleridge. Is he, in fact, a relative, Coleridge?'

'Er, vaguely, sir.'

'Good. Then please do *Kubla Khan* for Saying Lesson next week.'

Then, the next term, the same thing would happen with a different teacher. And then again. I'm still word perfect. 'But oh! That deep romantic chasm which slanted / Down the green hill athwart a cedarn cover!' et cetera, et cetera.

A distant cousin, F. J. R. Coleridge, was Vice Provost of the school, a towering, formidable, senatorial figure in his mid-sixties, former housemaster and renowned sportsman. Towards the end of my first year, Fred Coleridge and his wife, Julia, kindly invited me to tea in the Vice Provost's Lodge.

'Have you been rowing for your house junior bumping four?' he boomed at me.

'Er, I'm afraid not, sir.'

'Well then, did you play for your house first year Field Game side?'

'Er, sadly not, sir.'

At this point, I could see on his face the panicked look of someone who has entirely run out of conversational leads, and is casting about for anything at all. Fortunately, Julia, a talented watercolourist, invited me out of pity to view some of her recent paintings of Cannon Yard and Lupton's Tower, so the tea party was partially retrieved.

★

Around the time I turned sixteen, my Eton career started to pick up. Having struggled through O Levels, and thus able to jettison all the subjects I was bad at, it turned out I was quite good at the remaining three. Almost overnight, I transformed from dimwit to clever-dick intellectual and, with all the zeal of a recent immigrant assimilating to a new culture, I embraced my new status. I started writing for the school magazine, the *Eton Chronicle*, in those days a weekly newspaper printed on yellowing faux-parchment. I joined the Debating Society with Craig Brown, which met amidst the panelled splendour and classical busts of Upper School, and where the perennial motions for debate were: 'This house would ban fox-hunting' and 'This house would ban tailcoats as school dress.'

Craig and I joined the school debating team, along with Oliver Letwin★ and Charles Moore,† competing for some South of England Rotary Club schools debating trophy. We cruised without effort through the first few rounds of the competition. Oliver had a reputation as the cleverest boy in the school; Charles was a quixotic intellectual with a deep fringe of black hair who laughed easily. Our rival in the finals was Wycombe Abbey, the serious and brainy girls' school, and we travelled over to Wycombe in a Transit van, jotting down a few random notes for the debate as we went.

As we approached the school, we noticed a team of brick-layers raising the height of the perimeter school wall; if you know Wycombe Abbey, it is a very long wall, a mile at least. The Headmistress explained, 'We have had a *most unfortunate incident*

★ Tory MP for West Dorset. Chancellor of the Duchy of Lancaster (2014–16); Cabinet Office Chief (2015).
† Editor, *The Spectator* (1984–90), *Sunday Telegraph* (1992–95), *Daily Telegraph* (1995–2003). Biographer of Margaret Thatcher.

involving *lewd young men* from the town. They parked a lorry against the wall, stood on the roof, and wolf-whistled at our girls playing netball. We had no option but to build the wall higher.'

There was a judging panel of ten judges, all dignitaries of the Rotary Club – actuaries and county solicitors, local councillors and Lady Mayoresses.

The motion was 'Coca-Colonialism. This house regrets the baleful influence of American popular culture upon Western civilization.' The Wycombe Abbey girls were up first. They were disconcertingly well rehearsed, arguably a bit dull, but word perfect, having learnt their speeches by heart, sing-song fashion.

Next came Eton, amateur, facetious, extemporizing. Letwin was bafflingly intellectual, interrogating the very concept of Western civilization, standing the motion upon its head. The panel of Rotarians deliberated for all of twenty seconds before delivering their damning verdicts in turn: Wycombe Abbey, Wycombe Abbey, Wycombe Abbey . . . Eton lost ten votes to nil. I cannot pretend we were surprised or particularly mortified.

Not long afterwards, Craig and I won a newly established school cup for debating – the Jeremy Thorpe Cup, named after the Old Etonian Leader of the Liberal Party. (It seemed no sooner had we won it than Thorpe was prosecuted for the alleged attempted murder of a boyfriend, the male model Norman Scott. The cup was hurriedly renamed the Eton Debating Cup. 'Winner of the Jeremy Thorpe prize at Eton' felt like a liability on a CV.)

One evening, while watching *Top of the Pops* on the giant TV set in Rowlands, David Bowie appeared on screen performing 'Starman', with his spiky orange hair and Kansai Yamamoto bodysuit. The tuck shop was filled with Etonians, many returning from cricket matches in cricket whites, staring stupefied at the television. No one had seen anything like it. Despite a groundswell of derision and booing ('Who the hell is this poof?'), I found him mesmerizing.

It was the start of a lifelong fandom, and the very next day I bought at Audiocraft, Eton's record shop, the entire back catalogue: *Hunky Dory*, *Man Who Sold the World*, *Space Oddity*, all of them. On Christmas Eve, I went with Craig to see Bowie in concert at The Rainbow, Finsbury Park; an outing necessitating a complete change of clothes − sailor-suit top, silver satin strides − in the train lavatories between Haslemere and Waterloo. I remember being more convinced by Bowie than Craig was − I had drunk the Kool-Aid hook, line and sinker, while Craig remained sceptical. He always had a keen nose for anything pretentious.

Craig was a talented playwright and satirist, with pitch-perfect ear. Aged fourteen, he could parody the literary styles of authors and public figures as adeptly as his *Private Eye* satires forty-five years later. We put on plays together. *Sinderella* (with an S) was billed as 'Eton's first pantomime', to be followed by a multi-cast rock musical mocking the impending royal wedding of Princess Anne to Captain Mark Phillips. It was a bonus when *The Sun* newspaper devoted most of page three to the supposedly scandalous production: 'Eton boys in a royal howler ... Queen "deeply offended" say palace insiders.' We loved it, we were publicity whores.

We set up a club to invite celebrities to the school, lent fig-leaf respectability by its lofty name, 'The Contemporary Arts Society'. For additional gravitas, the society was given a Latin motto − *Lumines Nomine Noscere* − which translates as 'To get to know the stars by their Christian names'. Brian Eno, lank-haired genius of Roxy Music, was the first guest, followed by Angie

Bowie, wife of David, who ate asparagus in a thrillingly sexy manner in The Cockpit, a teashop on Eton High Street.

We spent our days feeding 10p pieces into coin-box telephones, pestering publicity girls at record labels and befriending celebrities' PAs, wheedling our way into their diaries.

Eventually, Elton John was signed up. He was already an A-list star and arrived in a gold Rolls-Royce, which made a lap of honour around the parade ground, much envied by all, not seen as remotely vulgar by the boys. As our guests were forensically interviewed by Craig and me onstage, the two of us basked in the reflected glory. There is a historic photograph of Elton standing on the steps of the school theatre, surrounded by a throng of random Etonians. In the picture, I can be seen with a boscage of curly hair, next to an already almost-bald Elton. Over time, Elton's hair miraculously regrew, while mine gradually evaporated. My hair in the photo looks like an ungroomed cat ready to leap from my head onto his.

Craig and I took over the *Eton Chronicle* and edited it in succession. The yellow parchment paper and letterpress were replaced by white stock, the pagination doubled, sports reports and obituaries of dead beaks were ruthlessly cut back to make space for gossip columns, celebrity interviews and tabloid-driven editorials in the style of the *Daily Express*'s Jean Rook. There was a censor, a Classical civilization master named Pete Needham, who was supposed to vet the articles in advance and suppress contentious material. We avoided this by the simple ploy of removing from his pile of proofs anything likely to offend him, until it was too late. His bald head, criss-crossed with knotted veins like electric cables, trembled with fury at each new issue.

'Why was I never shown this *seditious garbage*?'

'I've no idea how that happened, sir. It must have slipped through the net in the production process.'

I became political, canvassing for the Liberal Party in Slough at the 1974 General Election. This was entirely due to Charles Moore, then a proselytizing Liberal whose father wrote Jeremy Thorpe's speeches, and who recruited Craig and me into the cause.

Slough was a rock-solid Labour seat, with the fiery Socialist Joan Lestor its unassailable MP. The Liberals fielded Philip Goldenberg, a bearded local councillor of zero charisma. Every afternoon, we bicycled to a different inner-city hotspot, delivering leaflets and sweet-talking the voters. Many had chained Rottweilers in their front yards, all had red Labour posters in their windows. The appearance of three Eton boys on their doorsteps, however persuasive, made zero impact on their voting intentions, and Joan Lestor sailed back to Westminster undented.

A crucial part of my Eton was Tap, the school pub, which occupied half of a Georgian house on the High Street, with a narrow back garden. I went most days. It was run by an imperious landlady (never barmaid), Mrs Moulton, and opened its doors for drinks at 11 a.m., so you could have a pint or two of Carling at elevenses, in the break between lessons. This surprising tradition continued for decades until some killjoy noticed it was odd to be serving alcohol to sixteen-year-olds so early in the morning.

The food in Tap was magnificent: avocado and prawns, smoked salmon on rye, a 'long egg' (open bridge roll with scrambled egg and cress on top). Furthermore, you didn't need to pay at the time. 'Down on the National Debt, Coleridge?' Mrs Moulton would ask, adding it to a tab.

Everything about Tap in the seventies seems impossibly swanky and privileged. And it was so. My sons report that, today, the only food available is microwaved cheeseburgers and crisps, Mrs Moulton has been succeeded by an ex-policeman, and boys must be fingerprinted before each drink order, triggering a computerized record of consumption.

Late one evening, I was strolling back from Tap to my boarding house and noticed two hooded figures wrapped in overcoats, attempting to sleep outdoors under the stone porch of the school library. They turned out to be exceptionally pretty girls aged thirteen, who had missed their coach back to their boarding school, Heathfield, and had no money for a cab. I suggested they might be more comfy dossing on a sofa in Baldwin's Bec, and sneaked them inside. Pandora Stevens and Laura Leatham became good friends.

Pandora was the daughter of Sir Jocelyn Stevens, owner of *Queen* magazine and Chief Executive of Beaverbrook newspapers, who was to have an immense impact on my career. Pandora was warm, funny and beautiful, with blonde bobbed hair, huge eyes and freckles. She looked in those days like a perfect cross between her three famous daughters, the Delevingne girls: Chloe, Poppy and supermodel-turned-movie-star Cara, my god-daughter.

She had a gift for making everyone in her orbit fall instantly in love with her, and want to help her. Through Pandora, I soon met her circle of friends – Laura Leatham's twin Alice, and a girl named Birdy Rose, who wore Japanese geisha make-up. We hung out at Françoise, a basement nightclub in the King's Road, opposite Peter Jones, and at the Stevens' houses in Chelsea and Hampshire. Pandora's mother, Janey, wrote the shopping column for *Vogue*, and I remember spotting a stash of *Vogue* writing paper on her desk and being weirdly impressed. It held an almost totemic allure, and I longed to be the sort of person who kept *Vogue* stationery in their study.

On the terrace at the Stevens' enormous Queen Anne country

house, Testbourne, on a bend of the River Test, with an ever-hovering butler named Vipers, was a set of twelve green canvas director's chairs, each with the words 'Jocelyn Stevens, Editor-in-Chief' stencilled on the back. I was fiercely envious of these chairs, recognizing something to aspire to in their tycoon swank.

Returning to our house in West Sussex, which always seemed to have shrunk after a visit to Testbourne, I described the chairs over supper in awed admiration. My mother declared, 'Goodness, they sound rather show-offy to me.'

Shortly afterwards, I was invited to Pandora's sixteenth birthday dinner at San Lorenzo in Beauchamp Place, then the most fashionable restaurant in London.

Twenty-five teenagers had been asked to the dinner, seated at one long table in the main dining room, surrounded by tables of other customers. Jocelyn was a charismatic, impulsive, matinee idol, leading member of the Princess Margaret set and cameo attraction in every gossip column. At the end of dinner, he stepped up onto his chair, silencing the entire room. 'Ladies and gentlemen,' he boomed. '*I am Jocelyn Stevens*. Tonight is the birthday of my beloved daughter, Pandora, and I want everyone – *everyone in the whole restaurant* – to drink a toast to her. Lorenzo, Mara . . . bring champagne, champagne for every table. Pandora, happy birthday! Happy birthday!'

I was impressed to bits by this glorious, confident bravado. I remember thinking: this is the last thing on earth my own parents would do, stand on a chair ('I am Jocelyn Stevens') and order champagne for multiple strangers.

I realize that I have not, thus far, given any proper description of my father and mother. All parents create a particular microculture of their own which delineates the boundaries and expectations of family life, and our family microculture was a very happy one.

My father had an unusually calm and consistent personality; one of the kindest of people, who I never saw agitated at any time in his life. Mathematically astute (he could calculate figures in his head to four decimal points), he was intellectually idle, reading only one book a year, generally the latest blockbuster by Wilbur Smith, poolside on his summer holiday. He almost never referred to his work at Lloyd's, and had less personal vanity than anyone I've met. I can see, now, how unusual that is amongst prominent businessmen, who generally bore-on about their accomplishments and define themselves by them. When my father became Chairman of his firm, Sturge, then the largest Lloyd's underwriter, and simultaneously Chairman of Lloyd's of London, it came as quite a surprise to his children, since he had never mentioned such a possibility before. He always preferred to ask other people benevolent questions than to talk about himself. I think he genuinely considered his job uninteresting to others, and did not wish to inflict it in conversation. He had the gift of being able to speak to anyone, with ease and without condescension. He loved jokes, especially long-running ones. An instinctive Conservative, his only vehemently held views were negative ones about Labour politicians ('Healey is a *ghastly* man', 'Gordon Brown is *perfectly useless*', 'Tony Blair is the *worst Prime Minister since Lord North*', and so forth).

He told his sons, 'I don't mind what you decide to do when you grow up. Do any job you like, whatever you enjoy doing. Don't feel you have to go into the City. But one thing I *do* mind about. You have to get a job, any job, and turn up, not lounge about in bed all morning.'

Wonderfully relaxed in his own skin and in every conceivable social situation, he felt no need to impress. He adored my mother, loved his sons, loved his garden and his azaleas, enjoyed ordering claret from The Wine Society and mixing Bloody Marys with the full set of ingredients. The life created by my parents was one of complete order, comfort and certainty, meticulously planned, often months in advance. 'Do you know if you're coming to us for Christmas this year?' my mother would ask in, say, February. 'I would like to know, I'm starting to make plans.'

Inspired by my mother, my parents are alarmingly punctual on all occasions, and this became a family thing. If, say, a church service at South Harting was at 11 a.m., and it was fifteen minutes' drive from home, we would agree to assemble, ready to leave, at 10.30. But at 10.15, everyone was ready and waiting. Any family member assembling at 10.20 would be considered late. To this day, I am seldom late for anything.

My mother was the engine of the marriage, the person who initiated plans, chose holidays and our daily food, organized dinner parties, remembered birthdays, oversaw decorating schemes (the sofa covers at their houses were in perpetual process of upgrade). She noticed everything, and this is a habit (for better or worse) I have inherited from her – noticing entertaining oddities of dress and speech, a tilted lampshade, a rumpled rug. She has a great horror of unplumped sofa cushions, relishing the sensation of entering a perfectly fresh drawing room or study, with no evidence of recent prior occupation. She is unexpectedly well-informed on subjects which interest her, being an attentive reader of modern novels and glossy magazines, which she studies closely. Brought up in Knightsbridge, her London consists of a tiny and civilized triangle bounded by Sloane Street, the King's Road and Brompton Road, with Chelsea Green at its epicentre.

As a parent, she instinctively prioritized her children over everything else, seldom accepting a dinner party invitation during the school holidays, or going on a holiday that wasn't a family one. The things she dislikes are bad manners, thoughtlessness to staff such as cooks and cleaning ladies, tattoos, piercings, men considered 'too pleased with themselves', new technology (my parents have no email, my mother not knowing 'where one would put one of those ugly computer things' in their large house) and grandchildren who don't write thank-you letters. Perhaps it is her influence that none of her children or grandchildren have either tattoos or conspicuous piercings.

Our home life at this point was divided between a long, narrow, tile-slung house in Sussex, from which my father commuted to London each morning by train, and a small flat in Cranmer Court, a mansion block on Sloane Avenue largely inhabited by elderly Tory-voting widows. My parents had had a third son born thirteen years after me ('our afterthought'), my brother Christopher, who was at nursery school in Midhurst, thus leaving the run of Cranmer Court to Timmy and me. It quickly became a dosshouse for friends, sleeping on every sofa and spare inch of carpet.

Timmy, considered handsome, was cat-nip for Tudor Hall and St Mary's boarding school girls in skin-tight jeans, Alice bands and velvet jackets, who shrieked and yelped at the slightest provocation, causing a stream of complaints from our geriatric neighbours.

Once, after a particularly rowdy Pimm's-fuelled party at the flat, ten girls squeezed into the tiny lift. Already inside was a uniformed Cranmer Court porter, accompanying a long, narrow canvas bag. Only halfway down was this revealed to be a body bag, concealing the just-dead Brigadier from the flat upstairs.

Our social life on the West Sussex–Hampshire borders was comprised of gloriously juicy convent school girls, leavened by bohemian Bedales' sixth-formers.* My school friends Craig

---

* The Blacker sisters of Liss and the Steels of Odiham were leading local attractions.

Brown and Napier Miles lived nearby, and we met up at The White Hart, a pub in South Harting, or at The Three Moles in Selham, having driven over on mopeds (mine was bright orange). It was our custom to minutely analyse and critique the characters and appearance of all the local talent, and so engender a happy feeling of superiority and male bonding.

In the days before mobile phones, it was a complicated business to ring any girl at all. Most families we knew in West Sussex had only one landline extension, positioned in the hall or sitting room. There was no privacy to place or receive calls. If you wanted to speak to a girl, you dialled their number while your own telephone was unwatched. You heard it ring.

'Hello. Fernhurst 212.' A haughty mother's voice.

'Er, hello, can I speak to Miranda, please?'

'Who is this speaking?'

'Er, Nick Coleridge.'

'What are you to David and Susan?'

'They're my parents.'

'Well, do please give them my love, and say we'd adore to see them sometime, we really would. Now, Miranda is out riding her horse at the moment. But I shall tell her you telephoned, and I shall ask her to ring you back before lunch, at twelve fifty . . .'

In our immediate vicinity, there were two sorts of teenage parties: the flashier ones centred around the Cowdray polo set at Easebourne; others, more parochial, over the Surrey border into stockbroker country towards Haslemere. Here the girls were less polished, often day pupils at local convent schools, and regarded as more promiscuous when warmed up.

Drinks at these gatherings consisted of a wishy-washy punch served in a metal cauldron, known as a 'witches' brew', comprising one part cider to three parts orange juice and a gallon of soda water. The challenge for guests, of course, was to find means of tipping as much brandy, rum, gin, vodka, tequila, anything alcoholic, into the bowl to get the party rocking. The final record of the night was always 'A Whiter Shade of Pale' by Procol Harum, the snoggers' call to action.

One of my early romantic episodes took place at just such a party, held in a stockbroker Tudor-style mansion on a Haslemere road. Behind their house, our hosts had a brick Victorian game larder, filled with several dozen dead pheasants, partridges, duck and hares suspended from metal hooks, bounty from recent shoots. As the party unfolded, I found myself with a hefty, predatory girl in a black lace blouse; she must have been fifteen, with conspicuously large bosoms. When she suggested we 'get away from this party for a bit', I was only too willing to go along with the plan. It seemed rather flattering. Though I became dubious when she led me towards the brick game larder. 'Don't worry, I have a key.'

Once inside, she immediately peeled off her blouse and black bra. I stared, mesmerized, at the massive, swollen mammaries being presented: I had, quite literally, never seen anything like them before.

'Don't you want to touch?' she asked, impatiently.

Staring down at us, on all sides, were dead birds and ground game, impaled on their grisly hooks. Gingerly, I reached towards a nipple, which stood out like a plastic thimble. At that moment, the face of our stockbroker host leered at the tiny, misted-up window. 'Stop that *at once*,' he commanded, 'and *unlock this door*.' The girl was promptly led away and sent home, while I was free to rejoin the party.

When my father came to collect me at midnight, the stockbroker explained. 'No hard feelings, and Nick wasn't in any way to blame. We'd been warned in advance about this girl.

Suffice to say, she has serious mental issues. I was asked to keep a close eye on her, which fortunately I did . . .'

These county jamborees were all very fine, but the parties we wanted to be at were the London ones – gatherings of a thousand or more guests, like the annual Feathers Ball at the Hammersmith Palais, at which the cream of the nation's posh teen talent congregated for a mass groping session. Here was the pick of the crop, stir-crazy from a term in purdah, desperate for human contact and completely undiscriminating. In a way, events like the Feathers Ball anticipated, by several decades, speed dating and Tinder, with their emphasis on instant connections based solely upon first appearances. The deafening music, the shrillness and excitement of the guests, made all conversation impossible.

Afterwards, boys would ask each other, 'Did you enjoy the Feathers? Any luck?'

'Yah . . . five.' (That meant five snogs with five different girls over the course of the four-hour event.)

'You?'

'Nine.'

'Christ, that's obscene, Johnnie! Really?'

'No swanks.'

There were other lesser balls too, generally held in aid of some comically inappropriate medical charity, such as throat cancer or gynaecological research. I wonder whether the distinguished professors and pioneering fertility doctors realized the degree of louche behaviour which lay behind the raising of their vital research funding?

I remember going to just such a party at the Rubens hotel, opposite the Victoria and Albert Museum, staged in aid of breast cancer. After the ball, half a dozen Eton boys had been invited to sleep on the floor of a friend's flat, an Edwardian mansion block on Campden Hill Road. We were having a final nightcap before turning in, when the mother of the house entered the room with a plate of warm mini-quiches. She was rather a prissy lady, who spoke with carefully enunciated vowels.

'Would any of you young gentlemen like a *little warm tart* to take to bed with you?' she innocently enquired, handing them round.

We fifteen-year-olds rolled about in hopeless mirth, unable to stop, tears flowing from our eyes.

The first glossy magazine I ever opened was a copy of *Harpers & Queen*. I was sixteen at the time, ill in bed, and borrowed a copy from my mother who was a subscriber. That first couple of hours with a glossy changed my life. I was mesmerized by the wit, by the blend of serious journalism and trivia, by the glamour of the fashion photography, sheen of the paper, gentle waft of fragrance from the advertiser's scent strips, punning headlines, understated snobbery, zeitgeist-interrogating social commentary . . . all of these things I found spellbinding, and I knew in a heartbeat I wanted to make a career in glossy magazines.

As a glossy-mag virgin, touched for the very first time, it occurred to me that if I could somehow write an article for this magazine, and have it published, I might somehow enter this tantalizing through-the-Narnian-wardrobe world that magazines seemed to offer. So as my quarantine dragged on, I scratched out 1,500 words on 'How to survive teenage parties', then trudged the half-mile to the post box at the end of our lane and sent it off. Handwritten (how amateur), addressed to The Editor.

And, lo and behold, they bought it and printed it, and the typography and glossy paper made it look ten times better, and

I had a byline. And, not long afterwards, the magazine invited me to a party at the Park Lane hotel, filled with 300 of the most glamorous, semi-famous people – writers, fashion designers, socialites, politicians and models – not one of whom I knew but several of whom I had read about in Nigel Dempster's *Daily Mail* gossip column (he was also a guest). It was Xanadu. Certainly several steps up from the game larder.

Meanwhile my happy school life continued. I considered myself lucky to have Giles St Aubyn as my Eton housemaster. A distinguished historian and author, eccentric, complex and not without his demons, his non-sporty, mildly sophisticated house suited me. His study displayed glorious paintings of St Michael's Mount, the St Aubyn family island in Cornwall, where he had grown up, and outside Baldwin's Bec were parked an astounding collection of cars – Aston Martins, Mercedes, Bristols, two Bentleys, and for a while a Rolls-Royce. Not the cars of visiting parents, but Giles's own cars.

He invited amusing bachelor friends to lunch – the Queen's Private Secretary Sir Martin Gilliat, the *Sunday Telegraph* diarist Kenneth Rose, the artist Derek Hill. The Queen Mother came as a guest to house plays more than once. And Giles was not above a little harmless showing off from time to time.

As a housemaster, he found conversation at lunch – 'Boys' Dinner' as it then was – excruciating, and who can blame him, eating with the same group of adolescent louts day after day? Sometimes he ran short of things to say.

On such occasions, he would announce a competition to the table. 'In my pocket, I have a certain sum of money,' he would say (much jangling of coins). 'I do not myself know precisely how much money. I would like everyone at the table to make a guess, but first you must weigh the probability. I am well known to be quite a rich man, the richest housemaster. So, I could reasonably have a very LARGE amount of money upon my person. On the other hand, rich men seldom carry much cash. You should take both these facts into consideration.'

About fifteen boys then had to guess, their estimates noted down by the House Captain.

'Er, two hundred pounds, sir?'

'Er, one pound, seventeen shillings and sixpence, sir?' and so on.

Nobody ever got it right. Had you done so, you were promised to keep the money. Thus lunches were occupied at Baldwin's Bec.

There were all sorts of early legends about Giles, which people repeated as fact, thus adding glamour and lustre to his personality. It was said that he'd been a great 'deb's delight', as a young master in his youth, who would turn up to teach wearing white tie and tails, having come directly from dances in London. It was even said that he'd once been lined up as a possible husband for Princess Margaret. Frankly, by the time my year group arrived at the house in 1970, it was hard to visualize our intelligent and urbane but intensely private and sometimes diffident housemaster as a dashing deb's delight . . . but perhaps it was so.

He had the most distinctive of signatures: like a coil of barbed wire above a First World War trench, with a great rococo flourish at the bottom, swirling and looping back and forth. Everyone in the house spent months learning to forge it. Thirty years later, a group of us had dinner with Giles at the restaurateur Gavin Rankin's place, Bellamy's of Mayfair, and all had a crack at doing his signature on paper napkins, with Giles judging which looked authentic. It felt desperately radical to be forging his signature in his presence, under his eagle eye.

He taught me the history of the Victorian Church and the Tractarian Movement for A Level, part of the Divinity courses. Attentive readers will recall that Scripture was my strongest academic suit, though its name kept changing: Bible Study becoming Scripture becoming Divinity becoming Theology and Comparative Religion.

Craig (another Theologian) and I took pleasure in inventing entirely new verses and texts from the Old Testament and the Synoptic Gospels and slipping them into essays, banking on no teacher bothering to check. It was satisfying to find a big tick alongside a fictitious manufactured quote from Isaiah or Ezekiel.

In the holidays, I did social work on a project for underprivileged children in Southwark, consisting mostly of teaching five-year-olds how to swim in a municipal baths and hanging out at an adventure playground. Charles Moore and James Leigh-Pemberton★ were my fellow volunteers. It seems strange today that we would be put in sole charge of forty inner-city kids at a swimming pool, with no background checks at all, but it was so. In the evenings, we sought out authentic pubs in South London, led by Charles who was an unlikely champion of the Campaign for Real Ale. We hung out in a pub called The Black Dog in Vauxhall, drinking Old Speckled Hen and Charles Wells Bombardier, while Charles lectured us on the excellence of Jeremy Thorpe and his imminent political breakthrough, then an almost-credible proposition.

Recently, I found a cache of forgotten photographs from this period, including one with fifteen of my school contemporaries

★ Sir James Leigh-Pemberton CVO. Investment banker, CEO Credit Suisse, Receiver-General for the Duchy of Cornwall, Executive Chairman, UK Financial Investments.

hanging out at some school event: Craig (now the *Private Eye* satirist), John Scott (Islamic expert, living in Istanbul), Trelawny (financier), Napier (medical negligence barrister), David Ogilvy (musician), Gavin Rankin (nightclub manager turned restaurateur), Charles Moore (Editor and biographer), James Baring (estate agent, musician), Christopher Figg (film producer), Oliver Leatham (food entrepreneur), Geoffrey Adams (knighted Foreign Office mandarin and ambassador), David Shaughnessy (Los Angeles TV soap director), Kio Amachree (Nigerian rock composer), Rupert Forbes Adam (muralist, died young), James Rankin (criminal law barrister). It surprises me how many of them I still see, and like seeing, either by design or because our lives overlap. Numerically, perhaps a quarter of my closest friends are Old Etonians, but their networks are as deep and pervasive as Japanese knotweed.

As the end of my Eton years loomed, I had no idea what I might do next. John Scott was heading to the Courtauld to do History of Art, Craig to Bristol to do Drama, Trelawny to university in a Confederate American state where you couldn't even buy a beer. For me, the future was wide open. Not for the first time, Scripture came to the rescue. Charles Moore was off to Cambridge, to Trinity, and suggested I do the same. 'You should enter to read Theology,' he advised. 'You can always change later. Anyone can get in, if you apply for Theology.' I took the backhanded compliment on the chin.

According to Charles, there were at least five Theology dons at Trinity, all with endowed sinecures, who were crying out for pupils, it being vaguely embarrassing to have nobody to teach.

A couple of weeks later, I was sitting in a set of rooms in Great Court, being interviewed by Bishop John Robinson, a notoriously trendy bishop whose book *Honest to God*, questioning the existence of the Almighty, had made waves at the time.

He could not have been more genial, offering me a thimble of Madeira and a place to read Theology next October, in that order. The whole interview took forty minutes.

'I shall look forward to seeing you,' he said, as I strode out into the sunshine of Great Court.

4.

I had read somewhere, probably in Evelyn Waugh's *Scoop*, that the best route into journalism was to start as a tea boy on a national newspaper.

So the week I left school, as my gap year before university began, I posted off a letter to the first newspaper Editor I could think of, who was John Junor,* Editor of the *Sunday Express*. At the time, he was the towering laird of Fleet Street: Scottish, trenchant, cranky, the author of a widely read column of opinion, and famous for proclaiming that only homosexuals drank white wine. It was to Junor I addressed my job application to push the tea trolley.

Amazingly, he replied. I was summoned for an interview at his office off the newsroom in the Beaverbrook Building. Sir John was sitting behind his desk, wearing a white nylon shirt through which you could see the contours of a string vest. He was holding my letter and shaking his head. 'I've read your letter, sonny, but you can never be a tea boy here. The unions won't wear it. You have to be the son of a tea boy to be considered, or a nephew. If I so much as suggest it, they'll down tools, we couldn't get the paper out . . .

'But I'll tell you what,' he went on. 'I can send you to the *Falmouth Packet* as a trainee reporter. It's a local rag down in Cornwall, one of ours. We can pay you fourteen pounds a week. That's if you want the position.'

* Sir John Junor, Editor *Sunday Express* (1954–86). Sage of Auchtermuchty. Inventor of the phrase 'Pass the sick bag, Alice.'

As I left the building, down half a mile of linoleum-covered corridors reeking of printer's ink, I passed a trundling tea trolley laden with a steaming urn and china mugs. I glared at the young lad pushing it along, whose family connections had denied me my big break. Instead, I was relocating to the deep south-west.

The *Falmouth Packet*, named for the eighteenth-century steamships which plied the Atlantic, was one of the most profitable local newspapers in the country. It had the highest penetration of sold copies to population: virtually everyone in Falmouth read it. The Editor of the *Packet* was in no doubt why this was. He sucked on his pipe and disclosed to me his secret recipe. 'Mention as many names as possible in your copy, young man. Each name printed is a sold copy. When I send you to cover a school Sports Day, don't come back with fewer than a hundred names – kids, parents, teachers, all of them. If it's a council meeting, name-check everyone, they're the worst, the councillors, vain to the bone. If I send you down the marina, mention every boat – dinghies, yachts, tubs. Remember, every name printed is a sold copy . . .'

I lived with a landlady on a street lined with palm trees. The going rate for my tiny bedroom was £2.20 a night, but I was offered a weekly rate of £14, to include breakfast, and access to a lounge where the TV was permanently on and travelling salesmen watched sport in mournful silence. In the mornings, a dainty display of tinned prunes in a crystal dish, cereals and a jug of tinned pineapple juice were showcased on a dresser. My landlady presided over the dining room: 'When you've finished your juices, I'll bring you your breakfasts.' Every morning I enjoyed a gargantuan fry-up, with a bonus smoked kipper nestling between the eggs, bacon and beans.

On my second day, the Editor loomed over my desk. 'Alright,

young man, I'm giving you a big story to get your teeth into. This has front-page potential, so I'm taking a risk here . . .' His dentures rattled. 'British Rail has announced they're adding Cornish pasties to the buffet on their south-west routes. I want you to ring all the Cornish Members of Parliament for a reaction.'

It felt like a daunting assignment. Would MPs want to speak to me? Having obtained the telephone number of the House of Commons from Directory Enquiries, I rang the seven Cornish MPs in turn – the MP for Camborne and Redruth, MP for Truro and Falmouth, MP for St Austell and Newquay . . . Most were Liberals. All took my calls at once; I sensed they were sitting in their offices, gloriously unoccupied. And all revered the Cornish pasty. 'The Cornish pasty, in my highly partial opinion,' said one, 'is the finest culinary invention on God's good earth. I have campaigned ceaselessly for this day. I know I speak for every one of my constituents when I say if I had to eat only one dish for the rest of my natural life, it would be the Cornish pasty.'

Soon I specialized in covering silver and golden wedding anniversaries of Falmouth citizens. I would be sent round on my moped (the orange moped had come with me on the train) to interview the anniversary couple in their front rooms.

'May I ask, what is the most exciting thing that has ever happened during your wonderful long marriage?' I would enquire, notebook in hand.

The couple exchanged glances. 'I don't think anything exciting has happened, not really. The birth of our daughter, Jeanette, I suppose. We've led a quiet life.'

'And have you planned any special celebrations for your big day?'

'No, nothing planned. Just a normal day really. Our daughter may pop round.'

My piece would be headlined: 'Falmouth couple celebrate 60 years of quiet marriage. Nothing planned in celebration.'

Knowing nobody who lived within fifty miles of Falmouth, I ate alone most evenings in a Chinese restaurant named Ming's Garden, where I was generally the only customer. During these solo dinners, I read the complete works of E. M. Forster, in chronological order, beginning with *Where Angels Fear to Tread* and ending with *Maurice*.

Fresh from the *Falmouth Packet*, I set off on an adventure with my school friends John Scott and Trelawny Williams. I can't now remember how we hit upon the idea of crossing Russia by train to Iran, and then hitch-hiking back to England overland from Isfahan, but it was to be the first of many such expeditions. This first one was notable for an almost total lack of preparation, beyond buying flights to Moscow and, at the Soviet Intourist office in Piccadilly, reserving Third Class train tickets from Moscow's Paveletsky terminal to Tehran, a ten-day journey covering (very slowly) a distance of approximately 3,000 km via Tbilisi. John's mother, the Duchess of Buccleuch, organized a weekend at their Northamptonshire house, Boughton, at which various distinguished experts were assembled to offer us advice. The Russian-born Byzantine art historian Tamara Talbot Rice, already very old, briefed us on the Seljuks of Asia Minor, and must have been aghast at our level of ignorance. She cautioned us against travelling on foot in Eastern Turkey at night, owing to rabid Anatolian dogs.

In those Soviet days, the only practical way of entering Russia was on an organized tour, which we would join for two weeks before striking out on our own. So we were shepherded in and out of coaches around Moscow and St Petersburg, accompanied by guides who kept a beady eye on us at all times.

One problem, as a group of three friends, was that each night one of us had to share a bedroom with another single man on the trip. This rule could not be relaxed. The single man was a 74-year-old British union official, a steel worker from County Durham, whose life ambition had always been to visit the USSR, a country he worshipped from afar. His hatred of England and admiration for Russia was compounded by acute respiratory problems, probably due to asbestos.

All night he coughed up phlegm from deep in his lungs, and fulminated against the ruling elite of Great Britain. Everything in Russia delighted him. The breakfast buffet, consisting of slices of cardboard cheese and vile chalky coffee, thrilled him. 'You could never find a spread like this in England.' The Soviet space programme dazzled. 'You can't see the English putting a feller into outer space.'

On our final day in Moscow, a group of officials showed up. 'I am sorry, it is forbidden to travel by train to Tehran. Your tickets are invalid, you will fly instead.'

'But we want to go by train, we have our tickets already.'

'Flying is better for you. You will prefer.'

'We insist upon the train. We have paid.'

The officials disappeared to confer. Eventually, 'Okay, you may go by train. But you will have different tickets.' We had been upgraded from '3rd class hard' to First. Quite how lucky this was, would soon become clear.

I have always loved railway sleeper carriages. The First Class compartments on the Moscow–Tehran Express had deep Tsarist sofas with antimacassars, steaming samovars and brocade curtains. For ten days, we would be cocooned in splendour, cutting through the birch forests and endless lakes of central Russia. Only when the train pulled out of the station did we discover one crucial drawback . . . there was no dining car, nowhere to buy food on the train for a week and a half. Through the open doors of adjoining compartments, we saw passengers surrounded by picnic baskets. They glared mulishly. As often happens when food is unavailable, we suddenly felt incredibly hungry.

For twenty hours, the train rattled through snow-covered forests, never stopping. Trelawny found two hard-boiled eggs at the bottom of his rucksack, and these were much enjoyed.

In the middle of nowhere, the train slowed at a deserted platform, with a megalithic statue of Stalin on a hilltop behind. In a trice, hordes of old ladies – babushkas – staggered out of the shadows with baskets of produce: tinned sardines, black bread, lemons, knobbly cucumbers . . . We bought armfuls through the windows. Each day, the process was repeated. As we neared Tbilisi, Georgian champagne was on offer and Sulguni cheese in brine.

One evening, we strolled the entire length of the train to find the '3rd class hard' accommodation. There must have been a hundred carriages, and the closer to the back of the train, the less salubrious they became. 'Third class hard' was a barrack hut on wheels, eighty wooden berths per compartment, occupied by Soviet soldiers returning home, plus a healthy selection of Kazakh and Azerbaijani predators, who visibly perked up at our arrival. I remember us declaring that we were furious with the Intourist officials for denying us this more 'real' encounter with the country and its people, but it was a pleasure to slink back into our imperial seclusion.

At the frontier with Iran – then the most sensitive border crossing in the world – the train halted for a day for the wheels to be changed on every carriage to the narrower gauge of the Persian railway, then edged, with infinite slowness, across a mile of raked sand, heavily mined, while Soviet troops faced backwards on the roof to prevent their citizens doing a runner. From watchtowers,

American soldiers and the Shah's border guards followed the progress of the train towards them. Only four passengers by now occupied the 100 carriages – John, Trelawny and me, and the Director of the Moscow State Zoological Museum. Thus we arrived in Iran, where several hundred hawkers immediately boarded the train selling Coca-Cola and kebabs, and postcards depicting the Shah, Reza Pahlavi and Empress Farah and their family. The Pahlavis seemed highly popular rulers.

The weeks that followed were revelatory for me. The intense dry heat of the country, Islamic architecture, the mosques of Isfahan, Yazd and Shiraz, hitching long distances in blinding sunshine . . . all of these experiences were formative. Despite (or perhaps because of) living in four stately homes of unrivalled magnificence, John sought out the cheapest, roughest hotels in every town, and if we could barter down the price from 30 rials a night to 15, we would devote as long as it took. All night through the hardboard-thin walls of the Abadeh flophouse or the Fasa hotel, we could hear the violent throat-clearing, retching and spitting of our fellow guests, mainly truck drivers, interspersed with random angry shouts and sobbing. Recently, I found the diary I had kept on this trip and was struck by the distances we covered, the number of sites we visited each day, and the negligible sums of money we lived on.

In every shop and bazaar, framed photographs of the Shah were displayed; I'm sorry to say we had no inkling of the revolution waiting to erupt, barely a year later. Our interests were, anyway, architectural more than political. The mosques in Yazd lay in ruins, the mud walls of the old city collapsing. Persepolis had yet no giant coach park, and the ruins of Xerxes' palace were unfenced and free to clamber over. I think we fancied ourselves as travellers in the grand tradition of Robert Byron and Fitzroy Maclean, dawdling in the crucible of ancient civilizations.

It was while hitching from Yazd on the roof of a petrol tanker that I fell off onto the road, my rucksack following close behind and landing on my spine. I did not actually hear the slipping of my disc, but felt it soon enough. The excruciating pain drew a line under the trip, as I was invalided home in agony to King Edward VII's Hospital, in Marylebone.

My back remained a problem for ten years, despite the attentions of the most distinguished and expensive back doctors the length of Harley Street. It would only eventually be cured, in two minutes flat, by a peculiar faith healer in a furry-hooded anorak . . . but that miracle lay far ahead into the future.

Discharged from hospital, limping and brimming with painkillers, I embarked upon an Italian Grand Tour with Craig Brown and Guy Lubbock, meeting up with John on his return leg overland from Iran. We drove in a dark green Datsun Cherry, loaned by Guy's mother, the actress Moyra Fraser.★ In the boot were two small tents, in which we proposed to sleep.

It was unfortunate that, two days into the trip, all our luggage and money were stolen while we swam off a Porto Ercole beach. We now had only the clothes we stood up in. Craig wore his seersucker dungarees for the next two months.

At this moment of crisis, Guy declared, 'We've been sort of invited to stay with Lady Melchett in Porto Ercole if we want. Well, her daughter Pandora Mond once said we could, at a party . . .'

We were sceptical. Did we really want to stay with some stuffy titled Brit we hadn't met?

'The daughter's fun,' said Guy.

Sonia Melchett's pink villa overlooking the sea was film-star

---

★ Actress (1923–2009). *Airs on a Shoestring*; *Bell, Book and Candle*; Lady Ottoline Morrell in *Bloomsbury*.

magnificent. If she was surprised by the arrival of four complete strangers, teenagers without luggage, she hid it well.

Outside on the terrace, we found the publisher Lord Weidenfeld and the novelist Edna O'Brien, and a host of other alluring guests, including Pandora – who was every bit as fun as advertised.

Sonia Melchett – London's primary hostess, presiding over a soirée of politicians and authors at her Tite Street home – was the most generous and tolerant of people. We couldn't believe our luck. George Weidenfeld told long, long stories about his Nobel Prize-winning authors and friends; the worldly Italian foreign correspondent Paolo Filo della Torre taught us the proper way to cut a peach (sideways, parallel to the stalk) for easy removal of the stone. The sun beat down.

After a week, we reluctantly peeled off to see Florence, Siena and Urbino, sleeping one night in the tents on the central reservation of an autostrada, with three lanes of traffic rushing past on each side. But we soon returned to the Melchetts' for a second bite of the peach. Edna O'Brien was rather taken with John, and spent much time giving poolside reflexology to his feet. The novel she was writing was called *Johnny I Hardly Knew You*.

Craig was beside himself. I remember going to post postcards with him in the port, and our messages home all began, 'You won't believe who else is staying in the same villa . . .'

Embarrassing how celebrity-struck we were.

5

The room assigned to me in my first year at Trinity, in the optimistically named Angel Court, was in a late-fifties concrete-and-brick annexe cunningly concealed behind Great Court. One minute you were standing in Cambridge's most glorious quadrangle, with its cobblestones, chapel and fountain, the next you were slinking down an alleyway into the back end of a municipal centre with multiple fire doors and orange wood corridors.

My room – my suite – consisted of a sitting area with desk and pinboard, and a bedroom just large enough for a single bed and a basin, regularly used by visitors to pee into. From my window, if you clambered out onto the ledge, you could see Trinity Street and Heffers bookshop below, and a panorama of spires and rooftops.

It must be firmly stated that Cambridge was much easier to get into in the seventies than it is today. Trinity wasn't yet accepting women, which doubled your chances by definition, nor did many students apply from Europe or Asia, other than the son of the Singaporean Prime Minister, Lee Kuan Yew, whose room was further along my corridor. The Cambridge I found was still almost entirely a university of white, British men, mostly public and grammar school; such girls as there were, were cocooned in women-only colleges, and the gates of most colleges were locked at midnight (with a well-policed postern gate) and overnight visitors forbidden.

I made my five best friends at Cambridge in the first fortnight, and they remain friends to this day. Twice a year for thirty years we have held a reunion lunch in the same Chinese restaurant in London – the Jade Garden in Wardour Street – one of the dimmest dim sum joints in town. From time to time, someone suggests we really ought to raise our game and go somewhere nicer next time, but they are overruled: the Jade Garden it is. But I am getting ahead of myself by several decades.

On my first day at Cambridge I was walking past Magdalene College when an alarmingly tall man in a suit loomed above me. He was at least six feet seven, maybe taller, I couldn't see that far up.

'Are you Nick Coleridge?' he languidly enquired. 'I believe we may have friends in common.'

It never occurred to me he could be a student; I assumed he was a don, possibly Dadie Rylands or Maurice Bowra, or some distinguished aesthete from the Brideshead era.

'Come and have tea in my rooms tomorrow at four thirty,' he said. 'The Porter's Lodge will direct you.'

Nothing about the Hon James Stourton's* set of rooms indicated he wasn't a well-established senior don; through a half-open door from his panelled sitting room, with its bay window overlooking a garden, I could see an equally large panelled bedroom, and a bathroom beyond. Furthermore, the rooms were hung with prints by John Piper and mezzotints of stately homes, and armorial shields, and bookcases filled with art books and first editions. On a sideboard stood decanters and ecclesiastical candlesticks. Every other Cambridge room I visited had Pink Floyd posters and Athena art posters Blu-tacked to the walls.

---

* Chairman, Sotheby's UK (2006–12). 2nd son of Charles Edward Stourton 23rd Baron Stourton, 27th Baron Segrave, 26th Baron Mowbray. Author, biographer *Kenneth Clark* (2016).

We talked at cross purposes, excessively polite and formal. Slowly, very slowly, it dawned on me, from certain remarks about gap years and working in Chinese casinos in Aberdeen, that James was actually a contemporary, who had only arrived at Cambridge two days earlier. I could not have been more surprised. Confusion sorted, he quickly became one of my closest friends. In the intervening years, he has looked exactly the same, while the rest of us have aged and overtaken him.

James's cousin Edward* was on my staircase at Trinity – handsome, chunky, mature, already with a telegenic anchorman's face. In the next room was Nick Allan,† who I knew from school – punky, cooler than the rest of us, he ran a discotheque named Roxoff in the Chilterns. Along the passage was Peter Pleydell-Bouverie,‡ a scruffy Harrovian with floppy fringe and infectious laugh. The sixth member of the future Jade Garden dim sum set was Kit Hunter Gordon,§ an enviably handsome artist who owned a lighthouse on a remote rock off the Scottish coast, to which potential girlfriends were lured with the promise of a nude portrait of themselves.

At the end of the third week, we held a joint pyjama party with sedative-strength White Lady cocktails in James's senatorial set of rooms; at least 150 girls,¶ largely gathered from sixth-form colleges and typing schools, were squeezed in, wearing pyjamas and

---

* Broadcaster, author. Presenter BBC Radio 4 *Today* for ten years, presenter *Sunday*. *Absolute Truth: The Catholic Church Today* (1999); *Cruel Crossing: Escaping Hitler Across the Pyrenees* (2013).

† Asian hedge fund manager. Co-owner Indian hotels, Raas Jodhpur, Raas Devigarh, Raas Kangra. Deputy Chair, English National Opera.

‡ Japanese fund manager. High Sheriff of Wiltshire (2007).

§ Entrepreneur, venture capitalist, artist.

¶ I feel sure Miss Rose Scott, Miss Mary Iliff and Miss Mary Mowbray were in the throng.

nighties. It was a glorious bonding experience and rather set the tone thereafter.

If proof was needed of how old-fashioned and un-PC Cambridge was at the time, consider this strange episode. The Master of Trinity was Rab Butler – the Tory grandee who had so nearly become Prime Minister. His charming wife, Mollie, was a member of the Courtauld family, which explained why the Master's Lodge was filled with museum-quality Impressionist paintings as well as Tudor portraits of past Masters.

Each year, Lord and Lady Butler gave three separate drinks parties to welcome 'freshmen' arriving at Trinity, on three consecutive evenings.

To the first party, they invited alumni from the top public schools, along with many of the Butlers' own smart friends from Cambridgeshire to jolly things along. Champagne was served. To the second party, they invited second-division public school and top grammar school men. Dons and Fellows were invited. Red and white wine was served.

The third party was a beer and cider gathering for the remaining state sector, with junior tutors and research students.

It says a lot about us – and nothing good – that I don't remember any of us finding anything odd in this arrangement. It was interpreted as 'putting people at their ease'. Today, of course, Rab Butler would be pilloried by the *Sunday Times* and *Daily Mail*, and obliged to resign.

It is probably no coincidence that I have got a thousand words into this Cambridge chapter without once mentioning my academic course; I'm afraid it was only periodically I remembered I was there to study Theology. The Divinity schools – with their gaudy Tractarian architecture by Basil Champneys – were barely a stone's throw from my window, but this did not make them any more alluring. Having fallen into the habit of skipping lectures, I soon stopped attending them altogether. The only other religiously minded student at Trinity was Justin Welby, an always-smiling, conspicuously spiritual figure, later Archbishop of Canterbury, who could sometimes be glimpsed crossing Great Court holding a coffee and walnut cake from Fitzbillies teashop, en route to a God Squad prayer meeting. How I passed my first-year exams (an essay about early Celtic Christianity on the island of Iona was part of it) I have no idea. But, by then, I had switched to History of Art, my Scripture days behind me.

Arriving at Cambridge, we almost at once began launching and editing student magazines. The main protagonists were the Jade Garden set, with guest appearances by Charles Moore, Wesley Kerr (a Jamaican friend of particular fascination, being every possible minority all at once: a gay, black, Roman Catholic, orphaned Wykehamist), Harry Eyres on wine, plus my old friend Craig Brown contributing (from Bristol) a twisted story about a peeping Tom father at a Hampshire party. Pandora Stevens and Alice Leatham wrote about fashion.

The funding for this magazine, named *Rampage*, which ran for several issues, came from two sources only: from Jocelyn Stevens, who took advertising for the Express Group, and from tandoori and balti restaurants in the town. Looking at these ancient issues now, I rate them 9 out of 10 for quality of contributors, 2 out of 10 for design. It is striking how words-first we were, and how little attention we paid to layout. The pages were created with scissors and Cow Gum on Edward Stourton's floor, with bottles of wine tipping over onto finished artwork, all produced in a thick fug of cigarette smoke. These precarious paste-ups, full of in-jokes and borderline libels, were carried to a backstreet printer on the Trumpington Road, which turned them into pages. The issues sold like hot cakes, and we soon accumulated quite a large profit in our account.

Rampage was not the only show in town, and fierce rivalry simmered between competing magazines, like New York newspaper wars in the 1940s. We were not above pressurizing local newsagents, Mafia-style, to refuse to stock our rivals. Robert Harris,* then a leading Fabian, ran *Stop Press* (the official student rag) and was a vicious opponent in those days, though later became a friend. Meanwhile, the intellectuals of Trinity – Oliver Letwin, Noel Malcolm,† Charles Moore – published their own high-minded magazine, *Definite Article*, from G2 Great Court, of superior worth, but lower sales.

My Cambridge was half self-consciously cool, half defiantly traditional. Still in the thrall of David Bowie and glam rock, Nick Allan and I hennaed our hair bright orange, and my room was plastered with Ziggy Stardust and Roxy Music posters, and crayon pictures of sailors in the style of Jean Cocteau by Lindsay Kemp,‡ Bowie's mime tutor, with whom I took lessons at a church hall by Battersea Park. Pages from *Vogue* and *Harper's* were pinned everywhere.

But I was also a member of the Pitt Club, with its neoclassical portico and enfilade of club rooms with leather sofas and armchairs, like a St James's club. Its membership – men only – wore suits with ties or tweed jackets, and a pair of comically subservient staff, Dick and Mr Harborne, shuffled to and fro delivering Bloody Marys. Members ordered Veuve Clicquot at lunchtime, which was signed for by chit, and added to accounts that were only presented for payment after the end of the term. It was no

---

* Novelist. *Fatherland* (1992); *Enigma* (1995); *Archangel* (1998); *Pompeii* (2003); *Imperium* (2006), et cetera.
† Sir Noel Malcolm, academic, historian, political journalist.
‡ Choreographer, mime artist (1938–2018). Mentor to Kate Bush. *Flowers, Salome.*

surprise that the Pitt Club almost went bankrupt, saved only by being partially turned into a Pizza Express.

On my first visit to the Pitt, I was introduced to an older member, Nicholas Shakespeare,* who was wearing a flamboyant silk cravat.

'Nicholas Shakespeare meet Nicholas Coleridge,' said a friend. 'You should know each other, you have similar literary names.'

Shakespeare gave me a haughty appraisal. 'I think we can all agree that Shakespeare was a rather greater talent than Coleridge.'

It was my Pitt Club friends from Magdalene who invited me to the annual 'Wylie Practice', a fixture which seemed to belong to an earlier age. An eighteenth-century Magdalene alumnus, Sir Joshua Wylie, had supposedly left, in his will, a great fortune in trust, the interest from which should be blown on an annual party in his memory. Twelve Magdalene 'Trustees' wore morning coats and circulated around a walled garden with jugs of lethal cocktails – 80 per cent vodka, 20 per cent grapefruit juice – challenging guests to 'bumper' pints in one. It was the shortest party ever. Within twenty minutes, most guests had passed out, comatose on the grass. It was a much-anticipated summer event.

My days followed a full-on itinerary of urgent time-wasting. Not one moment was left unoccupied. At 8 a.m., I would have breakfast in Hall, up with the lark; afterwards, I would have coffee in the rooms of a succession of friends, gossiping and planning articles; before lunch, I might stroll to WH Smith in the market square, to see if any new glossy magazines had been delivered; then lunch at the Pitt or a pub, perhaps at the Pickerel opposite Magdalene; then a nap, followed by a play rehearsal (I was in the Footlights with Nick Hytner,† Griff Rhys Jones

---

* Novelist and biographer. Former *Telegraph* Literary Editor (1988–91).
† Sir Nicholas Hytner. Artistic Director National Theatre (2003–13).

and Rory McGrath), pre-dinner drinks, dinner in Hall, a debate at the Union, some parties, bed.

Of course, there were variations. The Gardenia Greek restaurant in Rose Crescent was a favourite. Sometimes we drove out to Shelford and The Tickell Arms, to be berated by the cantankerous diva of a landlord: 'Don't play with the candles, girls, you're not in your convents now,' he would bellow across the bar.

Sometimes I would linger all afternoon in the room of Nick Allan, drinking wine and speculating about girls Nick thought he quite fancied, or we bunked off to the cinema to watch *Saturday Night Fever*. Edward Stourton insists we once drove to Little Gidding, near Huntingdon, and read aloud T. S. Eliot's *Four Quartets* in the churchyard there. I suppose it is possible, though I don't remember it. The pretentiousness of the idea lends credibility. I used to go to a lot of debates at the Union, especially when Edward became President, having inherited this lofty position from Andrew Mitchell, last seen as the Ashdown House Stamp Club Secretary.

History of Art – in my case, the history of 18th- and 19th-century neoclassical and Gothic architecture – consisted largely of sitting in the dark watching slide shows of English country houses. I was taught by two great figures: David Watkin★ – a legendary don from Peterhouse, distinguished, dainty, the authority on Sir John Soane and champion of the fightback against modernist architectural dogma – and Gavin Stamp,† original model for the Young Fogey movement and a contributor to *Harpers & Queen*. On one occasion, I was travelling back

---

★ Architectural historian (1941–2018). *Morality and Architecture* (1977); *Radical Classicism: The Architecture of Quinlan Terry* (2006).

† Architectural biographer (1948–2017): Sir Edwin Lutyens, Alexander 'Greek' Thomson, George Gilbert Scott.

to Cambridge by train and quietly copy-editing the proofs of a
Gavin Stamp article for the magazine; further along the carriage, I spotted Gavin himself, correcting one of my essays. I
kept my head down.

Although I did shamefully little work for either of these
impressive scholars, I was certainly influenced by them, at least
up to a point. One of Dr Watkin's stranger initiatives was
screening the film *Triumph of the Will*, Leni Riefenstahl's 1935
propaganda movie showcasing the Nazi architecture of Albert
Speer, which he admired. My essays were generally delivered
late. I think I had a philosophical blind spot about researching
and writing long unpaid essays to be read aloud to an audience
of only one person – my supervisor – which was the Oxbridge
system. I preferred to write paid articles to appear in *Harpers*, for
an audience of 100,000.

Cambridge History of Architecture exams consisted in part
of writing short essays about photographs of country houses
and architectural details. You opened an envelope to find half a
dozen black and white pictures, labelled A–F. If you were
clever, you'd write: 'Picture A is the side facade of Chipstead
Hall, near Grantham, with portico by Robert Adam, wings by
Samuel Pepys Cockerell and a later neo-Gothic oriel window
by Norman Shaw . . .' and so forth.

If you were less clever, you wrote: 'This is a neoclassical
house, er, inspired by the Parthenon in Athens . . .'

As our Finals exam envelopes were handed round, we took a
quick shuffle, then turned to one of our friends and gave him a
cheery thumbs-up. He looked blank and confused.

Afterwards, we said, 'God, some people have all the luck.'

'Er, what do you mean?'

'Picture D . . .' (colossal pile in East Anglia).

He was none the wiser.

'It's your own house, isn't it?'

His face fell. 'Christ, that's embarrassing. Oh bloody hell . . .' Then he said, 'Actually, I do see where it is now: round the side, down near the kitchens. And in my defence, I haven't been down there for ages.'

During the holidays, I worked as an intern at *Harpers & Queen*, writing and sub-editing, enthralled by the inner workings of glossy magazines and the wider ecosystem of fashion, culture and society they showcased. My mentor at *Harpers*, to whom I owe so much, was the idiosyncratic Features Editor, Ann Barr – who had acquired my original unsolicited article, commissioned a dozen more and gave me work experience in the office.

I started dating a *Harpers & Queen* fashion editor, Sophie Hicks, who was wonderfully attractive in a gamine, boyish sort of way. She wore sailor suits and drove a Morris Traveller. She came to stay often at Cambridge, where she was strongly opposed to the custom of peeing in basins, and brought a dash of metrosexual glamour to the tweedy world which hung about the university.

Harpers & Queen was positioned in a particularly sweet spot at the time, in part because there was so little competition. Aside from *Vogue*, it had the upmarket all to itself. *Tatler* was moribund; *Elle, InStyle, Vanity Fair, Condé Nast Traveller, GQ, Esquire, The World of Interiors, Wallpaper** . . . none yet existed. The consumer and fashion boom of the eighties, which was to usher in the thirty-year golden period for glossy magazines, was still in its infancy, but already the glossies were fattening up with advertising. Not yet hemmed in by rival niche titles, *Harpers & Queen* could be all things to all women – and men too, the men's market not yet existing. Ann Barr gave me – the intern – a book of stories by Susan Sontag. Opening it at random, I found one which stated: 'Look at all this stuff I've got in my head: rockets and Venetian churches, David Bowie and Diderot, nuoc mam and Big Macs, sunglasses and orgasms . . .' It felt like a manifesto for *Harpers & Queen* itself – the intuitive, dysfunctional editorial alchemy which permitted political and sociological articles to exist alongside defiantly conventional ones, and treat them with equal value. Ann was only in her forties but to me she seemed ancient, with her dyed orange hair, deceptively dithery manner, Thea Porter jackets, velvet knickerbockers and concurrent admiration for intellectuals and Sloanes. She encouraged all types of disparate people to hang out in the office: drunks, punks, George Michael and Andrew Ridgeley from Wham! You never knew who'd show up.

She was a brilliant line editor; handing in an article, I would hover beside her at her desk as she read it. Her busy pen struck out superfluous adjectives, while she muttered, 'So much cleverness here. So clever, so *clever*. How do you even know all this?' She had a theory that every 'standfirst' (magazine introduction to an article) must contain a new or arresting fact. To Ann, an example of a bad standfirst would be: 'Best parties of 1978 – who came, who shone, who dazzled.' She preferred: 'Best parties of 1978 – the year charity ball inflation took tickets to £40 each for the first time.' If she felt uncertain as to whether a particular idea was any good, she rang her sister, Deirdre, in Kent for a second opinion. 'We'll see what Mrs Average thinks.' And then, 'Mrs Average says yes.'

The Editor of *Harpers & Queen* was Willie Landels, Italian, sophisticated and effete, an art director by background. He not only edited the magazine but laid it out; disdaining paragraph indentations as ugly, every article was 'ranged left', which looked chic on the page but was harder to read. Ann hated it. 'Willie isn't a reader,' she would fret. 'He *doesn't even read the articles*.' While Ann busied herself commissioning zeitgeisty articles and essays about Sloane Rangers, Willie took care of the fashion, decoration and design sections.

'Oh, my *God*,' he would declare in his camp Italian accent, 'I do dislike Ann's Sloanes . . . too awful for words, those people.'

I was once with Sophie Hicks in Venice, heading from the Giudecca to the Zattere on a vaporetto, and we spotted Willie and his wife, Angela, strolling along. Willie was thirty paces ahead, draped in a pashmina, cooling himself with a Chinese fan. Angela trudged along behind, laden with six heavy bags of groceries. I had never seen Willie so carefree.

Even as an intern, I realized that one had to take sides: you were either a Willie person or an Ann person. Peter York, Andrew Barrow, Paul Levy and a host of random contributors were Ann people; the fashion and beauty departments plus Loyd Grossman were Willie people. With Sophie a Willie person and me an Ann person, I just about managed both sides at once. Ann would grizzle, 'That Willie! He is so lazy, so lazy.' He wasn't, but she didn't see it.

A fellow intern, destined to become a great friend, was Alistair Scott. He was the son of two doctors from Leeds, and we hit it off at once. He was a vehement foodie, already intensely greedy aged twenty, and we hung out in Soho brasseries gossiping about journalism, Peter York and Wilfred De'Ath. (Alistair was harsher on our colleagues than me, but we both relished the process.)

One evening, lingering late over drinks in the office, Alistair became hungry. Finding no snacks available, he hit on the idea of raiding The *Good Housekeeping* Institute on the floor below – he had heard they possessed industrial-sized fridges and kitchens filled with grub. During the day, one regularly spotted *Good Housekeeping* cooks bustling to and fro outside their test kitchens, large women in white aprons, bearing dishes of food.

Ten minutes later, Alistair returned looking shifty. He was carrying a two-tier cream and marzipan gateau covered with maraschino cherries and candied lemon peel. We polished it off in one sitting.

The next morning, an enormous fuss erupted. A security guard repeatedly broadcast a message to all staff over the intercom. 'This is an important announcement . . . a fancy cake has disappeared from The *Good Housekeeping* Institute. It is required immediately for a photographic shoot. If anyone has any information regarding its whereabouts, please ring security.'

The foil cake base was still on our shared desk in plain sight, covered with crumbs. Panicking wildly, we wrapped it in newspaper and dumped it in a builder's skip several Soho streets away.

As Cambridge wore on, we moved rooms. James Stourton found another magnificent set in Thompson's Lane, which he painted Pompeiian red and commissioned a mural by Alan Powers★ of the sculpture gallery at Arundel Castle. It was officially unveiled at a launch party to which numerous ancient grandees were invited.

Kit Hunter Gordon had moved to a converted artist's studio off the Huntingdon Road, to which all our loveliest contemporaries were drawn in succession like bees to honey. It was envy-making. I, meanwhile, had moved to digs in Portugal Street, to a terraced house run by a retired Trinity porter, Mr Dunn. I shared it with Harry Eyres, a wine connoisseur. However inconspicuously you tried to enter or leave the house, there was Mr Dunn at the foot of the stairs, keen for a chat.

'Did I ever tell you,' he would ask, daily, 'about the time His

---

★ Cambridge contemporary. Author, expert on twentieth-century architecture. *Eric Ravilious: Imagined Realities* (2003).

Royal Highness the Prince of Wales came to take breakfast here in your very rooms?'

'Actually you have told me that excellent story, Mr Dunn.'

'Oh goodness me, what a day that was. Mrs Dunn prepared eggs, bacon, sausages, fried bread, mushrooms, a choice of tea or coffee, toast, marmalade . . . Normally, of course, Mrs Dunn doesn't do breakfasts, but this was for The Prince of Wales, of course.'

'How fantastic, Mr Dunn.'

'Oh yes, he was the breakfast guest of Lord Alexander Russell, who used to occupy your rooms . . .

'At the end of breakfast, The Prince of Wales turned to Mrs Dunn and said, "Thank you very much, Mrs Dunn, that was an excellent breakfast." '

I must have heard that story thirty times, quite feasibly fifty. Later in life, I became friends with Alexander Russell.* He wasn't, as it turned out, a Lord at all, but he confirms the breakfast menu.

Sophie Hicks became a participant in a *Harpers & Queen* article named 'Lifeswaps'. The idea was that ten people would trade their lives, jobs, homes, friends with somebody else for a month, and write about what it felt like being the other person. Sophie was to swap with Bob Colacello, the Editor of Andy Warhol's *Interview* magazine in New York, work with Andy at The Factory and inhabit his magnificent Manhattan apartment. Bob, in return, would get to live with Sophie's parents in Kensington, sleep in her narrow childhood bed, and spend weekends with her current beau, i.e. me.

The Lifeswap experiment coincided with the Trinity May

* Consultant, Sotheby's Europe. Car-wash executive. Married to Libby Manners, garden designer.

Ball to which I invited Bob as my partner. The dress code was white tie and tails, and he turned up looking as slick and oiled as a gigolo on a Hollywood red carpet.

Whether it was the sight of so many beautiful girls, or indeed beautiful boys in white tie, at the May Ball, or delayed jet lag, he hit the cocktails hard. Soon he was a liability. I realized I had to get Andy Warhol's right-hand dude out of there fast.

I gingerly drove him back to London in my dented yellow Ford Fiesta. As the journey unfolded, he became sleepy, resting his head against my shoulder, then dozing with his face in my lap, so it became hard to change gear. Arriving outside Sophie's house in Brunswick Gardens, I asked if he had his house key.

'It's in my trouser pocket . . . please help me find it.'

I fished away around his groin, and eventually retrieved it. Unlocking the door, I pushed him inside. As I pulled the door back shut, I heard Bob Colacello collapse onto the doormat, and the sound of violent retching.

My housemate, Harry Eyres,* was an exceptional scholar with a serious disposition. It was perhaps no surprise, then, that he was approached one day by a particular don, and sounded out to become a spy in MI6. Trinity was a rich recruiting ground, and Harry had a first-class brain. Over drinks that night, he told me what had taken place and swore me to secrecy.

I respected the spirit of his confidence by telling only one other person, Edward Stourton, who was a model of discretion, telling only a couple more. We all loved the idea of Harry as James Bond, heavily disguised as a spice salesman in Istanbul keeping watch on the Soviet Embassy. Within a week, the news went viral, everyone knew. The recruiter don withdrew his job overture.

---

* Journalist, writer, poet. 'Slow Lane' columnist, *Financial Times* (2004–15).

Several vacations I spent travelling in Eastern Turkey with John Scott; we did four long trips in all, hitch-hiking from Diyarbakir to Lake Van, Kars and Trabzon. Crossing the plain of Troy in a tinny white hire car, we were pursued for five miles by a giant, loping sheepdog, half wolf, half mastiff. It eventually bounded onto the bonnet of the car, snarling and frothing from its jaws, and cracked the windscreen with the iron spikes of its collar, before eventually limping off.

Other holidays, I went to Venice with Sophie, to stay with Rupert Forbes Adam in the burnt-out shell of the Palazzo Dario on the Grand Canal, where he lived with his girlfriend Anya Hillman, a reformed groupie for The Byrds. From the top floor, the palazzo had the finest view of the canal in the city, directly opposite the Gritti Palace hotel. We used to dance vigorously to a track called 'Lucky Number' by Lene Lovich, with the windows wide open and the volume turned up to maximum. ('I'm having so much fun / My lucky number's one / Ah! Oh! Ah! Oh!') It must have been intensely annoying for the gondoliers down below, and the Gritti guests opposite, trying to sleep.

While in Paris, Rupert Forbes Adam took Craig Brown, John and me to lunch with Diana Mosley at the Temple de la Gloire. She was one of the Mitford girls and widow of Rupert's grandfather, Sir Oswald Mosley, the brown-shirted leader of the British Union of Fascists. Within the curtilage of its walls, the Temple was the most beautiful place I had ever visited: a Palladian folly near Orsay, their exquisite place of exile. Diana Mosley could have been any charming aristocratic widow of a certain vintage. She questioned us sweetly about school and university, and spoke about her sisters Nancy, Debo and Unity growing up in Oxfordshire, and how she used to keep her own hand cream in the ladies' powder room at Claridge's. On a table in the blue-painted sitting room was a wedding photograph of the Mosleys' wedding, held at the home of Joseph Goebbels, with Adolf Hitler gracing the line-up. When we departed, she stood on the front steps to wave us off, flanked by a butler and a sinister manservant in beige linen jackets.

My back and slipped disc, damaged in Yazd, continued to give me pain, especially in cold weather, and I hobbled around Cambridge with a stick when the Siberian winds blew in. Sometimes it was fine for months, then the sciatic nerve became inflamed, and it was torture.

One such attack coincided with my Finals and I was rushed to the Edward VII hospital, injected with painkillers and put in traction. Unable to sit all my exams, there was some doubt over whether or not I would be awarded a degree. My college tutor rang the four dons who had taught me, to get their take on my likely grade, and it was unfortunate that two of them had never met me at all, since I'd skipped all their supervisions.

Fortunately, I had completed my dissertation, written in the National Art Library at the Victoria and Albert Museum, on the subject of the eighteenth-century Indian paintings of Thomas and William Daniell, and their influence upon Mughal-neoclassical architecture in England at Sezincote, Daylesford and the Brighton Pavilion.

After some anguished discussion, I was given an aegrotat degree (aegrotat being the smart word for 'sick note'). To this day, I don't actually know if I'm a BA or an MA.

My friends joked that the slipped disc was lucky timing, as a means of avoiding Finals. Fortunately, I had conclusive X-rays of my back as collateral. It was just as well.

But, by now, I was craving to get on with life as a journalist, and Cambridge and degrees already felt like stale news.

6.

Tina Brown was not yet The World's Most Famous Magazine Editor she was destined to become, but I had been reading her pieces for several years in newspapers and admired her. The week I left Cambridge, I spotted in the *Evening Standard* her appointment as the new Editor of *Tatler*, and I needed a job. I applied at once. I was interviewed at the terraced house she shared with her boyfriend, Harry Evans, Editor of the *Sunday Times*.

We sat in her kitchen. Tina was twenty-seven: blonde, foxy, watchful. Spread out on the table between us were thirty or so party photographs, taken at the recent eighteenth birthday party of the Duke of Rutland's daughter Lady Theresa Manners at Belvoir Castle. Peering at the pictures through a loupe, Tina asked, 'Do you know who any of these chinless characters are?'

I did. 'Actually I was at that party.'

'I need a headline,' she said. It was a test. 'Something snappy.'

'Saturday Night Belvoir?'

I was hired on the spot. (Note: the headline 'Saturday Night Belvoir' is a near-perfect example of early eighties glossy magazine wit, being both a pun on a recent film title and deliciously excluding. Only in-the-know readers who realize that Belvoir Castle is pronounced 'Beaver' and not 'Bellvoir' would get it. So at least half the paying audience would miss the joke, and the in-crowd feel smug. Which was the implicit editorial mission.)

Tina was wisely conducting her interviews at home, thus preventing applicants from encountering the *Tatler* offices until it was already too late. Lurking behind an impressive heritage address at

15 Berkeley Street, a stone's throw from the Ritz, were offices of unmatched decrepitude. You went up to the fourth floor in a jerking, pre-war lift with brass gates, walked up a further flight, passed by the offices of a debt collecting agency, and entered the tiny sloping catacomb that was *Tatler*'s global headquarters.

Tina occupied a windowless Editor's Office at the back, the other ten of us hunkered down at a mishmash of Edwardian school desks with antique Bakelite telephones and forty-year-old editions of *Debrett's* and *Who's Who*. It didn't require the services of an actuary to figure out that *Tatler* was teetering on the brink of bankruptcy. In actual fact, the magazine had been fighting for survival ever since it had been launched in 1709 by the Irish playwright Richard Steele in a St James coffee house. Every previous proprietor lost money, year after year, century upon century, until they gave up the fight and sold it on. Successions of aristocrats, industrialists, social climbers: all had a crack. Perhaps they reckoned there was some social cachet attached to being the publisher of *The Tatler & Bystander*, though looking around the offices it was impossible to say what. Elton John's manager, John Reid, had been a recent transient owner; the current proprietors were a claret-faced flâneur named John Elliott and a tiny, wiry Australian property tycoon, Gary Bogard, who had recently moved to London, bought Mozart's house in Ebury Street and been sold shares in the magazine. To have joined Tina's *Tatler* as Associate Editor at this hour was the luckiest break imaginable.

On my first morning in Berkeley Street, a photographer from the *Evening Standard* arrived to take a picture of Tina's New Team. We were a ramshackle bunch: Tina herself, glamorous in the front row; Georgina Howell, fresh out of *Vogue*, standing birdlike and anxious at her side; Michael Roberts, the louche fashion director, with a cynical glint in his eye; me looking oddly like an Arab terrorist with staring deep-set eye sockets. A selection of adorable Surrey secretaries, journalist deadbeats and borderline-bonkers paste-up artists completed the troupe.

Tina gave the assembled team her vision for the new-look *Tatler*: out would go photographs of galloping majors at point-to-points and hunt balls, out would go the wedding portraits of pudding-faced Herefordshire debutantes; also for the chop were pictures of glass-eyed backbench MPs at the annual parliamentarians' tug-of-war (then an annual *Tatler* fixture), and anything else elderly, dowdy or staid.

Instead . . . readers would be treated to sexy London 'It' girls, philandering men about town, disgraced dukes, libidinous novelists, upwardly mobile hostesses and knighted thespians. The new cast of characters was to hover somewhere between the scurrilous end of *Burke's Peerage* and Nigel Dempster's *Daily Mail* Diary.

'It's an upper-class comic,' declared Tina.

We shuffled out of Tina's office (in my case with a distinct spring in my step) to encounter an unseemly fracas in the lobby. A disgruntled former contributor had turned up, wearing a trilby, claiming not to have been paid for an article he'd written several years previously about racehorse genealogy. He had been wrangling for a cheque ever since. Joining him in the queue of debtors were both our printer and paper supplier, threatening to withdraw their services.

Tina, meanwhile, was planning a no-expense-spared relaunch party at the Ritz, to which 700 of Britain's Most Wanted were invited. It was a spectacular gathering with wall-to-wall duchesses, newspaper editors and pretty girls; still the benchmark recipe for a successful *Tatler* party.

My job description soon accrued three distinct duties. The first was to write at least four articles a month, under multiple pseudonyms. Unable to pay many outside contributors, I would write two under my own name, then several more as Marcus von Trout, Harry Haviland, Percy Peverel and so forth. After the painstaking fact-checked pieces I'd done for *Harpers & Queen*, it was fun to speed-write *Tatler* articles with buccaneering brio. Tina Brown had the shortest attention span of anyone I'd met. She would commission an article but be bored of the idea long before it was delivered; I quickly learnt to file copy only on deadline, so she didn't become tired of it. I learnt from Tina that to be boring was the cardinal sin: an article had to grab you from the first paragraph and hold on to you. Some magazine writers (particularly when writing cultural profiles) feel obliged to insert italicized paragraphs of their subject's CV in the middle – lists of books, lists of films. Tina struck out everything that wasn't fun. I wrote articles for her in those days with titles like 'Villa Bodies – the most comfortable and uncomfortable private holiday villas in the world'. The owners of the so-called uncomfortable ones were enraged. 'You haven't even visited our villa in Corfu,' they thundered, entirely reasonably. 'And never will either!'

Tina loved it. We christened it 'shoot-from-the-hip journalism'.

My second role was to sell the review copies of books for cash. *Tatler* was sent numerous expensive art volumes, and these we augmented by ringing round the book publishers and pretending we were planning a big feature on the best new illustrated books. They would courier these round on motorbikes. My job was to take them by taxi to a second-hand bookshop named D. Levin of Grape Street in Covent Garden, and flog six large boxes of them. The £300 of cash I would hand to Tina, who passed it straight to the novelist Julian Barnes, our restaurant critic, who spent it on reviewing Langan's Brasserie or The Savoy Grill.

My final task was to personally collect the monthly column

of Margaret, Duchess of Argyll, who lived all alone in a rococo-and-chintz service flat in the Grosvenor House hotel. She was still notorious as the protagonist in the 1963 'headless man' scandal, when she'd been photographed through a keyhole performing a sexual favour on an unnamed gentleman with an obscured face, but visible dick, in the drawing room of Inveraray Castle. *Tatler* was rehabilitating her reputation by commissioning a social column of unparalleled drivel, named 'Steppin' out with the Duchess of Argyll'.

Each visit, I was made to sit alongside her on a sofa, while I copy-tasted (speed-read) her latest effort. Her blind French poodle, Alphonse, perched on the other side, snuffling.

The Duchess sat disconcertingly close, leaning across to ensure I'd fully appreciated some witticism or name-drop, though the column was sadly short on both. Her claw-like hand rested on my knee.

'One evening when you have more time, we must drink cocktails together in the suite,' she murmured.

Although the dramatic turnaround of *Tatler*'s fortunes is now the stuff of legend, it is a miracle it survived at all. The first eight issues weren't much good and the queue of creditors grew longer. A new accountant named Bill Pickup (actual name) was hired to do precisely the opposite; he seldom picked up any invoice if he could avoid it. As the roster of contributors and photographers grew starrier and more distinguished, embarrassment increased. Michael Roberts specialized in writing caustic 'spinelines' (the motto along the binding of a magazine): '*Tatler* – the magazine that bites the hand that feeds it.'

So ashamed were we of the issues in the early days that we lived in a bubble, having dinner together most nights at San Lorenzo or Mr Chow, often with the Turkish designer Rifat Özbek, and Nadia and Swami La Valle who owned the Spaghetti boutique on Beauchamp Place. We drank Bloody Marys by the gallon, and ate bowls of *crudités con bagna cauda* (raw vegetables with anchovy sauce). My school friend Napier Miles was frequently part of these outings too, bringing his own misanthropic perspective to the scene.

My relationship with Tina hovered somewhere between teenage crush and low-level terror. She was mesmerizingly witty and sweetly ruthless. Her editorial yardstick was whether or not a contributor 'delivered' – nothing to do with the physical 'delivery' of an article, but whether the copy 'delivered' punch, caused trouble, stitched up the subject, betrayed confidences. If you could deliver what Tina wanted, you basked for a while in the gorgeous, almost sexual glow of her approval; if you didn't or couldn't, you quickly disappeared like a member of Idi Amin's cabinet floating face down in Lake Bugondo. Failures were kissed off with the phrase 'he's a busted flush'. As more senior staff members disappeared, I rose in the vacuum. At editorial conferences, we competed to suggest stories to delight Tina, the more lascivious the better: British dukes with the biggest dicks . . . posh wives who had started life as escort girls . . . the most unctuous royal courtiers. Poor, high-minded Georgina Howell, hired to propose cultural articles, would say, 'Bridget Riley has a retrospective of her stripe paintings coming up at the Tate. Should we perhaps photograph her artist's studio?' And the rest of us would roll our eyes, and cut in, 'Hey, Tina, what about a piece called "Hot Cross Nuns" about the sexiest nuns at Catholic convent schools, St Mary's Ascot, et cetera? An alternative title could be "Dirty Habits".'

I had moved out from home to a tiny basement flat in Chelsea, off the King's Road, at 57a Radnor Walk. It was eccentrically arranged, in that the only way to reach the kitchen was through the bedroom, though this was actually convenient, since I seldom cooked. Two doors away was a perpetually empty Italian restaurant, San Quintino (now the perpetually full Ziani's). I would ring through my supper order, and a waiter traipsed down the basement steps to my flat carrying a plate of lamb cutlets, mashed potato and peas, which I ate in bed. I was allowed to pay the next time I was in the restaurant.

In the sitting room, Michael Howells★ painted a mural of a neo-Egyptian fireplace with sphinxes, with faux party invitations and spoof wedding invitations painted along the top. A giant pop art canvas by Duggie Fields, of French hookers and sailors, completed the look.

The Embassy Club had opened on Bond Street and this became my number-one hangout; it appeared to own only one record – Donna Summer's 'I Feel Love' – which was played over and over again. I've always been a bit of a 'two restaurants person', going to the same ones all the time, and these were Eleven Park Walk (chrome-chaired Italian) and Foxtrot Oscar (club dive on Royal Hospital Road). At weekends, I headed home to Sussex, still the focus of family life, where my father mixed big jugs of Bloody Mary for his elder sons. My brother Timmy was working as a names agent at Lloyd's and playing low goal polo at Kirtlington; our cheerful 'afterthought' brother, Christopher, now aged eight, was at a prep school in West Sussex, and kept everyone young and amused with his jokes.

Tatler's finances remained precarious. I flew to Florence to interview the aesthete Sir Harold Acton† at the Villa La Pietra,

---

★ Production designer (1957–2018) for John Galliano at Dior, Jean-Paul Gaultier, Christian Lacroix. TV and ballet designer: Ballet Rambert, ITV's *Victoria* (2016).

† Scholar, aesthete (1904–94). *The Last Medici* (1932); *The House of Bourbon* (2 volumes, 1956–61).

with strict instructions to spend as little money as possible. I stayed the night in a YMCA next to the railway station and met up at lunchtime with Joan Haslip,★ the very grand historical novelist, who was to escort me to her friend Harold Acton's Renaissance palace.

'I have booked a table at rather a lovely restaurant,' she declared. 'It's *very spoiling*, but we *are* on the *Tatler*'s expenses.'

She ordered three courses, the most expensive on the menu. 'Ah, white asparagus and truffles . . . and a peach Bellini . . . and do I espy the first wild raspberries of summer over there on the trolley? I'm sorry, I cannot resist. After all, we are on the *Tatler*'s expenses . . .'

I ordered the cheapest pasta and a glass of San Pellegrino, praying I had sufficient lire to pay the bill. I did, but only just, so left no tip. A phalanx of waiters glared mulishly at the door.

It was during this period that I first encountered Nicky Haslam, the celebrity decorator, wit and tastemaker. Initially I found him an alarming figure, omnipresent, impossibly well connected, razor-sharp, judgemental. Tina Brown and Michael Roberts worked him up as a figure of fun in the office, and he appeared as a regular walk-on part in *Tatler* articles of the period. Nicky was particularly furious at a '*Tatler* Christmas Panto-mime' feature, written in rhyming couplets, featuring him as the Fairy Godmother.

With Sophie Hicks, I used to visit his eighteenth-century folly near Odiham in Hampshire, The Hunting Lodge, the for-mer home of John Fowler. I remember always feeling slightly wrongly dressed for lunch there, either too smart or not quite smart enough or insufficiently cool. His lunches were filled with

★ Popular author specializing in historical novels about European royalty: Lucrezia Borgia, Marie Antoinette, Catherine the Great.

people named Guinness or Lambton (generally several of each) and I didn't yet know how they all slotted together.

Nicky vaguely resembled Liberace, with bouffant grey hair, simultaneously louche and proper. This was long before his various Bowie-style transformations and reinventions of his appearance, from Noel Gallagher to Oliver Twist, which has made him seem younger and younger with each passing decade. Over time, he became someone I liked a lot, and whose advice, when I sought it about magazines and life, was invariably right. Whenever I spot him at a party, which is often, I brighten up.

I wrote an article for *Tatler* about the Tsarist Russian scene in London, which led to a particularly surreal legal action. Somewhere in my piece, I had interviewed a Russian doctor named Dr Gherkin, a St Petersburg émigrée, whom I referred to as 'Dr Gherkin (pronounced *gherkin*)'. A long and furious solicitor's letter arrived, protesting that their client was most certainly not pronounced gherkin, and demanding a retraction and suitable compensation. Letters were exchanged back and forth for several months. Then, one day, her solicitor muddled up his post, and we were mistakenly sent a letter intended for Dr Gherkin. It read 'Dr Gherkin, we do not recommend making too much of the pronunciation issue, since we understand that your name is, in fact, pronounced gherkin.' The Gherkin-not-pronounced-gherkin episode petered out at this point.

Meanwhile, in the parallel world of illusion, *Tatler* parties became ever more frequent and glamorous. Minor royals, major tycoons, nightclub greeters, social astronauts, posh teenagers and serial seducers like Dai Llewellyn, Sir William Pigott-Brown and Rupert Deen defined the guest list. *Tatler* was buzzing.

It still sold shockingly few copies, but the advertising department spun it as a slam-dunk success, and so it was perceived. Tina wrote a pseudonymous column, 'Rosie Boot's Guide to

London Bachelors', and returned from these lunchtime encounters with playboys fired up with disparaging descriptions; she had a theory that dull men invariably order cheese soufflé, the preparation of which entailed an additional twenty-five minutes in their company.

It was the arrival of Lady Diana Spencer on the scene which finally saved *Tatler*. Her combination of London Sloane, Northamptonshire blue-blood and princess-designate played to all the magazine's core competencies at once.

A special *Sunday Times*-style *Tatler* Insight team was set up at a designated Diana desk, with every detail about Lady Di amassed and tabulated. I was proud to serve on it.

The Coleherne Court mansion flat, where she lived with her three flatmates, was permanently staked out by *Tatler* staff, her hairdressers, school friends, car mechanic, dry cleaners, a local newsagent, all ruthlessly monitored. As the whole world yearned for more and more Diana Spencer information, *Tatler* become the go-to source. My 5,000-word article on the 'Lady Diana Set' began: 'There are still a few girls left in Britain who haven't been to bed with Jasper Guinness and all of them are friends of Lady Diana Spencer.' It was a good example of the sort of knowing, insider, slightly irritating writing style we all relished.

Circulation soared. The magazine was suddenly the toast of the town. Assigned to cover the royal wedding at St Paul's, I was driven the entire route from Buckingham Palace to the cathedral by Sophie in a chauffeur's cap in her yellow open-topped jeep, while a million jubilant spectators waved Union Jack flags at us.

The *Tatler* party was truly rocking . . . which is always the perfect moment to slip away.

7

It is rare to get two job offers in one evening, but that is what happened.

An *Evening Standard* friend, the gossip columnist Richard Compton-Miller, known as 'The Brompton Gorilla', asked me to dinner at his Fernshaw Road flat. The Editor of the newspaper, Louis Kirby, was also a guest that night, as was the paper's famously camp astrologer, Patric Walker, who wrote the horoscope. I hit it off with both of them.

Louis Kirby was a textbook newspaper man: gritty, northern, a production technician who could design pages, write headlines to fit, turn stories around in a heartbeat. He was very charming. He had recently moved from the *Evening News* to take over the editorship of the *Standard* from Charles Wintour (father of Anna Wintour, later of American *Vogue*). He was in hiring mode.

At some point over supper, he said, 'You should write a column for us, Nick.' He was typically precise. 'What I'm looking for is a Monday column to fill the centre double-spread. A bit of fun, surprising, man-about-town stuff, stunts to entertain the commuters. Bags of personality and bravado. Let's say an eighteen-hundred-word main piece, a secondary story of five hundred words, then a foot-of-page teaser of, shall we say, a hundred to a hundred and fifty words. Your audience will be three million Londoners.'

He mentioned money and it sounded agreeably more than *Tatler*.

I was heading home after dinner when Patric Walker said, 'Nicholas, this may sound crazy, but I've received a message from above. From the planets. We can't speak here, but drive me to my hotel, sweetie, I'd like to buy you a nightcap . . .'

I drove him to Mayfair, to a chi-chi boutique hotel on Chesterfield Street. 'Come sit in the snug,' he said. 'It's cosy. We won't be disturbed.' He ordered whiskies.

Patric was the most celebrated and successful astrologer in the world, his daily horoscopes syndicated from Hong Kong to the States, earning him millions; he was regarded by devotees as uncannily perceptive. He was tall, mannered and confiding, with the suspicion of a comb-over about his hairline.

'Listen, Nicholas,' he said, edging closer. 'I don't mean to alarm you, but I've had a message from my celestial guides. It came during dinner. You are going to be my successor, my disciple and my heir.'

'Goodness,' I said. 'I don't really read horoscopes.'

'What is your star sign, Nicholas?'

'Er, Pisces.'

'Of course, I knew it. Your lack of knowledge doesn't concern me, I can teach you. You will inherit my books, my astrological library. And eventually my business. You will come with me to Greece, to Lindos where I have a house, and I shall teach you everything . . .'

Probably Patric knew my decision already, and I joined the *Evening Standard* the next month.

The Black Lubyanka building at 120 Fleet Street (now headquarters of Goldman Sachs) was the same building in which I'd been interviewed six years earlier by Sir John Junor; it had not changed one bit in the meantime. Tea boys still rattled trolleys along corridors reeking of printer's ink.

The editorial floor of the *Standard* was immense, with several hundred journalists bent over typewriters or monitoring juddering telex machines. I was ushered to a chair at a bank of desks where Max Hastings was composing an op-ed at breakneck speed. Across the room I could see Milton Shulman banging out a theatre review, the Londoner's Diary team transcribing titbits of gossip over the phone from paid informants and, in the far distance, the City and Sports desks.

The literary editor, Valerie Grove, took me on a brief tour, and attempted to introduce me to a semi-retired features executive named Marius Pope, who was slumped over his desk, head in his hands. 'He's asleep,' Valerie said. 'It's normal, you'll meet him later. After lunch at El Vino's.'

Returning from lunch, Marius hadn't moved an inch.

'Marius? Marius?' said Valerie. '*Marius?*' Now she was concerned. '*Oh no* . . .'

Marius had suffered a massive coronary five hours earlier, after breakfast. He was heaved away on a stretcher by several burly men from the post room.

I believe he recovered.

Three days to go before my first column, I still had no idea what to write. With typical hyperbole, the paper was already trailing their new hire ('This brilliant, fresh, 23-year-old talent'), which made things much worse. I was sick with lack of inspiration. The centre pages loomed empty as the Sahara. I walked round and round my flat, sometimes kicking the sofa, with not one decent idea for a debut column. Periodically, a features person from the paper would ring, asking, 'Any idea what your first splash is about? Picture desk is asking.' It was terrifying.

At the eleventh hour, a brainwave. The next night was Prince Andrew's twenty-first birthday ball at Windsor Castle. A few friends were invited to it, but what intrigued me was the simultaneous 'Chauffeurs' party' that the royals were putting on for guests' drivers, taking place in the cellars beneath the castle.

A friend agreed to sneak me in as their chauffeur, and I borrowed a uniform and peaked cap from my father's driver at Lloyd's. No one batted an eyelid as I deposited three pretty girls in puffball dresses at the castle door.

The cellar was thronged with chauffeurs, holding their caps in one hand, soft drinks in the other. Some of the caps had plumes. Several drivers wore knickerbockers. A lavish buffet featuring pork pies, sausage rolls, coleslaw and potato salad was on offer. Distantly, you could hear the discotheque from the ball. 'Making Your Mind Up' by Bucks Fizz.

Nonchalantly, I struck up conversations with my fellow drivers. This one drove the Duke of Here, that one drove the Earl of There. Others drove foreign heads of state, ambassadors, tycoons, Grade II royals and celebrities.

'I don't think much of the spread, do you?' said one. 'I'll bet they're doing better for themselves upstairs, it'll be champagne and lobster all the way up there.'

It is amazing what insights you can garner from a cellar full of chauffeurs as they gossiped and carped about their bosses. It made for electrifying copy. As I left the ball at 4.30 a.m. to deliver my passengers home, I remember thinking: well, that's week one in the can. What on earth is next week's column?

For the next four years, I somehow managed to fill the space, often by the skin of my teeth. Happiness was having ideas for two weeks in advance; the opposite was agony. Louis Kirby and his two features chiefs, Dick Garratt and Nigel Turner, loved stunt journalism, so I arrived at casinos dressed as an Arab sheikh in flowing robes, to test the reaction at the roulette table, or worked as a waiter in San Lorenzo to discover which celebrities left the best or worst tips (Dustin Hoffman was a generous tip-per, I do remember that).

Another column involved turning up at poetry clubs in Earl's Court and Fitzrovia, clutching my intentionally bad verse, and seeing what the other thirty attendees thought of it (they loved it – 'so sensitive').

The department which wrote the *Evening Standard*'s bill-boards at the station kiosks came up with a cringeworthy new slogan: 'NICHOLAS COLERIDGE EVERY MONDAY – the man who gets under the skin of London living.' It sounded like a virus. Luckily they soon dropped it.

An abuse scandal broke out at a boarding school in Suffolk, run by a sadistic-sounding headmaster with a fat, sweaty face. I think the *News of the World* had exposed the story, and parents were urgently withdrawing their children from the place; every newspaper in Fleet Street was desperate for an interview with the Head. Unsurprisingly, he wasn't talking.

I had the idea of ringing the Admissions Office and pretend-ing I wanted to put my nephews down for the school, and please could we look round. I took a friend, Lily Johnson, disguised as my wife, with a borrowed wedding ring. The school was excited at the prospect of new pupils, since their numbers were in free fall.

We arrived at the school gates and were pleased to be waved in, past an encampment of rival journalists from the *Daily Tele-graph* and *The Times* dawdling about outside. It was the grimmest of schools, popular with the sons of army sergeants posted overseas. Our tour culminated in an audience with the Head in his study, a bull of a man in a pinstripe suit. His lardy, jowly face encased lips with an unpleasant curl to them. The room was alleged to be the setting for monstrous beatings and mistreatment.

By this time, we had refined our cover story. I explained that my elder brother and sister-in-law had died in a recent car accident, leaving my wife and I with unwelcome responsibility for my nephews. It was vital they went to boarding school without delay. Wife Lily nodded along.

I added, 'I did notice some nonsense in the newspapers, which I'm sure is very much exaggerated, in the irresponsible way these journalists behave. It occurred to me you might have vacancies for two chaps, they're nine and eleven. To start next week.'

The headmaster was only too pleased to offer places, sight unseen. He also had plenty to say about discipline, self-reliance and the mollycoddling of children. I encouraged him with my questions, but was terrified that at any moment our cover would be blown. His hatchet-faced secretary had been glaring at Lily on the way in, and I felt she might have seen through us. By the time we departed, we were sweating, and the secretary tried to sting me for a term's school fees up front.

My article, titled 'The day I put my boys down for St Whacko's' was a great scoop. The Head resigned soon afterwards.

As fate would have it, I was mooching about in an antiques shop in Pimlico a month or two later when, to my horror, the headmaster of St Whacko's entered the shop. We stared at each other. His eyes bulged with fury. 'You!' he bellowed. '*You!*'

He began chasing me round the Georgian chairs and marquetry tables. He was like Spode from *Jeeves and Wooster*. Fortunately, the owner appeared out of his back office, and I sped swiftly away.

As an occupation for your early twenties, a column on the *Evening Standard* was hard to beat. I briefly became quite famous amongst the taxi driver community, who were heavy readers of the newspaper and, it seemed, my principal audience.

Meanwhile, the features editors and copy editors taught me

tricks of the trade. One was to remove the word 'that' when-ever possible from every sentence. 'He knew that the Queen was attending.' The 'that' adds nothing, they insisted: it's a road block, slowing the reader down. I still do regular 'that' checks.

My London life centred around my old school and university gang, plus various alluring new girls like Nicky Shulman,★ Evgenia Citkowitz and Amanda Grieve,† witty and pretty, who got photographed all the time for *Vogue* and were dated by my friends in rotation. Sometimes I dated dangerous magazine girls, sometimes I dated endearing, loyal Sloanes. I don't think I ever knew which of these options I preferred, each speaking to a different part of my personality. Perhaps I still don't.

I developed a hopeless crush on Evgenia, boho daughter of the novelist Lady Caroline Blackwood, who was seventeen and had the most beautiful soulful eyes. *Tatler* had described her as having 'a mouth like a bruised peach'. When you took her out to dinner, she barely spoke a word, just stared at you dolefully, obliging you to do all the talking yourself, like a visit to the psychiatrist. She must have found my constant chatter oppres-sive because she once slipped off to the restaurant loo in the middle of dinner, clambered out of a back window onto a Ful-ham mews, and escaped home by cab. It was twenty minutes before I began to wonder where she had got to. A search party was sent to look for her. Eventually a waiter reported, 'The kitchen porter, he saw the lady climb out of window, she gone.' Demoralizing at the time.

★ Biographer, journalist. *A Rage for Rock Gardening* (2002); *Graven with Dia-monds* (2011). Married to 1. Edward St Aubyn, 2. Marquess of Normanby.
† Creative consultant associated with John Galliano, Karl Lagerfeld. Mar-ried Francis Ormsby-Gore, Lord Harlech.

Evgenia wrote an adorable letter the next day, explaining she'd simply run out of conversation and was embarrassed.

My friend Napier Miles, who had lost an eye in a skiing accident and wore a black eyepatch, cut a dashing figure. His cheek was slightly scarred, like a duelling gash, and he cultivated a world-weary cynicism. He had a flat in Flood Street, round the corner from mine in Radnor Walk, and we hung out at bars and nightclubs like Zanzibar and The Titanic several times a month, and had dinner together incessantly, generally at Foxtrot Oscar in Royal Hospital Road or at Ziani's. It remained our custom to analyse and dissect the characters of the various girls we liked – Evgenia, Nicky, Amanda, Sophie, Nenna Eberstadt,★ Flora Fraser† and some others. Periodically, Napier would exclaim, 'Aaaah, *bloody women*!' and shake his head and grimace, as if suddenly recalling some romantic disappointment. I found these dinners intensely enjoyable. By tradition, Napier drank whisky and ginger ale, and we both drank sambuca.

Sometimes we visited a girlie dive in Soho, the Pinstripe Club on Beak Street, where pay-as-you-go hostesses, many of them achingly beautiful and from Wolverhampton, made themselves friendly over bottles of extortionately priced champagne. Our purpose was fun, bravado and, I think, an impetus to encounter a different cast of women. The girls at the Pinstripe were mostly called Kelly or Scarlett. The girls were trained to ask, 'Mind if I order cigarettes, I've just smoked my last one?'

'Sure, that's fine.'

When the bill arrived, you discovered they'd ordered a carton of 400 Marlboro and a bouncer with a broken nose was standing over you, ensuring you paid up.

★ American novelist. *Low Tide* (1985); *The Furies* (2003).
† Biographer: Emma Hamilton, Pauline Bonaparte.

I wonder what the sexy hostesses thought of Napier and me in their club? We were aged twenty-four or twenty-five. The other customers were thirty years older and from out of town, attenders of business conferences on the razzle. Men from Manchester and Preston, who had heard about the Pinstripe Club from their hotel concierges. What did Kelly and Scarlett really think of us? Probably they found us ridiculously naive and circumspect. And a novelty. And perhaps they cut us some slack for being young and funny. The Pinstripe Club has long gone. It has become an eco-health shop now.

With Napier, I went to stay in a riad in the Ourika valley outside Marrakech, belonging to a cousin of his, the aesthete and antiques dealer Christopher Gibbs. The house lay in the foothills of the Atlas Mountains, with a steep ravine on one side and views across an endless, empty Berber plain. All day we lounged on the flat roof, wearing dressing gowns and fezzes, eating oranges. The house came with a major-domo named Moulai Kabir, a grand housekeeper who had only two occupations. By day, he tried incessantly to sell us Moroccan slippers supplied by his family; by night, he noisily seduced the cook, Fatima, in the adjacent kitchen. ('Fatima, oh Fatima. Come to me, Fatima . . .' and so on.)

Tokyo Joe's, a shiny new Mayfair club where Charles Finch★ and my friend Kathryn Ireland† ran the guest list, was another haunt. It played 'Celebration' by Kool & The Gang on a loop: 'Celebrate good times . . . *come on! Let's celebrate.*' As a PR stunt for the club, Charles and Kathryn became engaged to be married, which secured a useful plug in Londoner's Diary but was a

---

★ Public relations expert, film producer. Son of Hollywood actor Peter Finch.
† Los Angeles-based interiors and textiles designer. Presenter, *Million Dollar Decorators*.

shock to Kathryn's mother when she read about it in the evening paper.

London in the mid-eighties was emerging from a protracted recession which had lasted more than a decade. You could see the change everywhere: new restaurants springing up, Italian and French designer labels brought to Bond Street and Sloane Street by fashion entrepreneurs, everything in the world I inhabited felt shinier and glossier, magazines thicker in pagination and advertising. A new type of charity ball was invented, some with punning names like the Snow Ball and the Abomni-Ball, and others to raise funds for military escapades overseas: the Falklands Ball, the Freedom Ball and the Afghan Ball (we were supporting the Taliban against Soviet Russia at the time).

The *Evening Standard*'s Londoner's Diary gossip desk, with its staff of about a dozen hacks, was positioned close to my own desk at the newspaper. It became a bone of contention that I didn't feed enough stories to the diary, and at least once a week the diary editor would mince over and ask, 'Any juice for us? It's been a while . . .'

One evening I went to a soirée in Tite Street given by Lady Melchett, our old Porto Ercole saviour. The first-floor drawing room was jam-packed with politicians, authors and TV stars, including many of the protagonists in the prevailing TV-am saga, when the five famous anchor-people at the breakfast TV station had been abruptly fired by the Chief Executive, Jonathan Aitken MP, and replaced by the glove puppet Roland Rat. At Sonia's party, Anna Ford (one of the Famous Five) suddenly and dramatically threw a glass of wine in Aitken's face, in a moment of furious revenge.

The next morning, I went into the *Evening Standard* as usual. As I strolled past the Londoner's Diary desk, I mentioned, 'Here's something which might possibly make an item for you . . .'

Within seconds, pandemonium had broken out. Three news reporters were gathered round my desk, notebooks in hand. The Editor was clearing the front page, the cartoonist JAK was starting again. Within an hour, pages 1, 3, 4, 5, 6, 7, 12, 15, the leader, the cartoon, all were devoted to Anna Ford's coup de théâtre. The women's section contributed an instant article on how to remove red wine from a suit. The courtroom artist produced an impression of Sonia's drawing room, complete with guests, sofas and the mid-stream wine.

I was never sure whether to be proud of my scoop, or embarrassed to have been so casual in passing it on.

My Radnor Walk flat took a leap upmarket with the employment of a cleaner. My first charlady was the actor Rupert Everett,* the second the fashion stylist Joe McKenna.† Neither was much good at housework. I would return home to find the telephone dragged to the full extent of its cord to my bedside, and a deep hollow on the bedspread where they'd been gossiping on the phone. I assumed to LA.

My friend Pandora Stevens, along with so many others at the time, became addicted to drugs. Nick Allan and I used to drive to visit her at a rehabilitation clinic named Broadway Lodge in Weston-super-Mare, where she was trying to kick the habit. On visits, we were made to join 'family and friends group counselling sessions', with twenty-five visitors and inmates sitting in a glum circle on plastic chairs.

'Please tell Pandora and the group everything she has done to

---

* Golden Globe-nominated actor, author. *Another Country* (1984); *My Best Friend's Wedding* (1997); *The Happy Prince* (2018).
† Fashion stylist for *American Vogue*, *Paris Vogue*, *W*, Calvin Klein, YSL, Giorgio Armani.

disappoint and hurt you,' instructed the counsellor. 'Tell us everything harmful, all the misery she has caused . . .'

'Well, none at all to me actually,' I replied. 'She's a lovely friend, loyal, great fun, always remembers birthdays . . .'

The counsellor looked disappointed.

Tessa Dahl, Roald Dahl's daughter, became a friend. She was nineteen and mesmerizingly beautiful and I used to meet her in a nightclub named Wedgie's on the King's Road, where she was pursued by strings of playboys including Dai Llewellyn, always described in gossip columns as 'The Seducer of the Valleys' (he was Welsh). Tessa adopted me as a courtier, we shared the same taste for the absurd, and she would invite me down to Gypsy House in Buckinghamshire for lunch.

Roald wrote in a hut in the garden, with a rug over his knees, but generally made an appearance to say hello. Each time I left, he would lope up to my car with a huge pile of books, foreign editions of his works. 'Here you go,' he'd say. 'A Polish edition of *Charlie* for you . . . Japanese *Matilda* . . . Korean *Mr Fox* . . . what's this one? Mandarin, I think. Or Bhutanese – that's Dzongkha correctly. A French *BFG*? Dutch *James and the Giant Peach*? There you go. Don't feel obliged to read them all.' Probably Roald's purpose was to clutter-clear his shed.

Somewhere along the line I started writing a novel named *Shooting Stars*, about drugs, love and Venice, which was published by David Godwin at Heinemann. An odd theme to choose, it could be argued, since my entire life experience of drugs is confined to being offered a single line of coke in a Manhattan apartment: it looked so potentially life-enhancing that I chickened out, fearful of where it might take me.

The novel was typed out by my friend Prue Murdoch, eldest daughter of the media mogul. I can't now remember why Prue ever agreed to take on such an unrewarding task. Perhaps I bought her lunch?

Mark Birley, founder of the Berkeley Square nightclub Annabel's, was being courted to open a branch of his club in the Philippines, in Manila. President and Imelda Marcos thought it would bring prestige and sophistication to their bankrupt country if they had an Annabel's, so were all for it. Mark asked if I would like to accompany him on a trip, to check out the club scene and write something for the *Evening Standard*; the Manila Sound, he promised, was electrifying and about to become the Next Big Thing. Many people found Mark Birley difficult to talk to. He was famously handsome and well dressed, but forbiddingly tall and fastidious. I had witnessed rich American ladies, from Florida and Nassau, gibbering and gushing around him in panic, because he didn't give much back in conversation.

On our Manila trip, Mark was conviviality itself, as he took me to watch the Juan Dela Cruz Band and a Filipino group named Hotdog. Afterwards, we went to nightclubs with various shady members of the Marcos family and their entourages. Our hosts wore those elaborately embroidered Filipino shirts called Barong Tagalog, with dark glasses and pistols in holsters.

During the day, I had nothing whatever to do except sunbathe by the swimming pool of the Manila Hotel or sit on my balcony. One afternoon, I was reading a novel when I heard voices from the next-door room, drifting across the balcony. As I listened, I began to recognize the voices as friends I knew from university. I also heard young Filipina women's voices, and giggling. It became clear there was a foursome in progress.

It was impossible to ignore. Stepping across the shallow fence between our balconies, I tapped the spine of my book against the window. 'Can you keep the noise down in there, please?'

'Fuck, Nick. What the *hell* are you doing here?' they exclaimed, seeing my face peering in.

The foursome was suspended, while my two friends came over to the window to chat, towels wrapped round their waists. We made plans for dinner. Unfortunately, while we were talking, the two Filipina girls made off with their wallets, and scarpered. The dinner was on me.

The treadmill of producing a weekly stunt column took its toll, and it was a relief to dream up a Big Idea which I reckoned could get me through twelve weeks at least. The ruse was to recreate the 'Around the World in Eighty Days' journey of Phileas Fogg from the Jules Verne novel, in which, for a wager, he sets out to circumnavigate the globe in less than eighty days without flying; it all had to be done by land and sea, beginning and ending at Fogg's club, the Reform on Pall Mall. Louis Kirby immediately embraced the idea, seeing it as a 'super-stunt with a London angle', and I was sent on my way with maximum fanfare, white suit, swordstick and a bon voyage party at the Reform Club.

It was unexpectedly enjoyable to embark on a mission at top speed during the grey London months of January to March. The journey itself, which is delineated in the Verne novel, combines mad dashes with gentler passages by sea; I had prearranged several legs by merchant vessels and container ships, with immovable schedules, but much of it was improvised on the hoof. The route goes Reform Club to Waterloo (by taxi), Dover to Calais (ferry), overnight sleeper to Brindisi via Paris, ferry to Alexandria, container ship down the Suez Canal into the Red Sea, calling at Aqaba and Jeddah, disembarking at Port Sudan. Then taxi through Sudan, Eritrea and Ethiopia to Djibouti, Arab dhow across the Gulf of Aden and Arabian Sea for five

NC aged five months, photographed in Carlyle Square, London, with his mother, Susan Coleridge.

Four grandparents photographed outside St Margaret's, Westminster, following the wedding of NC's parents, David and Susan: Guy Coleridge MC, the Hon Norah Senior (Joicey), Ronald Senior DSO, Cicely Coleridge (Stewart-Smith).

Entitled-looking children on Hampstead Heath, Timothy and Nicholas Coleridge on a Sunday walk.

Billie Williamson, caustic classicist and Headmaster of Ashdown House prep school, with inmates.

Dotheboys Hall: Lunch at Ashdown House circa 1966. NC is seated second from front. The menu appears to be mince and mashed potato, a recurring treat.

Jamming on South Meadow, Eton, circa 1973. Craig Brown on the left in bellbottoms, David Shaughnessy on the right. James Baring, centre, with red T-shirt and necklace.

A gathering of assorted Etonians, 1975, possibly to celebrate NC's 18th birthday. The throng includes Hugh St Clair, Craig Brown, Guy Lubbock, Geoffrey Adams and Harry Wyndham among others.

Pandora Stevens (now Delevingne) and Napier Miles, who had recently lost an eye in a skiing accident. Photographed in Sloane Avenue.

David Ogilvy and John Montagu Douglas Scott, photographed up a tower, Cortachy, Angus.

Strangely random photograph of Elton John and the chat show host Russell Harty, photographed at Eton during a celebrity visit. NC and Craig Brown front row. Back row includes Guy Lubbock, James Colthurst, Desmond Monteith, Jamie Robertson, Percy Weatherall, Chris Figg, John Montagu Douglas Scott. Photograph by Terry O'Neill.

Above: NC and John Scott in the Grand Bazaar, Isfahan, during a gap year trip. The ethnic shirts smelt like dead cat. *Above right:* Edna O'Brien, Craig, NC, John staying with Sonia Melchett, Tuscany. Edna is massaging John's foot. *Right:* NC in a hoodie in Red Square, Moscow.

NC, Craig Brown in Venice, 1976. Craig wore the seersucker denim dungarees for weeks at a stretch.

James Stourton in costume for a pirate party, Magdalene College, Cambridge.

Kit Hunter Gordon and Nick Allan dressed to pull, Trinity College.

Nick Allan, Alice Leatham, NC in Great Court, Trinity. The boys' hair was hennaed orange in tribute to David Bowie.

Sophie Hicks dressed for dinner, Bowhill House, Selkirk.

Evgenia Citkowitz, aged 17, reading *Harpers & Queen* in NC's garden. *Top right:* Napier Miles, tomato juice and Lindsay Kemp gouaches. *Above right:* Ann Barr, Georgie Hunter Gordon, James Stourton, Alice Leatham, Michael Howells, 57a Radnor Walk.

Lucinda Simms, later Lubbock, with Craig Brown and Rupert Forbes Adam, after dinner bopping at Bowhill, Scotland, staying with John Montagu Douglas Scott. The music was almost certainly Nina Simone's *Don't Let Me Be Misunderstood*.

The editorial team at *Tatler*, October 1979, photographed in the offices at 15 Berkeley Street. Tina Brown, front centre, clutching her first issue. NC in the back row with Georgina Howell and Michael Roberts.

Photographed by Snowdon, London, circa 1982. NC is twenty-five.

In matador kit, Sonia Melchett and Pandora Mond's black and gold ball. Photograph by Alan Davidson.

Team photograph at The Glen, Peeblesshire. Bella Pollen, Craig Brown, Adam Shand Kydd, Lesley Cunliffe, Napier Miles, Nicky Shulman, NC, Patrick Benson, Sophie Hicks. Photographed for *Tatler* by Victor Watts.

Befezed on the roof of Christopher Gibbs' riad in the Ourika Valley, near Marrakech, in the Atlas mountains.

Setting off on *Around the World in 78 Days* stunt from the Reform Club, Pall Mall.

Georgia, aged 18, backpacking around Rajasthan and being stalked by NC. Photographed at the Lake Palace, Udaipur.

NC under arrest in Jaffna, Sri Lanka, on suspicion of being a Tamil terrorist and spy. He was released after 12 days. It was surprising he could retain his camera in prison.

Five hired models make NC look a whole lot better in a 1988 publicity shot for *The Fashion Conspiracy – A Remarkable Journey Through the Empires of Fashion*. The photograph was taken by Clive Arrowsmith for the *Mail on Sunday's You Magazine*. NC was Editor of *Harpers & Queen* at the time. The current whereabouts of the models is sadly unknown.

Georgia Coleridge on her wedding day, photographed on the steps of St George's Church, Hanover Square, around the comer from Vogue House. The dress is by Alistair Blair. Photograph by Anthony Osmond-Evans.

Tina Brown, Editor-in-Chief of *Vanity Fair*, Bernie Leser, President, Condé Nast Inc., Anna Wintour, Editor-in-Chief, American *Vogue*, Miles Chapman, *VF* headline writing genius, at the Coleridges' wedding reception at Claridge's. 22 July 1989.

NC and a bunch of trusty ushers: John Montagu Douglas Scott, Edward Stourton, Napier Miles, Nick Allan, Kit Hunter Gordon, James Stourton, NC, Alistair Scott, Sebastian James, Tim Coleridge, Craig Brown, Nick Boles, Christopher Coleridge.

Georgia on Anjuna Beach, Goa, not long after she and NC were married. Photographs of Georgia on beaches in direct sunshine are rare. She has an English rose aversion to sunbathing.

NC in Ralph Steadman cartoon for *Private Eye*. It illustrated a review of his novel *With Friends Like These*.

David and Susan Coleridge at Christopher Coleridge's 21st birthday party, the Savoy hotel.

Finalists for Magazine Editor of the Year, British Society of Magazine Editors: Ian Hislop, *Private Eye*, NC, *Harpers & Queen*, Charles Moore, *The Spectator*. The very long dinner was held at the Park Lane Hilton hotel. The winner, by miles, was Hislop. The two runners-up are looking for inspiration from the victor. Photograph by David Montgomery.

Sophie, Freddie, Alexander and Tommy Coleridge in Famous Five mode. Photographed by Saddell's Beach, near Kintyre, Argyll and Bute. The Coleridges rented Saddell's Castle numerous summers from the Landmark Trust.

The hot-water bottle men on a Rajasthan trip; the filling and emptying of hot water bottles was their only job, expertly done. The tents are pitched below Mehrangarh Fort, Jodhpur.

days to Mumbai, a night at The Taj Mahal Palace hotel to get some washing turned round, then on to Chennai by rail on the forty-hour *Madras Mail*. It was during this train journey across the central plateau of India, in blinding sunshine, that I first fell in love with the country and everything Indian. It was the beginning of a lifelong love affair.

Arriving in Chennai, I caught, with only half an hour to spare, the MV *Chidambaram* (monthly passenger ship) to Penang, a ship to Hong Kong, another container ship from Hong Kong to Yokohama, ditto to Hawaii, then hitched a ride on a private yacht to San Francisco. Amtrak across the States to New York, train to Montreal, ice-breaker and container ship to Felixstowe, British Rail and taxi back to the Reform Club. It took seventy-eight days. Once or twice a week, wherever I could find a working telex machine, I filed my copy to the newspaper, which bigged it up splendidly. Periodically, out of the blue, an agency photographer appeared on a railway station or port side, and transmitted blurred pictures of me wearing an increasingly crumpled white suit, and carrying the swordstick, back to base.

Home in London, I found my celebrity status amongst cabbies had been further boosted, and Louis Kirby took me to the Savoy Grill for a celebration lunch. 'You can choose anything you fancy from the menu, other than the lobster and caviar,' he declared.

A few years later, Michael Palin made the same Foggian journey for a TV series, with considerable panache and to great effect.

I returned to the weekly grind of my column and was surprised to win a gong at The British Press Awards – Young Journalist of the Year – which led to a memorable prize-giving ceremony. The *Evening Standard* had three winners that year – Max Hastings was Journalist of the Year (the top prize of all), me as Young Journalist (the novice award) and a photographer from the sports desk was runner-up for Football Photographer. The Editor took us all on his table to the awards lunch at the Stationers' Hall, which was thronged with journalists from every paper.

During the lunch, much wine was drunk, and the wife of the sports photographer got increasingly agitated. As the awards were dished out, she became aware the prize cheques were for differing amounts – Max had won £5,000, I'd got £1,000 but her husband only £50. Suddenly, she lost it. 'How come the writers get all this dosh, when Garth only gets a measly fifty quid? This is effing typical, this is.' Her voice slurred. 'What's so special about writers anyhow? Nobody reads the words, they look at the photos. Garth works every Saturday afternoon in all weathers . . . and they give him fifty effing quid.'

The lunch broke up with the poor lensman trying to gag his wife, while Louis Kirby and the rest of us looked on.

James Stourton, Napier Miles and I had an idea to found a publishing house, but it only ever produced one book. It did, however, necessitate numerous jolly lunches and dinners to discuss such crucial matters as governance and the backlist. James was Chairman, I think. I was MD and Napier appointed Finance Director on account of being the most efficient. The book we compiled and published was named *The Long Weekend Book*, and contained many excellent pieces written by our friends, illustrated with photographs of more friends in weekend mode, including one of the future Home Secretary Amber Rudd wearing a suit of armour and carrying a Masai spear. Other contributors included Sky's Adam Boulton, Nicky Shulman, Sophie Hicks and my cousin Georgina Montagu. There was a long section in the middle of the book about how to concoct The Perfect Bloody

Mary, running to about sixteen pages of instructions. This section was typed out by Mary Killen, then a piecework secretary operating out of Lord Durham's flat at 123 King's Road, now the sofa-bound star of Channel 4's *Gogglebox*.

Revisiting *The Long Weekend Book* thirty-five years later, there is only one section I still find funny, called 'Directions to a Strange House'. It is supposed to be verbal directions to a house party, delivered over the telephone by the mother of a friend. It is hopelessly out of date now, but I reproduce it in full.

'Can you find Harrods? Well do so and turn left. Then carry straight on until you reach Exit 16. You'll come to a roundabout and there'll be a sign pointing to Stroud. For God's sake *don't take that* or you'll go *miles* off course. Take the road marked Tetbury – in fact it's not the way we go to Tetbury but that's not your chief concern. Stay on the road for four miles and on the left you'll see a hideous garage. Keep going straight on the same road past six pubs when you'll come across a rather pretty church. What you want is the turning *before* the church. Follow that road which will be signposted Burford and keep going. It's all single-track and very windy. Over a humpback bridge – careful – until you see a telephone box on your *left* and a sign saying 'Polo'. You can take that but best of all keep going until you'll come to a junction where you want to go straight on. In fact, it's a left and a right but I'm sure you'll see what I mean when you get there. Keep going. Keep going. You'll know you're getting warm when you see the start of the estate wall. Follow the wall for about four miles until you see a pair of Palladian lodges and iron gates. *That's not us!* We're the little white house just set back from the road. If you reach Preston Candover you've gone *too far*. What's your name again? Oh good! Does the name Izzy Cumming-Orphan mean anything to you? No? Well I've given her your telephone number and said I was sure you'll give her a lift from Oxford. Which means you won't be coming quite the same way . . .'

Today, of course, this entire conversation is obsolete. You would simply be texted the postcode and follow the sat nav.

The book sold briskly in the run-up to Christmas and, when the accounts were finally closed a year later, we discovered we had made a loss of only £200, which we considered a pretty impressive result for all that effort, but not so impressive as to persevere with the publishing house.

It may be something to do with being a Pisces, but I have an inbuilt quirk to my character which means I always half wish I was doing the exact opposite of whatever it is I'm doing at the time. When I'm busy, I hanker for solitude; when things get quiet, I yearn for stimulation, people and parties. If things become too luxurious, I crave a simpler, plainer life, and so on.

So I leapt at the chance of a sabbatical from the *Evening Standard* to become a war correspondent for a few months to make a TV documentary about the civil war in Sri Lanka. My sponsors were Lord Cranborne,* the Tory grandee, and Hugo Swire,† not yet an MP, who ran an independent production company making news segments for Channel Four. The fact that I had never previously visited Sri Lanka, and knew nothing whatever about the Tamil–Sinhalese conflict, concerned nobody.

'Your team will be two ex-SAS guys, Peter and Mike,' said Hugo, cheerfully briefing me in Foxtrot Oscar. 'They'll look after you. Great guys, hard as nails.'

---

* Robert Cranborne, 7th Marquess of Salisbury. Former Leader of the House of Lords.
† Sir Hugo Swire, Conservative MP for East Devon. Former Minister of State, FCO.

We flew to Colombo on tourist visas, camera equipment concealed in several bags of scuba-diving kit. If asked, we were going snorkelling off Galle.

Peter Jouvenal was officer class; he later became a distinguished expert on Afghanistan and Iraq. Mike Zalankus, heavily tattooed, had left the SAS to become a nightclub bouncer in Oxford at a joint called Downtown Manhattan.

We rented a large car from a travel agency in the lobby of a five-star hotel, which was later to become the cause of considerable embarrassment.

'You won't be driving north of Kandy?' asked the nervous travel agent. 'It is too dangerous.'

'No fear! We're heading south to the reef. Scuba. Manta rays.'

Heading due north for several hundred miles, sticking only to the back roads, we avoided the many military roadblocks and eventually reached Jaffna, in the heart of Tamil Tiger country. For a week, we interviewed Tamil leaders and drove around in the scrub filming burnt-down Tamil villages. The terrorist Tamils ran the whole of the north part of the island, with only one beleaguered army camp still held by the Sinhalese. It was surrounded on all sides by Tamil guerrillas.

It struck us as an intelligent idea to film the camp from the bushes, to illustrate how government troops were held hostage inside their own camp. Creeping forwards through scrubby jungle, the equipment was set up, and I began a whispery segment to camera. Suddenly, the camp gates opened, three jeeps shot out and we were surrounded and under arrest.

For several days we kicked our heels behind the camp's razor wire, before the Sinhalese flew us by helicopter to Colombo for interrogation. As the chopper gained height and circled the camp, I saw our rental car down below and wondered what would become of it. It's probably still there now.

Landing at a military base in Colombo, we were bundled into jeeps and jailed in Welikada Prison. Originally built in 1841 by the British during colonial days, Welikada has rather an elegant facade with a monolithic entrance like a Norman castle keep. Inside, seventeen hundred demoralized-looking inmates trudged round an exercise yard, watched over by baton-wielding guards.

I hope readers won't be too disappointed to hear we were housed in the hospital wing; less comfortable, for sure, than any hotel, but not intolerable as cells go.

Each morning, we were transported to the Internal Security Ministry and questioned about where exactly we'd been, and who we'd met, in the north. They hoped, I think, we would disclose the location of secret Tamil Tiger camps.

These interrogations lasted several hours a day, for ten consecutive days, with the same questions posed in multiple ways. Our interrogators were surprisingly insecure, and regularly asked, 'What are you thinking about our investigation techniques? Tell us honestly, please. All our procedures are based upon Scotland Yard methods.'

Mike Zalankus, the tattooed bouncer, replied, 'What do I think of your methods? You lot are about as much use as a one-legged man at an arse-kicking party.' It is an SAS saying, apparently.

Later, they asked, 'How are you liking Sri Lanka, gentlemen?' It was an odd question, seeing as we were detained in their maximum-security jail. 'And what are you thinking of Sri Lankan women?'

Once again, Zalankus shared his view. 'Sri Lankan women? About as attractive as a blind blacksmith's thumb.'

As our incarceration approached a fortnight, it became rather repetitive, and I started to wonder how long we would be held.

To make matters worse, nobody even knew we were there. I spent my days writing short stories, later published as *How I Met My Wife and Other Stories*. Or we played a makeshift game of bowls involving empty plastic water bottles and rolled-up socks.

Then a lucky thing happened. One of our jailors sold the news of our imprisonment to the local newspaper, from where it got picked up by a wire service and reported in the *Evening Standard*. My mother read the item at her hairdresser's in Walton Street. My father asked his PA to find the telephone number of Welikada Prison and put him through. A guard raced into our cell. 'Come quickly, come quickly, Mr Nicholas, you have long-distance telephone call . . . special trunk call.'

I lifted the receiver and heard my father's voice. 'Honestly, Nicky, what are you up to, you goof? Your mother's hysterical with worry.'

We were released the next morning and escorted to the airport. 'I hope you have favourable impressions of Sri Lanka,' said the Chief of Police. 'You must come back for holiday.'

I had been back in England for a couple of weeks when I got a call from *Harpers & Queen*. My old mentor Ann Barr had stormed off the magazine in a huff ('Lazy Willie!') and Willie Landels wondered whether I might like to return as one of his deputies. The idea seemed rather appealing. I was twenty-eight. I said yes. And so the newspaper years ended, and I returned to my first and truest love, magazines.

8.

After the boisterous burlesque of my newspaper existence, it was a relief to revert to the refined microculture of the glossies. I have always liked magazine people, with their defining characteristics of faddishness, alertness and a predilection for diva-like behaviour. My return to *Harpers & Queen* was the start of a thirty-year cycle in the Gloss Machine, which spun faster and faster as the decades unfolded.

The *Harpers & Queen* offices in Soho, at 72 Broadwick Street, occupied a large open-plan floor, divided by shallow, modular, grey plastic screens into departments for Features, Arts and Reviews, Beauty, Travel, copy editors and so forth. The fashion department, with its lockable closets, was rammed with clothes rails, from which hundreds of outfits by Chanel, Yves Saint Laurent and Valentino drooped from hangers in preparation for fashion shoots. Fashion was run by two perpetually exasperated and eye-rolling women, posh Vanessa de Lisle and Scottish Liz Walker, for whom everything was 'hideous' – that Escada blouse is 'hideous', the Jasper coat 'quite hideous', the Dior bag 'perfectly hideous'. They were assisted by variously beautiful and camp assistants including Amanda Grieve (later Harlech), Hamish Bowles and Camilla Nickerson.

In adjacent offices lived the advertising team, led by a young, vehement, socialist Irishman with red socks named Stephen Quinn, an orphan from County Kilkenny, who was destined to become my closest friend on the business side of publishing.

I inherited a desk from Loyd Grossman,★ by now a television star, in which I discovered, in otherwise empty drawers, a large manila envelope marked 'Strictly private – do not open'. Inside, were half a dozen black and white photographs of Loyd, stark naked, pretending to play an unplugged electric guitar, which only half obscured his sensitive parts. They dated from his rock star days as Jet Bronx, from Jet Bronx & The Forbidden.

Soon afterwards, I was paraded upstairs to meet Terry Mansfield, Managing Director of the National Magazine Company, who was keen to check me out. He was short, energetic, inclined to philosophize. He occupied a corner office of beige modernity, rendered somewhat incongruous by the presence of a Victorian grandfather clock, and a Georgian breakfront cabinet filled with silver trophies. Terry would eventually become my Number One sparring partner in the media world, a ruthless competitor; but, for now, he was conducting a post-factum interview.

Upside down on Terry's desk, I read a briefing note about me from Willie Landels, which was rather generous, and went on to say that 'it would be a political appointment that will please the staff'.

Terry said, 'I believe you are joining us as Political Editor. We haven't had one of those before on *Harpers & Queen*. I hope you are a Conservative. All our readers are Conservatives.'

He went on to share some of his insights into the magazine. These included: Mrs Betty Kenward's social column, Jennifer's Diary, is the main reason people buy the publication ('That's why they take it, Nicholas, not for the clever articles'); on all front covers, the models should be wearing earrings and other jewellery borrowed from advertisers, and never costume jewellery;

★ Television presenter, sauce entrepreneur, musician. *Through the Keyhole*, *MasterChef*. Chairman, Royal Parks.

our readers love the countryside ('Many have two homes – in town and country'); Her Majesty the Queen subscribes to the magazine, as well as many other members of the royal family ('So we should avoid any disrespect towards them at all times').

This final caution was to become rather significant in due course, as things transpired.

Working for Willie Landels was, as he would doubtless have phrased it, 'so amusing'. He barely interfered with the articles, and seemed to like the ones I commissioned. His terms of approval or disapproval were uncalibrated and delivered in his playful Italian accent. An idea or person was either 'so amusing' and 'quite chic, I think', or else it was 'perfectly ghastly, my dear'. There wasn't a lot in between. His great joy was personally supervising the jewellery and luxury watch shoots, in which Bulgari bracelets and Patek Philippe timepieces were photographed on kebab skewers, between gobbets of meat and onion, or upon king prawns and lobsters or bowls of purple radicchio.

Terry Mansfield hated them. He would come down to the editorial floor and announce, 'I was having lunch with David Morris, the jeweller, who books ten pages [of advertising] a year, and he complained he couldn't see the clasp of his diamond and emerald encrusted necklace under all that salad.'

Willie would roll his eyes. 'My dear Terry, it is really too ghastly to have to hear what some advertiser or other thinks . . . what do they know?' He much preferred lunching with Lady Diana Cooper and the nightclub king Mark Birley. 'Quite amusing, quite chic.'

Contributors like Olinda Adeane* and Victoria Mather†

---

* Suffolk- and Venice-based journalist.
† Travel Editor, radio personality. *Tatler*, *Vanity Fair*, *Loose Ends*, *Social Stereotypes*. Pug enthusiast.

became friends of mine at this point, though there was a mild risk in using Victoria, owing to a deep-set froideur between her and Mrs Kenward. Victoria had come to work for the legendary eighty-year-old social editor as her junior secretary, an exacting role, since Mrs Kenward was relentlessly correct in everything she did, expecting the highest standards of decorum and etiquette; she looked oddly like Raine Spencer, with her bouffant helmet of hair topped by a velvet bow. One evening was the annual Queen Charlotte's Ball, where debutantes in white dresses paraded around with a massive iced cake. Betty Kenward was seated at the top table, of course, with the Lady Chair and Ball Committee. Victoria, a deb that year, decided it would be a good jape to streak naked across the dance floor. Mrs Kenward was appalled to see the full-frontal vision sprinting towards her, and then to glance up and recognize the face of her own junior secretary. Victoria was sacked the next morning.

The National Magazine Company was booming. Advertising paginations were growing by 15 per cent a year, circulations climbing at a similar rate. *Cosmopolitan*, then the biggest monthly women's magazine, selling over half a million copies, was making a fortune and licensed to seventy markets around the world. The women who wrote the twenty or so sex articles per issue occupied the floor above our own: mostly single, as it happened. Craig Brown and I contributed a quiz – '30 ways to know if you're getting enough regular sex'.

Let's hope it was useful.

I became interested in the commercial side of publishing, inspired by Stephen Quinn's buccaneering salesmanship. I was struck by the power of an individual to make a decisive difference to an advertising schedule – I watched Stephen sell twenty-two pages of Chanel advertising into a single November issue of *Harpers &*

Queen – and to project a magazine brand into something indispensable. The Hearst Corporation's head honchos in New York, Frank Bennack Jr and Gil Maurer, who were the ultimate bosses of National Magazines, visited London regularly, and Willie Landels and I were paraded to share our vision.

Willie sent me to New York for a month to identify new contributors and meet photographers. On account of my extended stay, I was booked into the Hotel Wales at 1295 Madison Avenue and 92nd Street: a well-past-its-glory-days establishment, with enormous run-down suites. A lingering smell of room service permeated every part of the hotel, and giant room keys dangled from brass keyrings bigger than doorknobs. Mine was soon to come in handy.

Each morning, I strode down Madison Avenue for rendezvous with writers, fashion photographers and their agents. Graydon Carter, then Editor of *Spy* magazine, became a friend, and I was excited to commission several pieces from Anthony Haden-Guest, for which he secured a large advance but scarcely delivered any of them. Tina Brown and Harry Evans took me to a PEN International benefit at the Plaza hotel, where Harry surveyed the ballroom and declared, 'It's miraculous, Nick, this city. Look at these people: the most powerful, influential people on earth. All here in New York.' And, indeed, they were all out that night: Tom Wolfe and Gay Talese, Jay McInerney, Art Buchwald, Norman Mailer and Erica Jong, Kurt Vonnegut and Bianca Jagger, wherever you looked. I was the wide-eyed boy from freecloud.

The next day, the Hearst chief honchos took me to lunch at the Four Seasons Grill Room, the first time I'd crossed the threshold of that legendary media haunt in the Seagram Building on Park Avenue. It was exciting to spot Si Newhouse, the owner of our rival publisher Condé Nast, Norman Pearlstine of

Time Inc., Rupert Murdoch of News Corp., Alfred Taubman of Sotheby's, Clay Felker of *Manhattan, inc.* (then my favourite magazine), Oscar Wyatt and Sid Bass the oilmen lunching together, and to meet Leonard Lauder, CEO of Estée Lauder for the first time, all in one room.

After lunch, flushed with the conviction I had somehow penetrated the very Canaan and Elysium of magazine publishing, I returned elated to my fleapit, the Hotel Wales. Probably it was my state of over-excitement which made me fail to notice my bedroom door was ajar. As I approached my desk, the steel point of a knife dug into my ribs, followed by the instruction to raise my hands above my head and sit down very slowly on an upright chair. Only now could I see my assailant: an eighty-year-old white man, shockingly emaciated, wearing only a pair of red Y-fronts.

'Easy, friend,' he kept saying. 'Let's take this nice and slowly. I don't need to hurt you, if you do exactly as I say . . .'

Having got me seated on the chair, it gradually became clear he hadn't got any fixed further plans for me. He didn't want money: 'I have plenty of money.' He held the knife up to my throat from time to time, inviting me to respect the serrated edge of the blade. A housekeeper knocked, asking to replenish the minibar, and the man in the red underpants motioned me to tell her to go away. An hour passed, which felt longer, and I sensed a mounting agitation. It wasn't clear how this would end.

He said, 'I have to use the bathroom, don't even think of moving. I'm watching you.'

But he wasn't watching, he was peeing. The giant keyring with its doorknob-sized ball was within reach. As red-pantsman returned, I swung it like a mace at his head, heard the thud, raced for the door and out along the corridor.

The concierge in the lobby was organizing show tickets for an out-of-town couple. 'Everyone appreciates *Cats*, it's a great show . . .'

'Excuse me, but I've just been attacked in my room by a lunatic with a knife. In red underpants.'

'You on floor six, by any chance? That'll be Mr G. He's a long-term resident. This happens. You want me to tell anyone?'

One afternoon, back in London, I wandered into the *Harpers & Queen* office and met an intern. I thought she was incredibly pretty, and sweet to talk to about books and journalism. She was wearing a stripy Breton top and white shorts. She had left St Paul's Girls School a few days earlier. The next morning, I looked out for her again, but there was no trace.

'Is that work experience girl around, the one with dark hair who was here yesterday?' I casually enquired. I didn't remember her name.

'Georgia Metcalfe? Yesterday was her last day.'

I rang Personnel and blagged her number. The number I was given was answered by the woman destined to become my mother-in-law. 'Hello?'

'Can I speak to Georgia, please?'

'Who is this speaking?'

'Nick Coleridge.'

'Are you a friend of my daughter?'

'Yes, I am. We were talking yesterday.'

'Then I'm surprised you don't know she's gone to India. She's gone backpacking. She flew this morning on her own.' That was news.

'Yes, that's exactly why I'm ringing you. Georgia said you'd have her schedule, I might be in India myself soon, we have a vague plan to meet up,' I extemporized.

On a whim, I flew to India and accidentally on purpose ran into Georgia in the street, outside a backpackers' hostel. What an amazing coincidence! What a surprise! Almost unbelievable! She looked gorgeous in her cheesecloth shirt and bulging metal-framed backpack. Her spectacles had been stolen, she said, on a night train from Calcutta, when a child's hand had reached through a window from a platform and grabbed them off her nose while she slept. We travelled innocently around Rajasthan for a couple of weeks, and it was a golden time. Everything about it is vested with a special glow in my memory. There is a gentleness and spirituality about Georgia which I found mesmerizing. We both loved India. That first adventure from Jaipur to Udaipur via Pushkar set the tone for many more. As our journey progressed, she allowed me to book two rooms in nicer and nicer hotels, until the backpackers' dives became a distant memory. We courted in the Polo Bar of the Rambagh Palace hotel, with its many brightly coloured Rajasthani cushions, and margaritas with salted rims.

It was annoying when, from time to time, Georgia referred to a boyfriend back home in England; he was an unforeseen element. The stalker bided his time.

In October, Georgia went up to St Hugh's, Oxford, and we heard no more of any boyfriend. We started dating. Eight years older than her, and feeling vulnerably ancient around St Hugh's, I rented an icy-cold weekend cottage in the Cotswold village of Notgrove, from David and Elizabeth Acland, and packed it out with friends older than myself, to make me seem youthful in context. The cottage was romantic but primitive, with its thick stone walls and defunct night-storage heaters, perpetually damp except in high summer. In winter, the narrow lanes between Notgrove and Turkdean regularly became snowbound, and we could be stranded for days. We trudged through virgin snow on beech-lined tracks to Cold Aston and ate in the pub. We bonded over our shared passion for Kate Bush and Leonard Cohen.

Charles Moore was editing *The Spectator*, and I began contributing zeitgeisty cover stories about yuppies and the new City rich. Another one was about why Mrs Thatcher loved toffs. Dominic Lawson★ took over as Editor, and I continued writing more of them. Both Charles and Dominic were indulgent Editors, who laughed at my jokes. Sometimes I wrote the *Spectator* Diary, which provoked the great Daventry-pronounced-Daintree episode. I had been staying with my old girlfriend Sophie Hicks at her cottage in Northamptonshire and been dispatched on Sunday morning to buy lunch ingredients in Daventry, the closest market town. The only shop open was a particularly miserable convenience store, selling nothing but deep-frozen beef burgers and breaded scampi, neither of which featured on Sophie's shopping list. I wrote a sneery paragraph comparing it to a pre-glasnost Russian shop. All hell broke loose in the *Daventry Express*, soon taken up by every national newspaper. Photographs were printed of a glum Daventry butcher holding out a tray of pork pies, and a fishmonger with a cod (neither opened on a Sunday, of course).

A local reporter rang Charles Moore, announcing himself from the *Daventry Express*.

'Daventry?' replied Charles, compounding the insult. 'Isn't the town correctly pronounced "Daintree"?'

An editorial railed against 'this grave and unwarranted insult to Daventry's rich culinary heritage from a little-read Tory rag'. I have never dared revisit Daventry.

I started going to *Spectator* summer parties, held in the narrow

---

★ Columnist, polemicist. Editor, *Sunday Telegraph* (1995–2005). *Sunday Times*, *Daily Mail* columnist. Married to Rosa Monckton, jewellery expert.

back garden of the old Doughty Street offices in Fitzrovia. I found them mildly intimidating, with their hundreds of mostly very tall, sometimes rather grubby, right-wing men with enormous brains and enormous nostrils (there may be a correlation). Such was the press of people, all jostling for drinks, you felt like a piece of driftwood tossed upon a raging sea, drawn by the current in this direction or that. My technique was to work my way down to the brick wall at the end of the garden, touch it, then work my way back again. The journey took forty minutes in each direction, all the time dodging Paul Johnson, Auberon Waugh, Peregrine Worsthorne, Algy Cluff and the rest. The *Spectator* cook, Jennifer Patterson, who later found fame as one of the *Two Fat Ladies* on TV, was another lurking hazard. She had taken a slight shine to me, in her overpowering way, and would exclaim, 'I adore your *eyes*, Nicholas, you have *Persian* eyes . . .'

During my *Evening Standard* days I had written about the opening of Le Caprice restaurant in Arlington Street, behind the Ritz, and this became my favourite restaurant for the next thirty-six years. I was destined to have lunch there 560 times. Originally launched by Joseph Ettedgui, the fashion entrepreneur who founded the Joseph boutique chain, it rapidly closed down, before being saved by Jeremy King and Chris Corbin, and then for years was managed by Jesus Adorno. By the time I arrived at *Harpers & Queen*, Le Caprice had already become my unofficial lunchtime office: virtually every important decision, hire and celebration in my career has taken place there.

When I first started going to Le Caprice, there was a clear pecking order for the better tables, for the corner window table in particular. First call on the corner table went to Princess Diana, who ate there frequently in those days, with a detective stationed at the bar keeping watch. Second call went to Jeffrey

Archer, the novelist. Then Leslie Waddington, the Cork Street art dealer. And then me.

As time went by, by a process of natural attrition, my ranking rose.

The curious thing is, despite all my visits, I have never read down to the bottom of the Caprice menu. I'm not particularly interested in food, and have never regarded food as the main point of any restaurant. So I choose duck with watercress salad as a first course nine times out of ten, followed by steak tartare or a hamburger. For me, the object of lunch in a restaurant is to buy seventy uninterrupted minutes of my guest's time, and to focus on them completely. Frequently, I cannot remember whether or not I have eaten the first course, I'm so busy talking and listening. At lunchtimes, I like to drink a Bullshot (cold beef consommé and vodka) followed by tap water.

Between my duties commissioning articles for *Harpers & Queen*, I embarked upon researching a non-fiction book about the fashion industry, specifically about its global power, reach and excesses, then an emerging phenomenon. It was the moment when a whole cast of designers were buying palazzos, private jets, private islands and cowboy ranches from the profits of their branded labels. My thought was to explore the full sweep of the fashion world from the sweatshops of India, Bangladesh and Brick Lane, where many designer clothes were manufactured, to the forty or so Big Ego billionaire designers who dominated the industry, drawing in the fashion capitals of New York, London, Milan, Paris and Tokyo, and incorporating the key department store chiefs, Manhattan couture customers, Arab princesses, journalists and opinion formers who complete the virtuous circle. My book would be a cross between a travel journal and a high-low economic analysis, both serious and satirical. And I came up with a title: *The Fashion Conspiracy*.

Over the next two years, I interviewed more than 400 people. As I worked on it, I realized this was a very rich seam of copy, largely virgin territory, nobody had written a similar book before. It also entailed a large amount of hanging about.

My system was to fly into a city, stay with a friend, and begin the frustrating business of negotiating with designers' publicity people for interviews. In a world before email and mobile phones, this meant being tied to a landline, awaiting calls seldom returned. In Manhattan, I stayed with Nick Allan at his apartment on Sutton Place South, where he was working as a stockbroker. When I arrived, we had a drink in a bar and he mentioned, 'Oh, by the way, there's a girl staying with me at the apartment. We met at a party last weekend and, er, well, somehow, she's still here with me. I'm not sure how much longer she's staying. It's a bit awkward. Anyway, she's called Tara.'

For the next three weeks, Tara and I got to know each other quite well. She was English and very pretty, and fun to talk to. While I watched the phone, waiting for Calvin Klein or Ralph Lauren to ring back, Tara washed her hair. She washed it every day, winding it up in a turban of towels on top of her head to dry. This occupied much of the day, until Nick returned and we all went out to supper.

Three weeks after my New York trip, I flew to Tokyo and stayed with my friend Peregrine Hodson,* who was an expert on the Afghanistan Taliban, now turned banker and living in Nogizaka. I planned to sit by his phone and bug the designers Yohji Yamamoto, Rei Kawakubo and Issey Miyake for interviews. Perry met me at a bar close to his flat.

---

* Author, *Under a Sickle Moon* (1986); *A Circle Round the Sun* (1992).

'Oh, by the way,' he said, 'I've got another guest staying. An English girl I met at a party in London last week. I said come and stay if you're ever in Japan, and she arrived. So she's here. We're sort of together. She's called Tara.'

Each day, I sat by the phone, waiting for Rei Kawakubo's people to return my calls. Tara washed her hair, winding it up in a towel on top of her head. In the evenings, when Perry returned, we all went out to supper in sushi bars.

One night, Perry said, 'I am going to take you to my club for a drink. Tara, sorry, you can't come, it's men only.'

'Is it a girlie bar?' Tara asked, rolling her eyes.

'No. It's a place for bankers. My Japanese bank pays my membership.'

We arrived at the club in an office building, it looked like the Business Class lounge in an airport, grey carpet, grey armchairs and banquette seating, subdued lighting. Two dozen Japanese men-in-suits sat in corporate groups. Perry ordered whiskies. A waiter arrived with the drinks and meticulously placed two crystal tumblers on the table between us. He wore a blue kimono. He bowed. Then he balanced a chopstick between the lips of the tumblers. He bowed again. Then, suddenly, astoundingly, he whipped up his kimono and karate-chopped the chopstick with his cock. The chopstick snapped clean in two.

The kimono dropped back down, re-covering his semi-erect penis, and he bowed again. Then he delivered a bowl of Japanese rice crackers. The whole display had taken, at most, five seconds. Nobody at any other table looked round to watch. It was a club tradition.

'I thought you'd enjoy that,' said Perry. Then we drank our expensive whiskies.

With my favourite cousin, Georgina Montagu, I travelled to Kyoto on the bullet train and then further south, crossing by ferry to the island of Shikoku. There is almost nothing to see or do on Shikoku, so we stayed in ryokans and lounged about in scalding hot *onsens* – traditional outdoor Japanese bathtubs – wearing our bathing suits, to the disapproval of the locals who bath naked. Georgina was in her Japanese phase, teaching English in Tokyo. Not long afterwards, she entered her American outback phase, living first on the red desert plains of remotest Moab, then on the Utah-Arizona border at Allen Canyon, where her outdoors bathtub is greatly enjoyed, with or without swimming trunks.

The harder I worked, the more important holidays became to me. I've noticed I'm capable of working more intensely, and avoiding mental collapse, if I know there is a holiday looming at some point, however distantly. Down the Nile with Nick Allan, to Tuscany with Prue Murdoch and Sophie Hicks, along the Turkish coast in a gulet with Georgia and others on a trip curated by Kit and Georgina Hunter Gordon were three memorable ones. My perfect holiday has the following components: long views, ideally of brown dusty hills with sparse vegetation (Tuscany, Rajasthan and Turkey all provide this), transparent blue sea, intense sunshine, unpretentious outdoor restaurants with umbrellas (optional). Things I dislike: overcast weather, traffic, pretentious dark restaurants with multi-course tasting menus and *menus de degustation*, wine pairings and food delivered under metal cloches for a big reveal. I like sitting on a terrace, staring out at the view in a trance-like state, half working on a project, while the therapy of sunshine evaporates all anxiety and stress from my head. I like to be up at dawn and am content to spend all day gazing and writing; then, at six p.m., out of nowhere, a group of amusing old friends ideally shows up, full of joy, wit and cocktails. That is my idea of a holiday.

★

Willie Landels produced a summer jewellery shoot for the magazine, in which he had bought postcards of the royal family and superimposed photographs of earrings and necklaces loaned by Bond Street jewellers. They were cleverly shot. The Queen was certainly one of them, and Princess Anne, possibly Fergie and the Queen Mother. It gave the impression that the royals were modelling the Garrard and Cartier pieces, along with diamond chokers from Boucheron and Van Cleef & Arpels. Everyone was thrilled by the pictures . . . until they were published.

All hell erupted. The *Daily Mirror*, first out of the gate, presented it as a commercial con, for implying that the Queen was endorsing the jewellery. Royal Warrant Holders complained by the score, several more each day. People were squarer and snottier in those days, more cravenly respectful of the royal family.

Terry Mansfield was aghast. The jewellery shoot offended his two most protected groups: Bond Street advertisers and Her Majesty.

As the storm raged around him, Willie became hourly more nonchalant. 'Really, my dear Terry, I do not believe the Queen has even seen the photographs, let alone cares two hoots. She is far too sophisticated.'

But he was shaken by the criticism, and offended by it too. Not long afterwards, ringing the office from a phone box at Heathrow Airport before boarding a flight, Willie tendered his resignation to Terry's secretary. 'Please tell Terry I am so sorry but I cannot bear to stay one day longer.' He took off for an undisclosed destination, never to return.

Out of the blue, there was a vacancy for a *Harpers & Queen* Editor.

9.

Anybody succeeding the great, flamboyant Willie Landels as Editor-in-Chief risked seeming callow by comparison, and my own appointment was far from a shoo-in. For a start, I was twenty-nine, less than half Willie's age, and *Harpers & Queen* regarded as the stately flagship of Hearst, their classiest publication. The case for appointing a young, single man, who had never edited anything before, was not overwhelming, and for several weeks rival candidates presented themselves at Terry's door, in whose gift as Managing Director the coveted prize resided.

It was helpful (to me) that Willie's phone box resignation had been inconclusive and faintly embarrassing and so prevented a full and orderly search for a successor, since he had left no official resignation letter. Less helpful was the conviction of Betty Kenward, the magazine's social diarist, that I was 'far too young by at least twenty years, it would be perfectly ridiculous'. She had Terry's ear, and her disapproval counted.

But eventually, as weeks became months and Willie failed to surface, it became necessary to fill the void. Terry declared he would take a risk on me. It was good of him, and I am forever grateful. He added, somewhat forebodingly, 'I have to tell you, Nicholas, that Mrs Kenward has serious reservations about your appointment. It must be your first task to reassure her. This evening I am escorting her to a Grosvenor Furs fashion show at Harrods, and I suggest you come along too. I hear some of the fur "antis" may be present, holding a demonstration, which is most unfortunate. Many of them are Communists, you know, with a prejudice against mink coats.'

We arrived at the front door of Harrods to find a vocal band of protestors clustered on the pavement. Several held placards stating 'Blood on their hands'. It was risky, or brave, of Mrs Kenward to have chosen to wear her ankle-length mink in a show of support for our 36-pages-a-year fur advertiser.

As we stepped from Terry's Daimler, the booing and fist-shaking intensified. 'Would you wear *human* skin on your back, bitch?' jeered one.

'Nicholas, we must protect Mrs Kenward,' Terry said. 'I will cover her right side, you cover her left.'

Mrs K, with velvet bow in hair and mink coat swinging, glided towards the door, oblivious to the baying throng. Inside, in the Harrods fur department, a miniature ice-skating rink had been erected, upon which a dozen models glided to and fro on skates, each one in a mink jacket, or else fox pelt, ocelot or jackal. The models in no way resembled the cool, edgy super-models found on designer catwalks, these were genteel crooked-fingered mannequins with beehive hairdos.

Once we had paid due homage to the owners of Grosvenor Furs, Terry drew me aside, 'Nicholas, we have a serious problem. We cannot risk taking Mrs Kenward back past that rabble, she's too important to the well-being of *Harpers & Queen*.'

'Perhaps we could leave by a different door?'

'That is a very smart idea, Nicholas. I shall discuss it with the Managing Director of Harrods.'

We exited through an underground staff passage, beneath Knightsbridge, where the Daimler was waiting for us, ready and purring.

'Well done,' said Terry. 'Your suggestion came in very handy, Nicholas.'

'Goodnight,' said Mrs Kenward tepidly, in the last word she would address to me for several years.

Thus my first day as Editor drew to a close.

I set about hiring a team, one by one, and the cast of characters we assembled largely defined my working life for the coming few years. It was a crack squad. Let me introduce the band: on Feature writing, the witty and poised Miss Nicola Shulman . . . on the Literature desk, Lady Selena Hastings, distinguished biographer and consort of dukes . . . Features Editor, the substantial and always well connected Ms Meredith 'Minky' Etherington-Smith . . . on Interior Decorating, Notting Hill's Miss Caroline Clifton-Mogg . . . Shopping Editor, please show your appreciation for Miss Sue Crewe . . . on the Arts beat, give it up for Mr Rupert Christiansen . . . star restaurant reviewer, man about town and primetime television face, Mr Loyd Grossman . . .

I had inherited, as Managing Editor, Uta Thompson, who became a loyal supporter, as well as a particularly clever Chief Copy Editor, Anthony Gardner, around whom a posse of sharp and punning headline writers coalesced, including the author Ysenda Maxtone Graham. In the fashion room was Liz Smith, procured from the *Evening Standard*, who soon gave way to the foppish post-Raphaelite Hamish Bowles as Fashion Director. Andrew Solomon from New York was Office Intern, Raffaella Barker the Features Assistant, Julia Elliot my soignée PA.

That was the first wave. It took a little time to upgrade the Travel Editor, who was a curious Frenchman named René Lecler, author of an undiscriminating guide book, *René Lecler's 300 Best Hotels in the World*. He had earned the right, through decades of service, to be regarded as indispensable, though he was a terrible writer and freeloader. As a copy editor, I had frequently fretted over his toe-curling articles. One began: 'I think it was the gnarled old hands of the orange seller in the market place which made me fall in love with Marrakech all over again.' Eventually he retired to Turkish Cyprus to a bungalow with a corrugated tin roof, where the heat got to him; he wrote me a letter, out of nowhere, saying that he'd been completely cleared by the Cypriot police of any involvement in the death by suffocation of his wife, and anything I'd heard to the contrary should be disregarded. He was eventually spotted strolling down the Old Brompton Road in pyjamas and dressing gown, and had to be rescued by Terry's chauffeur.

The new Travel Editor was another legend, John Hatt, hitherto a distinguished publisher of vintage travel books. A man of abrupt charm and intensely held opinions, he was arguably an eccentric choice of travel guru for a glossy magazine. He held a deep-seated prejudice against all the Caribbean islands and most luxury hotels frequented by our readers, and an aversion to piped music ('the dreaded muzak') in hotel restaurants, bars or lifts. Large sections of his articles were devoted to this topic, and his writing was superbly trenchant. Terry Mansfield regularly shared with me his reservations about John; he had preferred René Lecler 'who had special relationships with the PRs, Nicholas'.

The *Harpers & Queen* of the late eighties was fat with advertising, editorially coherent and occupying a fertile space between *Vogue* on one side and *Tatler* on the other. Magazine DNAs are complex entities, built up over many years, ultimately defined by the expectations of readers and non-readers alike, but accruing competences in related fields; so *Harpers & Queen* was, at its core, a luxury and social magazine, but with acknowledged competence in fashion and beauty, and a parallel proficiency in literary and intellectual matters. The trick was to keep all these disparate audiences in play at once: the rich-bitch Knightsbridge lady who lunched, the Fulham and Parsons Green divorcée, country wives (for whom *Harpers* was their last umbilical link to metropolitan life), boho literati, hard-core fashionistas, metro-sexual cool-cats. Different groups found in its pages entirely different pleasures, focusing on the bits which interested them and quickly flicking over the rest. One reader (let us say a 65-year-old Gloucestershire grandee) scans Mrs Kenward's Jennifer's Diary, glances at the decorating pages, horoscope and a profile of a racehorse trainer, and feels well served. Another (27-year-old Ladbroke Grove singleton) connects with a Peter York style essay, Loyd Grossman bar review, modern furniture shoot and the fashion. It was the tension between all these elements which brought character and success to the title.

We spent much time compiling composite articles with social punch but geographical reach. All magazines devote dispropor-tionate space to London stories, since these tend to be shinier, more glamorous and happen underneath editorial noses. But half the readers of *Harpers & Queen* lived outside the M25 belt-way. So we invented pieces with non-London strands: the 100 smartest/most beautiful women in Britain, the 100 most com-fortable spare bedrooms, the 100 best-connected people (the barber at White's was No. 1, I think), Britain's 25 greatest life enhancers, the 50 coldest houses in Britain (with freezing rooms photographed by Christopher Simon Sykes, all with one-bar electric fires), Britain's most alluring teenagers and young mothers (two separate articles, not girls who were both). These were deemed 'heartland' pieces, reflecting the world of core readers back upon themselves. It is striking how little celebrity journalism we published – no Hollywood front covers, no PR-driven interviews with LA film stars, no pre-approved questions or deals with publicists. All this would come later, of course. For now, we were gloriously uncorrupted.

I learnt it was the most unexpected articles which caused most offence. The 100 most comfortable spare bedrooms in Britain was one such. It consisted of twenty-five lavishly photographed bedrooms of the sort we admired (four-poster beds, Roberts radios, sofas, Turner watercolours, trouser presses, et cetera), twenty-five illustrated with smaller photographs, and then a listing of the best of the rest, with a paragraph of description about each. One of these belonged to Lady Young of Graffham, wife of the Trade and Industry Secretary of State, David Young. She sent a blistering letter of complaint, citing unforgivable inaccuracies. 'The bedroom wallpaper is <u>not</u> red with white stripes; the wallpaper is in fact white with red stripes. Furthermore, it is not a "spare bedroom" as you state, it is a "guest bedroom".' I obtained a sample of the disputed wallpaper and, as it turned out, the red and white stripes were identical width. Nevertheless, we published a fulsome apology, which entertained all those who spotted it.

Another complaint arrived from the wife of a business tycoon. 'My attention has been drawn to a photograph in your current issue . . .' it began. The expression 'my attention has been drawn to' is a sure sign you've got a pompous bore on your hands. 'It shows my two sons, but they have been incorrectly captioned. Michael is miscaptioned as Robert, and Robert as Michael. Please inform me, as a matter of urgency, what steps you will be taking to correct this. And check your facts in future!!'

I turned to the page in question. The boys were identical twins. Presumably their mother could tell them apart, but no one else on earth. We republished the offending photograph and apologized for any embarrassment caused; it looked and read like a *Private Eye* spoof.

The life of an eighties magazine Editor followed an eternal routine of features meetings, sucking up to advertisers, lunches with contributors and, inter alia, attending fashion weeks twice a year in the various fashion capitals. Exactly like life in a medieval or Tudor court, there was a well-understood concept of turning-up and paying homage. If Giorgio Armani or Gianni Versace was in town opening a new store, you turned up; if Estée Lauder or L'Oréal opened a counter for a sub-brand at Harvey Nichols, or Cartier a new concession in Selfridges, you turned up; if Louis Vuitton opens a branch in Sloane Street, there you are again. It is the contemporary equivalent of kissing the ring, bending the knee, respecting the pasha. You needn't stay long: just time enough to bow low and get photographed. It was a rare evening when I didn't drop in – or 'fly by' – at two or three of these parties.

When the stationery brand Smythson launched a new shop on Bond Street it was, quite literally, a case of going to the opening of an envelope. But all this turning up had a purpose: to keep the magazine front of mind, and the advertising dollars flowing.

Although my days were largely devoted to editorial matters, the business side of publishing was never far away; on glossy magazines, the Chinese wall between editorial and advertising is less the Great Wall of China than a clackety bead curtain or rice paper screen. The Publisher (commercial chief) of *Harpers & Queen*, Stephen Quinn, was by now a close friend; a charming and mesmerizing huckster, one of the few Publishers in the business who read every word of every issue, to better project the brand. He had arrived alone in England aged sixteen, on a night ferry from Dublin, and never lost the passion which first drew him to publishing. He took it as a personal insult if any advertiser had the temerity to reduce their spend; a visit from Stephen at full throttle sorted them out.

Stephen and Terry were polar opposites: the Irish socialist firebrand in the Blazes Boylan tradition, fond of a drink, idealistic, always ready to boil over, versus the controlling but eager Essex CEO with establishment ambitions. Terry had begun his working life as a Redcoat at Butlins and still had something of the holiday camp cheerleader about him, beneath a driving energy and studied gravitas.

What they had in common was a deep, almost pathological competitiveness with Condé Nast, which was seen as the dark side of publishing: our reviled rivals. Anna Wintour had recently arrived at British Condé Nast for a brief stint as Editor of British *Vogue*, and this only ratcheted up the competition still further. I used to have lunch with Anna from time to time at Cecconi's, in the days before she began wearing dark glasses at all times, and you could look into the whites of her eyes and assess the competition. She was very determined. And easier around men than around women.

The two rivals – Hearst and Condé Nast – had plenty in common, but were diverging in ambition. Hearst was named for its founder, William Randolph Hearst, the punchy American businessman and newspaper tycoon, inspiration for Orson Welles' film *Citizen Kane*. His famous Californian fantasy mansion, Hearst Castle, stood on a hill above the Pacific Ocean at San Simeon. Condé Nast was founded by the French-American publisher Condé Montrose Nast, with the purchase of *Vogue* in 1909. It was bought in 1959 by the newspaper billionaire Samuel Newhouse (father of Si Newhouse) as an anniversary present for his wife, Mitzi, who was an enthusiastic *Vogue* reader.

By the time I entered the gloss machine, Hearst was consolidating its grip on the high-circulation middle market, while Condé Nast's acquisitions and launches were all in the luxury market, the kings of high gloss.

It was the conviction at Hearst that Condé Nast people were vainer, shallower and more arrogant than Hearst people. Perhaps, at some primal level, we were haunted by the possibility that they were also smarter and more glamorous?

'God doesn't read *Vogue*,' was Terry's daily catchphrase. 'Never forget that, Nicholas: God isn't a *Vogue* reader.'

Whether Terry was correct is another matter. Nobody knows whether or not they take glossy magazines in the afterlife but, if they do, it is highly probable that God reads *Vogue*.

The photographers working for *Harpers & Queen* during this period were stellar: Hamish Bowles had brought Mario Testino to the magazine, and all his early shoots were published there. Ellen von Unwerth, Paolo Roversi, Andrew Macpherson and Claus Wickrath were regulars. As the fashion pages became cooler and edgier, the Jennifer's Diary social pages remained gloriously unbothered, proceeding in their stately way. Despite being a friend of my maternal grandmother, Mrs Kenward succeeded in barely exchanging a word with me for four years; she lurked inside a tiny cabin, with a porthole window in the door, veiled against snoopers by a lace curtain. Inside, she compiled her twelve-page column with its lists of guests and idiosyncratic punctuation. Untitled guests were followed by a comma ('Mr and Mrs John Smith, Mr and Mrs Philip Jones,' et cetera). Titled guests got a semi-colon ('The Earl of Margadale; The Marquess and Marchioness of Pershore;') – the semi-colon signalling superior status, and allowing the reader to draw breath in wonder. Members of the royal family merited a full stop ('Her Majesty the Queen. The Prince of Wales.'). Jennifer's Diary was the only section of the magazine where puns were expressly forbidden, society being a serious business.

Elsewhere, puns proliferated and were often literary in inspiration. A fashion shoot of mothers dressed in couture, saying goodnight to their children, was titled, after Philip Larkin, 'They tuck you up, your mum and dad.'

The *Harpers & Queen* years were endlessly fun, and it felt inconceivable that I would ever leave.

Least of all to join the dreaded Antichrist, Condé Nast.

10

Georgia and I became engaged at the Tollygunge Club in Calcutta on 4 March 1989, my thirty-second birthday. We were
sitting by a polo field having an evening drink when I asked her
to marry me.

Luckily, she replied, 'Yes.'

The Tollygunge Club, sometimes called the Tolly, is the
Hurlingham of Calcutta, a glorious oasis of green in the heart
of the city, with golf course, cricket pitches, polo fields, banyan
trees, and run-down colonial bungalows rented to travellers at
appealingly cheap rates. It was outside our bungalow, overlooking a polo chukka, that I made my proposal. I must have been
feeling confident because I'd trudged round India with a bottle
of champagne in my suitcase, rolled up in a shirt, now cooling
in the minibar.

In those pre-mobile, pre-social media days, getting engaged
risked being an anticlimax. Today, we would have taken an
immediate selfie, posted it on Instagram and Facebook, got 300
likes in a couple of hours, and excitedly Skyped our families. In
1989 Calcutta, you had to place a telephone call from the Central Post Office, and wait twenty-four hours for a crackly line.

The manager of the Tolly strode by, a Jimmy Edwards-
moustachioed Brit who had stayed on after independence, and
become a pioneering tiger conservationist. We told him our thrilling news.

'You'd better come to dinner with Ann and me on our ver-
anda,' Bob Wright OBE declared.

When we arrived, he said, 'Thought it might be a bit dull for you, with just us oldies, so we've invited another young English couple. They're renting the golf caddie's hut, our cheapest accommodation.'

Hugh Grant and Elizabeth Hurley arrived five minutes later. Not yet famous.

Georgia and I had made half a dozen Indian trips by now, travelling around by Ambassador car, finding nicher and nicher heritage hotels to stay in, the more eccentric the better. The old palaces and guest houses at Ghanerao, Kumbhalgarh and Dungarpur were our favourites. And we discovered Goa, in the days when it was still a series of distinct villages along the coast, with a mile of palm trees between each, not yet coalesced into a continuous ribbon of villas and shops. Calcutta was a favourite city, we had made friends with Indian journalists like Vir★ and Malavika Sangghvi,† and the Bengal newspaper proprietor Aveek Sarkar‡ and his wife Rakhi, the art collector. The historian William Dalrymple§ and his artist wife Olivia Fraser¶ were old friends of Georgia's. Willie was thin as a rake back then, already wearing the flowing, homespun dhotis that would become his style trademark. He and Olivia were living in Delhi on daal and air. When we took them to dinner at the Bukhara restaurant in the Sheraton, Willie ordered every dish on the menu and had the leftovers put in take-home doggie bags, to last the week ahead. The Dalrymples' encyclopaedic knowledge of India, and

---

★ Editor, TV presenter, gourmet. Editorial Director, *Hindustan Times*.

† Journalist, gossip columnist *Mumbai Midday*.

‡ Proprietor *Anandabazar Patrika*, the Calcutta *Telegraph*. Founder Penguin Books India, STAR News India.

§ Scottish historian. *In Xanadu* (1989); *City of Djinns* (1993); *White Mughals* (2002); *The Last Mughal* (2006).

¶ Artist. Flower and chakra-related iconography.

Willie's bumptious enthusiasm, made them favourite guides and hosts; they could turn up anywhere in the country, like Madame Bianca Castafiore, the Milanese Nightingale from *Tintin*, bringing energy and commotion to the scene.

Georgia and I began collecting Indian miniature paintings. I can now see that our earliest purchases were mostly fakes, but we hang them side by side with genuine ones. I had moved in London to a cottage on the Chelsea-Fulham frontier, in Wandon Road. For this house we started collecting more grown-up pictures. Philip Mould, the art dealer, told me that he'd found, in the basement of Spink & Son, a long-forgotten life-sized portrait of a Maharaja from Bihar, which he thought I'd like. I did. It cost an astronomical £6,000 and I took a deep breath, and went for it.

The next day, the man from Spink's rang me at my office. 'I need to tell you we have another interested party for the Maharaja.'

'But I've already bought it, haven't I?'

'You have indeed, sir. But I promised this other gentleman I'd pass on the message. He would like to buy it from you for £12,000.'

It was tempting. Very. But I passed.

The next day, he rang again. 'The gentleman is most persistent, sir. He is now offering you £20,000 for the painting.'

'God, who on earth is this guy?'

'I'm afraid I cannot say, sir. But I can tell you he's an American client.'

'Banker?'

'Actually he's in the fashion business, but I really shouldn't have told you that.'

'Not Ralph Lauren? It is, isn't it? He wants it for his new Bond Street store.'

There was a long silence. 'Er, it is best if I don't actually confirm that, sir. But you are perceptive.'

I kept the painting, and love it still. The substitute picture hanging above the stairs in Ralph Lauren's Old Bond Street store is of a First World War British officer.

I continued researching *The Fashion Conspiracy*, which grew longer and longer. In a coffee shop in Madras I met a retail sourcing expert from New York who took me to several heart-breaking sweatshops, full of just-turned-teenagers at sewing machines turning out American sportswear brands. And in London, in the labyrinth of streets off Brick Lane, the neighbourhood representative of the National Union of Garment Workers took me on tours of gimcrack workshops I could never have found without his help. Meanwhile, the length of Park Avenue, I interviewed super-rich couture-wearers such as Nan Kempner, Anne Bass and Mercedes Kellogg, who kept fashion's cash tills ringing. And then in Kuwait City, I finally located a dry cleaner I'd heard whispers about, but which had proved so elusive, where the basement was filled with hundreds of the most expensive beaded couture and designer dresses, dangling forlornly from rails. They had been sent for cleaning by their Middle Eastern owners but never collected, because the new season's collections had arrived and there was no longer any need for the old ones. It was the elephants' graveyard of fashion.

The book came out and Harvey Nichols' boss, John Hoerner,★ gave a splashy party for 400 in the department store, and it went to Number One . . . for one week only, before tumbling back down the charts. It was published in the United States, and

★ American-born retailer. CEO of the Burton Group, Arcadia (1991–2000). Fashion boss, Tesco.

Leonard and Evelyn Lauder gave a launch party at Mortimer's, which they filled with Manhattan's finest. The American publisher, Harper & Row, sent me on a nine-city book tour from Detroit to Atlanta.

A few days before I set off, I had lunch with the novelist Jeffrey Archer at Le Caprice and was given the following advice, which I have never forgotten.

'Young man,' he said, 'when you have been on as many coast-to-coast book tours as I have, you learn the tricks of the trade. Whenever I arrive at any American radio station, I say, "I assume you haven't read my new book. No, please don't pretend. I'm making life easier for you. Here is my list of questions. Just read them out, and I'll give you good answers."'

'Don't they object? The interviewers, I mean?'

'Not at all. They appreciate me doing their job for them. My first question goes: "How should I address you, Lord Archer? Should I call you 'Your Lordship' or something?" To which I reply, "Certainly not! Call me Jeffrey. Here in the land of the free, the world's greatest democracy . . ."

'The second question goes: "Okay, Jeffrey, I hear that the Queen of England and Prime Minister Margaret Thatcher are both big admirers of your novels?" To which I reply, "Good God, *who told you that*? It's meant to be a secret. I shouldn't really comment . . . but seeing as we're in Kansas/Houston/Phoenix, I can confirm it is perfectly true, Her Majesty and Prime Minister Thatcher both adore my books . . ."'

One morning, not long after *The Fashion Conspiracy* was published, I received a handwritten letter from the Chairman of Condé Nast, Daniel Salem, saying some kind things about the book which he had evidently read rather carefully, and asking if I would like to have tea at his flat in Ennismore

Gardens. It was the most courteous of letters and it piqued my curiosity.

Daniel was the epitome of elegance: sophisticated, half French, half American, an investment banker turned publisher in his mid-sixties. His double-height-ceilinged flat was chic and restrained. And perched on one of several white sofas was a surprise extra guest: 'S.I.' Newhouse Jr, the billionaire owner of Condé Nast in New York.

As a double act, they were irresistible. Daniel was tall, relaxed, shrugged a lot. He reminded me of Babar the Elephant but with perfect tailoring. He said, 'You know, this may not remotely interest you, but we have an idea . . .'

Si (as he was generally known) Newhouse was short, delphic and cultured. He was in London, he said, for the day to look at a painting and, er, to meet you. He was complimentary about *Harpers & Queen*, and referred in detail to several articles we had published. It was clear he read the magazine closely, and he referred approvingly to photographers and writers we were using. Condé Nast, he explained, had recently launched the men's magazine *GQ* in Britain, which was performing strongly on the business side but editorially weak (I already knew this). *Tatler*, he went on, which Condé Nast had bought five years earlier in 1984, was underperforming. The Editorial Director of the company, Mark Boxer,★ had recently died young, leaving them with a vacuum. And furthermore, their Managing Director, Richard Hill, was strong with advertisers but had no editorial instincts. Might I consider moving to Condé Nast as the new Editorial Director of the British company?

'Please take your time to consider,' Daniel said. He made an

★ Publisher, political cartoonist, wit. Editor, *Tatler* (1983–88), Editorial Director Condé Nast (1987–88). Husband of Anna Ford.

elegant gesture with his hand, indicating a glorious lack of indecent haste. 'We need not speak of money, I am sure you would be well satisfied.'

On my way back to Broadwick Street, my taxi passed Vogue House in Hanover Square, the Condé Nast HQ. I peered at the revolving doors, through which I could see a procession of *Vogue*, *Tatler* and *House & Garden* staffers tottering about on Manolo Blahnik heels. I had always been curious about what went on behind those revolving doors, in the dark empire which, all of a sudden, seemed less forbidding than before.

There followed a month of most painful indecision. Perhaps I had already decided to leave, seduced by the alluring combination of sophistication and power? Nevertheless, I tortured myself, aghast at the thought of abandoning the team I'd assembled, quitting a safe job for what might prove to be a perilous one, in an organization I'd been trained to mistrust. A move from Hearst to Condé Nast was like defecting from Christie's to Sotheby's, or Rothschild's to Lazard's. Furthermore, Georgia and I were getting married in a couple of months' time. I had a wife to think about. The timing could scarcely have been worse.

I am by nature decisive, but found myself in a slough of sickening, stress-inducing confusion. Terry Mansfield, who knew nothing of the dilemma, rang to offer me the loan of the Hearst Rolls-Royce for my wedding, a generous gesture I could hardly accept while contemplating treachery. Stephen Quinn, already at Condé Nast to launch *GQ*, was the only other person who knew, and urged me to sign up.

Whenever I came into the *Harpers & Queen* office, I felt worse. The previous year, Hearst had dangled a New York Editorship in front of me; I had been flown to New York on Concorde and told only that it was either *Harper's Bazaar*, *Town & Country* or *Esquire* – they'd disclose which one after I'd accepted the post. I had declined: I had no wish to live in the dark canyons of Manhattan with a new wife. But Condé Nast was tempting.

I made the decision; my move was announced. It was alarmingly public, with long articles in the newspapers, and undeniably painful.

'What have you done?' asked one of my more candid friends. 'Are you crazy? The people who love you are furious with you for leaving, and the Condé Nast Editors are furious you're coming. None of them want you. I'll be surprised if you last six months in that snakepit.'

Georgia and I got married on the hottest recorded day of the 1980s, under a sweltering, cloudless July sky. It was so hot that the government issued warnings about melting tarmac on the roads, and dogs and the elderly expiring from dehydration. There were no specific warnings issued to brides.

The church we had chosen – St George's, Hanover Square – is barely a stone's throw from Vogue House, though that had not been a factor when we booked it. Our reception, held around the corner in the Ballroom at Claridge's, was a furnace; no London hotels had air con in those days, it wasn't yet a thing.

Our wedding is best described as the Full English: the stand-ard one-hour 3 p.m. Church of England job, choir, six child bridesmaids, a pageboy, big hats, tailcoats, 'Jerusalem' as the recessional hymn. St George's holds 600, which was the number of guests we invited. My ushers were a combination of school and university friends, plus my two brothers, Timmy and Christopher, sheltering under the portico of the church doling out service sheets. I didn't see Georgia or her dress until she appeared down the aisle on the arm of her father, George, and she looked magical: 'like the young Audrey Hepburn', as *Hello!* magazine rather sweetly put it. Trailing along behind the bride, carrying her Alistair Blair train, came Edward Stourton's daughter Eleanor, Pandora Stevens' daughter Chloe, Tessa Dahl's daughter Clover, Olinda Adeane's daughter Dorelia, and Georgia's youngest sisters Luisa and Portia, in bridesmaid dresses created from cream and gold saris with dark pink borders, and

Rajasthani ballet shoes. Georgia's brother Daniel was the pageboy.

Every last pew was rammed with friends from every part of our lives: our respective families filling the front couple of rows, parents, surviving grandparents, uncles and aunts, Georgia's sister Becca, our godparents, my mother looking incredibly smart in Hardy Amies, Georgia's St Paul's and Oxford friends, my old friends from each phase of my life, the entire staff of *Harpers & Queen*, and many more from Condé Nast where I was shortly to begin work. The Jade Garden set was out in force: James and Edward Stourton, Nick Allan with his fiancée Sarah, Kit and Georgie Hunter Gordon, Peter Pleydell-Bouverie with Jane. Craig Brown wore a tailcoat and looked almost the part. Napier Miles made it in from the Pinstripe Club. Alistair Scott wore a kilt.

Tina Brown from *Vanity Fair* and Anna Wintour from *American Vogue* both wore dark glasses the size of saucers throughout the service, and couldn't have seen a thing in the gloom of the nave. Ann Barr wore a Thea Porter frock coat; Sophie Hicks wore a top hat. The *Daily Mail* gossip columnist Nigel Dempster brought a portable TV into the church, set it up with headphones in a ringside pew, and watched the Diamond Day stakes from Ascot while we exchanged our vows. He won £600 on a highly geared bet and whooped in triumph. Daniel Salem and Terry Mansfield skirted elegantly around one another. Mrs Kenward in her best black bow broke the habit of several years and greeted the groom and his bride. Wherever you looked was a sea of enormous hats and morning suits.

As Georgia and I processed back down the aisle, and the faces of the congregation blurred into a single shimmering vista of smiles and goodwill, it felt to me like the closing credits of a film, during which the director has reprised highlights from the entire movie. Like a man plunging in an unopened parachute from a great height, my life flashed before me, the whole cast of characters – past, present and future.

I remember almost nothing about our reception at Claridge's, other than a phalanx of white-jacketed, white-gloved waiters standing in line with outstretched trays of champagne, and circulating with plates of canapés. My brother Timmy made an excellent speech as best man, as did Georgia's uncle Jeremy Metcalfe, and I suppose I must have spoken too. The temperature in the ballroom was so hot that consumption of champagne reached double the norm, as guests gasped deliriously for air and liquid. The jail-bound conman Darius Guppy, an Oxford friend of Georgia's, clicked instantly with a pretty guest in a hat, and rather stylishly booked them both an impulse bedroom upstairs. Our vicar, Adam Ford, brother of wine-throwing Anna, looked suitably dignified in the scarlet cassock of a Queen's Chaplain.

We left our reception through the front doors of Claridge's in a blizzard of confetti, were driven once round the block and re-entered the hotel through the staff entrance in Brook's Mews, past the clocking-in machines, and up the rear elevator to the Royal Suite.

'We hope you will be comfortable,' murmured the General Manager. 'King Juan Carlos and Her Majesty Queen Sophia of Spain altered their plans and left a day earlier than expected, so we have been able to offer you their favourite suite.'

12

I had never passed through the revolving doors of Vogue House until the day I started work there. The building is an early fifties construction, with an impressive facade and entablature, and long views over Hanover Square. Inside, the magazines occupied one floor each, with a distinctly different vibe to each title; as you moved about the building, you felt the shifts in culture, almost all conforming to stereotype.

So *Vogue* really was populated by skinny fashionistas in black, with killer heels. *House & Garden* employed Tory matrons and pretty country girls, sifting through boxes of fabric samples; most had grown up in Old Rectories in Gloucestershire or Wiltshire. *Tatler* was staffed by party-minded, treacherous socialites, *Brides* by adorable, gentle young women who knew everything about wedding dresses and wedding flowers. *The World of Interiors* was art school bohemian, the *GQ* floor a testosterone-fuelled fug of sport and menswear, girlie calendars, aftershave and business writers. And so on for several more storeys.

Just as you can never fully comprehend the internal dynamics of other people's marriages, so you cannot decode the DNA of a company until you experience it at first hand. From the outside, the Condé Nast of the late eighties appeared as sleek and smooth as a well-oiled seal. I had observed their commercial teams in action at parties, confident and assured. And their fashion editors were smart, haughty and frequently the mistresses of powerful men. From the inside, it was impossible not to notice the yawning chasm between perception and reality.

The Managing Director, Richard Hill, was a tall, undeniably dashing figure in his mid-fifties, with military bearing. His days revolved around taking the company's biggest advertisers out to lunch, to Mark's Club, Harry's Bar and The East India Club in rotation. 'It's good news you've joined,' he said, affably. 'We're banking on you sorting out *GQ*, it's a bit of a shambles down there, apparently.'

'Anything in particular you see as a problem?'

He shrugged. 'God knows, I don't read it. I'm not one of *those*, you see.' He lowered his voice and gave a meaningful nod. 'Queers.'

The Deputy Managing Director, Glyn Stanford, took me to lunch at Claridge's on Day One. He wore an unusual gold sig-net ring with a ruby set in the middle. He summoned the sommelier and ordered a bottle of claret of astronomical price. 'I think you will find,' he said, rubbing his hands together and casting his eyes appreciatively down the menu, 'that we do things with just a bit more style at Condé Nast than they do over the road at National Magazines . . .'

A tour of the building and meetings with the various Editors had been arranged for the afternoon; in theory at least, they now reported to me, and would play a big part in my life. 'I wouldn't bother seeing Liz Tilberis at *Vogue*, if I were you, old chap,' cautioned Richard Hill. 'Best give her a wide berth. She's none too happy at your arrival, to be perfectly frank. She's in a major sulk. Nothing to be gained by going there.'

Instead, I was introduced to Robert Harling. He was the 81-year-old Editor of *House & Garden*, something of a legend in the business though seldom glimpsed. He had been a close friend of the author Ian Fleming and was said to be the model for James Bond. He was certainly stylish enough, with his skin-tight black leather trousers and homburg hat. He lunched every single day at the same table in the Causerie at Claridge's, generally with his deputy.

I liked him at once, he had an alert, mischievous, craggy face. I made a remark about the smallness of the *House & Garden* editorial team, which then consisted of only 13 people (*Vogue* had 63).

'My dear fellow,' he replied, 'thirteen is the perfect number – the blessed Editor and his twelve apostles. All these other Editors, no names mentioned [he pointed to the ceiling with a bony finger, in the direction of *Vogue*], they like to aggrandize themselves with casts of hundreds. Pure vanity . . . that's all it is.'

'What if someone's ill? With such tight numbers?'

'Ill?' he boomed. 'Ill! Nobody on *House & Garden* is permitted to be ill. My young secretary came to see me last evening, saying she had a cold coming on, she might need to take today off. Imagine! She's only twenty. I told her, "My dear, there's nothing in life which can't be solved by a good fuck or a gargle. That'll sort you out."'

There was a job to be done on *GQ*. *Gentlemen's Quarterly*, not a quarterly at all but monthly and always abbreviated to *GQ*, had been launched in Britain six months earlier to great fanfare, the first overseas edition of the successful American men's magazine, and the first mainstream men's glossy on the British market. Many media commentators had been sceptical: they predicted it wouldn't work and, as issue followed issue, it was looking uncomfortably like they were right. The first issue, with the Deputy Prime Minister Michael Heseltine on the front cover, and the provoking cover line 'Britain's beautiful bad boy' had sold 50,000 news-stand copies. The second issue sold 30,000, the third 15,000. All around the building, Condé

Nast executives were adopting a nonchalant brace position, as the launch fell out of the sky.

It didn't help that the Editor, named Paul Keers, was the wrong guy. He also appeared paranoid. He refused to have a secretary (unheard of at Condé Nast), not wanting anyone else to read his post. And when he slipped out to the Gents, he locked his office behind him and took the key. The issues were dreary and flat.

Meanwhile, on the third floor, *Tatler* had problems of its own. Magazines quickly become prisoners of their positioning and, slowly but surely, the *Tatler* DNA had shifted from audacious wit to something more like *Mugger's Weekly*. Word had got round that, if you allowed yourself to be interviewed by *Tatler*, you would certainly regret it, the tone would surely be vindictively negative. 'Like a seal cull,' someone described it. 'They'll club you to death.'

Consequently, few dared to be interviewed: interviews became profiles, reliant upon hearsay and recycled old cuttings; fresh portrait photographs became photo library retreads.

The Editor, Winston Churchill's granddaughter Emma Soames, was a fine journalist but presiding over a bucking bronco. In my first week at Condé Nast, three separate libel suits arrived from disgruntled *Tatler* subjects; unable to defend them, we settled all three.

Upstairs on the fifth floor – the *Vogue* floor – Editor Liz Tilberis was more hostile than Cinderella's sisters at Prince Charming's ball. A gifted fashion editor with a chignon of grey hair, she did everything to confound and wrong-foot me while presenting a treacherous, assassin's smile.

My name was published on the masthead (cast of characters) at the front of *Vogue* in heavy bold type – **EDITORIAL DIRECTOR: NICHOLAS COLERIDGE**. Liz organized for the typeface to be changed to a lighter one – *EDITORIAL DIRECTOR: NICHOLAS COLERIDGE* – to signal her disapproval. Or she removed my name altogether from the masthead for an issue. Or went to extreme lengths to secure the best table for herself at a fashionable lunch spot, Caviar Kaspia, and the worst table in the place for me. Luckily the proprietor of Caviar Kaspia was Gavin Rankin, my old Eton school friend, who reversed the instruction.

It was uncomfortable having an enemy on the fifth floor, especially when that enemy was the Editor of *Vogue*. At every party I went to, someone would enquire, 'And how are you getting on with Liz Tilberis?' while adopting an innocent expression, pretending to be ignorant of the raging discord. It was obvious Liz was dissing and undermining me all over town – frequently to my friends, who reported straight back. But I parked direct confrontation until the moment was right, and built my power base. And watched, while a succession of poorly chosen *Vogue* front covers failed at news-stand, which further stoked Liz's paranoia, and strengthened my hand.

Fortunately, I had allies aplenty. There was the shrewd Personnel Director, Barbara Tims, a wartime codebreaker from Bletchley Park who gave me the lie of the land, and Sandra Boler, veteran Editor of *Brides*, the Condé Nast wedding magazine. Julia Elliot, my PA, had come in my wagon train from *Harpers & Queen*, and others soon followed. On the business side of the company, the Publishers and advertising men were divided between those who went horse racing midweek – the back seats of their Jaguars piled high with trilbies, racecards and binoculars – and those who sat at their desks doing crosswords. Only Stephen Quinn, Publisher of *GQ*, had fire inside him, and Annie Holcroft of *Vogue*.

★

The elegant Daniel Salem was retiring as Chairman to be replaced by a young cousin of Si Newhouse, Jonathan Newhouse, about whom nobody knew anything other than that he had been working at American Condé Nast on *The New Yorker*. Days before his arrival, a message came from Manhattan to be passed to the security team at reception, so they could recognize him. The message said: 'Mr Newhouse will be wearing a bow tie and suspenders.'

Not realizing that suspenders is American for trouser braces, there was much excited speculation. 'I hear the new Chairman is from *The Rocky Horror Show*,' said Peter on the front desk, shaking his head. 'They say he wears knickers and suspenders.'

Jonathan and I had lunch in the Japanese sushi bar under the office, and I liked him at once. He struck me as quirky, clever and perceptive. That was my first impression. Later, I would add a string of supplementary impressions: bold, impetuous, modest, indiscreet and generous. But I had thirty years to refine my psychological profile of the Condé Nast heir.

He had a head of curly black hair in those days (later, a buzz cut and Japanese Yakuza tattoo) and wore the bow tie we had been alerted to. Like many Newhouses, Jonathan could suddenly dry in conversation, when out of his comfort zone, but overcompensated with disarming warmth and humour. He had begun life as a crime reporter on one of the Newhouse newspapers, and appreciated good journalism. Alert to slights, he was loyal to those he trusted and who could make him laugh. I instinctively sensed he was someone I would enjoy working for.

The overseas division of Condé Nast was, at the time, a fraction of the size it would become: 40 monthly titles published in five Western European markets (France, Italy, Germany, Spain and Britain), and with barely a thousand staff. At its zenith, as the Glossy Years unfolded, there would be 140 titles in 27 markets, on every continent, and more than 4,000 staff, with dozens of spin-off businesses in digital, restaurants and events. But, for now, it had a creaky, hidebound air. Typed memos to Directors were painstakingly formal and old-fashioned: 'To Mr R. Hill, Mr G. Stanford, Miss S. Boler, Miss B. Tims' et cetera.

It was only recently that Condé Nast had removed the 'private income' question from job application forms. All candidates filled in a questionnaire for Personnel with details of their schooling and home address, and were then asked how much monthly income they enjoyed in allowances from kind parents or family trusts. Diversity meant: did you go to Heathfield or Tudor Hall?

And if a gossip columnist rang up for a quote, it was panic stations. 'We don't speak to the press at Condé Nast,' Richard Hill cautioned me. 'Never trust a journalist. That's my advice to you.'

Having got my eye in, I made rapid changes. Alexandra Shulman was appointed Editor of *GQ*; it was controversial to appoint a woman to a men's magazine, but we needed a professional. She was the elder sister of my *Harpers & Queen* star, Nicky, and our careers were to be entwined for the next three decades. Alex had long, untidy, gypsyish hair and a sexy, hippy vibe. She was also decisive and a proper journalist, both of which *GQ* urgently required. On *Tatler*, I brought in Jane Procter from *W* magazine, a risk of a quite different sort, but desperate times call for radical solutions, and *Tatler* was once again on skid row. Jane was tricky, insecure, attractive and aspirational, and I had a sixth sense these qualities might just do the trick. They'd better. Even the benign Newhouses, with their legendary patience and long-term outlook, were beginning to sound queasy as *Tatler*'s losses hit £3 million a year, and to wonder what had possessed them to buy it in the first place.

The great (and entirely unintuitive) advantage of glossy magazines is that, compared to digital, they can alter direction in a heartbeat. With no platform to rebuild, no Content Management System, no flowcharts or tech considerations, the content, typefaces and design of a glossy can turn on a sixpence. In no time, Alex's *GQ* and Jane's *Tatler* looked a whole lot stronger and, furthermore, circulation soared on both. Alexandra put a woman – Sharon Stone in a gaping fawn raincoat – on the front cover of *GQ*, and sales doubled. It was a clue: women sell. Jane produced a colourful, witty, celebrity-focused and borderline chavvy iteration of *Tatler*, which boomed. Princess Di became a default cover girl, and Jane, ahead of all others, championed the next generation of 'It girls', Tara Palmer-Tomkinson and Normandie Keith, who were remorselessly featured. Suddenly, *Tatler* was out of intensive care and strutting its stuff.

Tara P-T, meanwhile, became an unexpected friend. She used to turn up at Vogue House in the afternoon, unannounced and uninvited, and take a nap on the sofa in my office. I would return from lunch to find her there, curled up, dozing away. We had to whisper during afternoon meetings, to avoid waking her. She was sweet and funny and vulnerable, and brimming with life. This was before the twin evils of cocaine and fame made everything more difficult for her, and eventually contributed to her early death.

It is a delicate position being Editorial Director of a group like Condé Nast. You are, at once, responsible for everything and nothing. You are simultaneously dependent upon the talent of the Editors you bring in, and accountable for their success or failure, but also a backseat driver. No longer holding tight to the steering wheel, you are clutching on to the shoulders of the chauffeur – the Editor – periodically lunging forwards to alter the direction of travel. 'Look out, you bloody fool, you almost hit a cow.' But politer. Because you need them and respect them, and cannot do everything yourself.

My job as Editorial Director was to be guru, confidant and cheerleader. Often, I felt like a parent at Speech Day, urging my protégés on, longing for them to shine. But in the end, their editorial success is their success, their failures partly your own. Sometimes, in a way that is harder for an Editor, perpetually engaged in the fortunes of a single title, you can more clearly see the wood for the trees. I understood and loved the job. It was power without responsibility; responsibility without absolute power. On *Tatler*, they called me 'the Gloss Adjuster'.

Once a year, Si Newhouse, billionaire owner and *capo dei capi* of Condé Nast, landed in London in a private jet to review his British colonies. This royal progress culminated in a lunch at Wilton's fish restaurant on Jermyn Street, at which Si ate the new season's gull's eggs, and an inner circle of executives was granted face time. In my capacity as Editorial Director, I was by now a core member of this circle which comprised Daniel Salem, Jonathan Newhouse, Richard Hill and me.

At the time, it was being widely reported that the Newhouses were in the running to spend $550 million to purchase *New York* magazine, and I asked Si whether he was indeed interested in buying it.

Before he could reply, Richard Hill broke in. 'Don't be stupid, Nicholas, Si already owns *New York* magazine. He could hardly buy it, he owns it already.'

Daniel Salem was the first to recognize the ghastly error, and tried to cover for Richard. 'Richard, you must have misheard, Nicholas was speaking of *New York* magazine, not *The New Yorker* which Si, of course, acquired two years ago.'

'You mean there are two different magazines, *The New Yorker* and *New York*?' persisted Richard, incredulously. 'Well, that's very confusing. I mean, if you went into a newsagent's shop and asked, "Have you got *The New Yorker*?" they might easily hand you a copy of *New York* by mistake. It must happen all the time. Recipe for disaster. I'm sure the advertisers can't tell them apart either. I get sent one of them every week. Not sure which one it is. It arrives on my desk. The one Si already owns, presumably? Not that I read it, no time, it's far too wordy, it would take forever to read. I'm sure nobody reads it. Who could? We're all so busy. Anyway . . .'

Si Newhouse, peeling his new season gull's eggs, stared at Richard in appalled bafflement. The rest of the table stared down at our plates. It was a defining moment.

Si realized he had a blithering idiot in charge.

13

Georgia and I were living happily in our cottage in Wandon Road, near the Chelsea football stadium. On match nights, tens of thousands of fans streamed past the row of brightly painted cottages, pausing only to pee against our front wall or to kick empty, clattering lager cans down the street. At weekends, we often headed to my parents in West Sussex for a blast of country air.

My father mentioned one Sunday over lunch that he would become Chairman of Lloyd's of London the following year. The Lloyd's underwriter he chaired, Sturge, had grown to become the largest in the market and been floated on the Stock Exchange by Cazenove the previous year. Had it not been for reports in the financial pages, we would scarcely have been aware, since he continued to consider insurance a dull subject to inflict upon his children, so seldom referred to it. We were suitably proud of his great success, the Lloyd's of London global market having 80,000 staff at the time.

'I think it might get a little bumpy over the next year or two,' my father added, with glorious understatement. 'The results for syndicates will be hammered by provisions for American asbestos claims dating back to the sixties, the courts over there are awarding huge compensation settlements. So my timing as Chairman probably isn't ideal. But someone has to do it. Now, how is the magazine world? People still buying the odd copy now and then, are they?'

My brother Timmy worked at Sturge; our youngest brother,

Christopher, was at Oxford doing history at Exeter College. In a long-running family joke, we all pretended we thought he was actually at Exeter University, so questioned him constantly about walks across Exmoor and Dartmoor, and Devon cream teas.

At weekends, Christopher regularly invited one or other of his Oxford friends to stay, often George Osborne, a poised, unashamedly ambitious twenty-year-old, perpetually short of money. It was my job to drop him at the railway station at the end of visits. As we approached the station, I would hear the clinking and counting of coins in the back seat.

'Er, Nick, what do you reckon a single to Waterloo is going to cost?'

'Not sure. About a fiver?'

'I've got three pounds and seventy-two pence. Can you loan me the difference?'

This happened more than once. Surprisingly soon afterwards, George became Shadow Chancellor of the Exchequer and then, in a heartbeat, Chancellor. I always intended knocking my outstanding debts off my tax return, with the instruction 'Collect from Chancellor'.

Through Alistair Scott and Victoria Mather, we became friends with Carol Thatcher. She lived in a terraced cottage off the Wandsworth Bridge Road, decorated like student digs with makeshift bookshelves built from planks and bricks, and a Union Jack flag draped across a collapsing sofa. The sole indication that her mother, Margaret Thatcher, was Prime Minister was a reinforced, bomb-proof letter box, installed by the security services and impossible to open, so perpetually imprisoning her post. I thought Carol's decrepit cottage reflected well on the integrity of British public life; the daughter of most third-term heads of state would have been living in gilded luxury.

Carol made a living as a freelance journalist, and amused us with her stories of saving money. Sent to interview President Bhutto of Pakistan by the *Daily Express*, her newspaper supplied her with a First Class aeroplane ticket, on account of her being the Prime Minister's daughter.

'God, I cashed that in at once,' Carol said in her noisy, matter-of-fact voice. 'I said at the airport, "Bung me down in toilet class and give me the difference in cash," which they did. When we landed in Islamabad, the President had sent a whole reception committee to greet me – red carpet, brass band, limo, ministers. But when they saw I wasn't in First, they went away again. I got a tuk-tuk to the palace.'

Our circle of friends was getting married thick and fast, and the ones that hadn't yet, were looking. My friend Prue Murdoch, who had typed out my novel *Shooting Stars*, shared her dilemma over lunch at San Quintino's.

'You've got to advise me, Nick, I met three new husband prospects at a wedding reception last weekend, I can't decide which one to go for.'

'Describe them.'

'Well, the first one's in the army. Very fit. Gorgeous really. I don't mind telling you, I really fancied him.'

'Do you see yourself as an army wife? Living in barracks in Munster or somewhere? Not sure I entirely do.'

'Okay then, there was this other guy. A racehorse trainer from Newmarket. Not so tall, but definitely dishy.'

'The trouble with racing people is they go to race meetings every single Saturday. Lunches in private boxes with owners. Is that you, Prue?'

'No, definitely not, now you mention it. I'd hate that. The third guy works in finance, Crispin Odey. He was at Oxford, I think.'

'I know Crispin. Very nice guy. Clever and fun. Can't think of any negatives really.'

Prue and Crispin became engaged shortly afterwards, and Prue's father, the media tycoon Rupert Murdoch, gave a magnificent wedding dinner at a Piccadilly hotel. Her Australian godfather made a mesmerizingly dreadful speech, filled with terrible puns. 'Let's all drink to their happy *Times,* and hope *The Sun* will never set over their beautiful union. This wedding is certainly the *News of the World* today . . .' and so on.

I had asked Prue, 'Where's the honeymoon going to be?'

She shrugged. 'I don't know, Crispin wants it to be a surprise. I've been told to pack two suitcases, one for a hot honeymoon, one for cold. But I know it'll be a hot one. The Seychelles, I reckon. Or the Maldives. I've only really packed for hot. I'm craving sunshine. You know how much I love the sun.'

I asked Crispin at the reception. 'I hear it's a surprise honeymoon. Any clues?'

He said, 'Don't tell Prue, but I'm taking her to a fishing lodge in Scotland. It's where I used to go as a child. It's a bit rough and ready, and freezing cold, but beautiful. The bedrooms are a bit like school dormitories, with rows of iron beds.'

I feared the worst. Luckily Prue's second marriage, to Alasdair MacLeod, a fellow Ashdown House old boy, has been a resounding success. Crispin started a hedge fund and became a billionaire.

Meanwhile, our friend Tessa Dahl was marrying, unmarrying and becoming engaged again at an accelerating rate of knots. At her best, she was hypnotically beautiful with perfect cheekbones, and unfailingly witty; but when she fell under the spell of prescription drugs and instability kicked in, she was impetuous and unreliable. Twice she rang me in the middle of the night to tell me she was engaged. 'Do me a favour, darling,' she'd slur.

'Ring *Hello!* in the morning and offer them an exclusive on the wedding. See what they'll pay, you'll need to negotiate.' The first time it happened, the groom was the *Blow-Up* actor David Hemmings; the second time, it was a surgeon at the Cedars-Sinai hospital in Los Angeles. The surgeon had been operating on her bowel when they had first met, the previous week. It had been love at first sight.

We seemed to be attending Tessa's engagement parties very regularly. Her father, Roald, had died by now, but her children, Sophie, Clover and Luke, were generally present, and their saint-like Scottish nannie, Maureen. I sensed that these engagement parties were an end in themselves, since marriage plans generally petered out soon afterwards, and nothing was heard of the fiancé ever again. Tessa started dating a friend of ours; they lived in a huge Kensington house on Victoria Road, which belonged to Dustin Hoffman. During the early stages of their romance, their love-making was so frenzied that Tessa accidentally ripped his foreskin with her long talon-like fingernails. This necessitated a late-life circumcision in his mid-thirties, excruciatingly painful. Georgia and I were invited to kitchen-supper in Victoria Road, to celebrate his release from hospital. He sat, whey-faced, at the table, in a white towelling robe, with a special wire basket shielding his bruised penis, to prevent it from chafing. He was clearly in intense pain.

It was arguably insensitive of Tessa to serve sausages and mash for supper. Nobody could eat a thing.

We visited her at a succession of different hospitals and clinics, where her maladies, interrelated and intractable, became ever worse. When she married the banker Patrick Donovan, I made a speech at the wedding. Sadly, the marriage lasted less time than it took me to write the speech; it was over in months – before my godson Ned was even born. Ned is clever and delightful and a first-class journalist, so much good came of it all.

I began accruing godchildren in a rush: Helena Allan, Nick and Sarah's daughter, who later got into textiles in Africa; Ione Hunter Gordon, Kit and Georgie's daughter, who became a gifted artist like her father; Cara Delevingne, Pandora and Charles's daughter, and Edie Campbell, Sophie Hicks and Roddy Campbell's daughter (these two became supermodels, which greatly boosted my cred in Vogue House). Ewan Wotherspoon, Alice Leatham and Johnny Wotherspoon's son, has become an architect. Willa Petty, my cousin Georgina and William Petty's daughter, is at Georgetown University in Washington. It was probably the constant round of christenings around baptismal fonts which first planted the seed for my novel *Godchilden*. Cara's other godparents were a particularly high-octane bunch, comprising the actress Joan Collins,★ Baron Enrico di Portanova, the Texas oil heir, and Annette 'Scruff' Howard, chatelaine of Castle Howard, amongst others. But *Godchildren* (the novel) was still a decade into the future.

Alexander James Coleridge, our first child, arrived on 22 May 1991 at Queen Mary's Hospital, Paddington. I was taking part in a circulation review at Vogue House when the call came through that contractions had started, and Georgia had been rushed to hospital. Our Circulation Director, Vivien Matthews, by nature very thorough, never felt comfortable cutting a long story short. She was saying something along the lines of, 'The weekly figure for *Brides and Setting Up Home* magazine is three per cent

★ Dame Joan Collins, actress. By some peculiar algorithm of placement at large dinners, NC is regularly seated next to her. She masks her disappointment very professionally.

behind forecast but two per cent ahead year-on-year, but EPOS data is suggesting we might be ahead of that by one or two per cent in Tesco and Morrisons stores, and we have a special point-of-sale promotion running at WH Smith travel outlets, so . . .' when the second call came.

Alexander was on the move. I made it with minutes to spare.

He emerged, perfect, into the world. Georgia had done brilliantly. Soon the hospital room was filled with several sets of grandparents, brothers and sisters, aunts and uncles, all toasting his arrival, while relays of nurses delivered half of London's supply of orchids and cut flowers, mainly dispatched from Vogue House.

It was a joyous moment.

I was so overcome by the emotion of it all that I lay down on Georgia's narrow hospital bed for a quick nap, and slept soundly for several hours.

14

I was summoned to Paris for the day, to the Condé Nast *hôtel particulier* at 4 Place du Palais Bourbon, built on land first acquired by Louis Joseph, Prince of Condé, in 1769. Inside, in an office overlooking the magnificent square, sat the current Prince of Condé Nast, Jonathan Newhouse, then living in Paris. Behind him, on a shelf, was a display of tourist mugs bought in the cities he regularly visited for work – Milan, London, Madrid, and so on – in which he kept leftover lira, pound coins and pesetas.

No sooner had I entered than Jonathan asked if I would like to become Managing Director of the British company, while also remaining Editorial Director. He slid a sheaf of papers across the desk. These, he explained, were the results of a secret handwriting analysis he had commissioned from a French graphologist, based upon a letter I had written earlier in the year.

My letter must have been written early in the morning, with unstressed hand, because the analysis was, in parts, rather flattering. In other parts, chilling.

It began, 'Overall impression: highly independent in both thought and action, thorough, alert, quick to comprehend the whole picture, decisive but cautious in thought, sense of responsibility, externalizes himself in his work but is somewhat isolated deep down, scrupulous.'

It went on, 'The writer has the high level of intelligence of a decisive man whose mind is quick, incisive and shrewd in dealing with the problems in hand. He has an analytical mind, high ideals and rather a creative side. He is able to break down a problem into simple terms, and has quite a free imagination which is not hampered by prejudice. He is a man who very quickly goes for the main point. He is selective in his intellectual interests. Although he may not seem to take much time in examining projects proposed to him, this does not stop him from selecting what appears essential and profitable to him.

'He has a determined sense of enterprise. He does not hesitate to commit himself, and his dynamism is reinforced by his own sense of pride and competitiveness. He hates everything that is pre-established. He can be impatient. The writer has strong potential for renewal. His character is that of a man who is superficially sociable and charming, but in whom the solitary side can sometimes dominate. He is impulsive, and does not like to wait for an order to be carried out once he has given it. He has strong powers of persuasion, and is able to convince others with his well-chosen, incisive and irrefutable arguments . . .'

The French handwriting analysis continued in this vein for several hundred more words.

When I had finished reading it, Jonathan said, 'I should clarify, we haven't made our decision to offer you the job based only on your handwriting. But these things can sometimes be perceptive.

'Why not think about it,' he went on, 'for twenty minutes, then give me your answer. Take a walk round the block.'

Clearly, I had zero credentials for the job of Managing Director, knowing very little at the time about business or advertising, but it occurred to me that, if I declined, someone else would surely be brought in to do it, and perhaps I wouldn't click with them. Whereas if I replied yes, I would probably rub along perfectly well with myself. So I took the role, and held on tight for the next twenty-six years. It was kind, and brave, of Jonathan to give me the break.

★

It was decided I should be sent to New York for a month, to live at the Pierre hotel and undergo training at the Condé Nast headquarters on Madison Avenue. This consisted largely of having lunch at the Four Seasons Grill Room or the Algonquin hotel with a succession of different Editors, Publishers and executives. It would be an exaggeration to say that much actual training was involved.

I had been told to present myself, on my first morning, at the office of Si Newhouse, but no specific time had been mentioned. It was well known that Si arrived in the office each morning at 4.30 a.m., which raised the question of when I should show up myself.

I decided that 6 a.m. would look appropriately keen, so booked a wake-up call for 5 a.m. The sidewalks of New York were entirely deserted as I strolled the few blocks to 350 Madison Avenue. The Condé Nast offices were similarly deserted, every floor of them, still plunged in an eerie semi-darkness. A lone security guard dozed at reception.

I found Si's office on the corporate floor, and his senior PA, Ann Marcus, ushered me into the presence.

Si wore a grey sweatshirt and tracksuit bottoms. He must have been sixty at the time. He had assembled one of the greatest collections of modern art in America, but his office was austere. On the floor that morning were displayed seventy-two front covers – the past three years of American *Vogues* and American *Elles*, arranged in lines on the carpet.

'Er, Nicholas,' he said. 'Good, I've been waiting for you.' He glanced at his watch, indicating mild dismay at my leisurely timekeeping.

Attached to each front cover was a yellow Post-it note, showing the news-stand sale of each issue. 'I'm trying to figure out what sells,' he said. 'Can you deduce a pattern here?'

We stared down at rows of near-identical images. The *Elle* covers were all close-ups of gummy, smiling blonde models, with cover lines incorporating large unrounded numbers. 'Your 563 new fall essentials', '1021 winter trends you will LOVE . . .'

We hovered over the covers, analysing the performance of blonde girls versus brunettes.

Si said, 'With numbers on front covers, they work best if they are precise and uneven – readers trust them better. "1000 new trends" sounds like it might be exaggerated, but "1021 new trends" indicates value and service.'

The following morning, I reckoned I'd better raise my game, and arrived at the office at 5.15 a.m. The streets were full of stragglers, heading home from the night before. A black jazz trumpeter swayed by, carrying his instrument.

'Er, Nicholas, good, I was waiting for you, I want to show you something . . .' Si was sitting behind his desk, manually counting the advertising pages of the new issues – his own and the competitors. On a yellow legal pad, he made a pencil mark for each sold page, then struck a line through them for each fifth one. In a column, it said *Vogue* 471, *Harper's Bazaar* 312, *Glamour* 337 and so forth.

'Do you do this, Nicholas? I find it helpful.'

'Well, I don't count the pages by hand. Perhaps I should. Our media research department provides the data.'

'But not as quickly, I'm sure,' said Si. 'The new *Elle* came in last night, so I'll have these figures ahead of the *Vogue* Publisher. It sends a signal.'

Alexander Liberman, the legendary Ukrainian-born Editorial Director and Si's Svengali, took me to the Four Seasons Grill Room and discussed magazines in a mesmerizing, cultivated and discursive manner that positioned them at the fulcrum of all civilization. I sat in on meetings with Anna Wintour, Tina

Brown, Art Cooper of American GQ and Bernie Leser, President of Condé Nast in the States. A Publisher named Ron Galotti, with oiled-back hair and the demeanour of a Mafia don, told me that he'd recently had his sports car flown over to Aspen for a sales conference, and this had been highly motivating for his sales team, to see his high-performance convertible parked outside the hotel, as something to aspire to. Another Italian slickster, this one heftier, named Steve Florio, assured me he had personally and single-handedly saved *The New Yorker*, and then proceeded to undermine all the Newhouses, Tina, Anna, Bernie, everyone in fact, in succession.

Si Newhouse, with enormous generosity, invited me out to dinner with his wife Victoria, not once but several times, at his home and at the Italian restaurant in Greenwich Village he loved, Da Silvano. His home in those days, an Upper East Side brownstone, was entered through a high-security bulletproof-glass decontamination chamber, like on a submarine. You rang the front doorbell, entered a glass bubble which slowly closed behind you, sealing you in, until a second glass panel slid open in front. Through the glass, you could already see numerous paintings by Jasper Johns, Mondrian, de Kooning and Mark Rothko.

It was illuminating to spend time in the court of King Si, submerged with his numerous, perpetually warring, high-maintenance divas and dysfunctional barons. But it was also a relief to escape unscathed back to London, to the relative safety of Vogue House, and the bosom of wife and growing family.

Within a week of my appointment as Managing Director, the Editor of *Vogue*, Liz Tilberis, resigned to take a job in New York as Editor of *Harper's Bazaar*, working for Hearst. Whether it was my confirmation as her new boss, or the lure of the bumper American pay packet which decided her, was never spelt out, but it was certainly helpful. We spent the days following her departure ensuring that all the *Vogue* photographers remained onside, and wouldn't defect with Liz to *Bazaar*, and this largely worked. Condé Nast's not-so-secret USP was the ability to have first dibs on photographers, models and stylists, and this privilege was fiercely enforced.

You were either a *Vogue* photographer or you were not a *Vogue* photographer, you couldn't hawk your talent from title to title. Similarly, if you wanted to be a *Vogue* cover model, there was no point queering your pitch by fronting *Elle*, *Bazaar* or *Cosmopolitan*. Photographer's agents and model agencies had always understood this nuance, which very nearly but didn't quite qualify as restraint of trade. Nowhere was it written down, it was simply understood. An Editor murmured, 'Obviously it's entirely your choice where you want to work. It's a free world and up to you. It would just be very sad for *Vogue*, never being able to work with you again. Or any of the other international *Vogues*. But don't let me try and influence you. It's your call.'

Alexandra Shulman was doing a great job on GQ, and it was tempting to switch her to *Vogue*. She still looked slightly too hippy-chick to be a Central Casting shoo-in for *Vogue* Editor-in-Chief, but she was clever and understood the magazine. An interesting phenomenon about *Vogue* is that you receive fewer external applicants for Editor than for other titles. So revered is it, it deters most chancers from throwing their hats into the ring; they self-edit themselves from the running. This is the exact opposite of, say, *Tatler* or *House & Garden* where you might get ninety or more applicants for Editor. Anyone who has ever been to a party or bought a cushion or made a pair of curtains, sees themselves as a credible candidate.

Seeking an Editor for *Tatler* in the late nineties, I received an application from the ex-wife of a world-famous banker. She wrote, 'I have attended many of Europe's grandest parties and balls, and am experienced at dealing with staff. We had more than forty staff in our houses around the world.'

Alex took *Vogue* and ruled for twenty-six years. Stephen Quinn was Publisher, and it was one of the most successful double acts in magazine history, generating revenues of £500 million. We resolved early on to try and grow the circulation, which had stood at around 150,000 copies a month during the Liz Tilberis period, then regarded as a respectable number; it was the largest-selling premium glossy. But if we could find another 50,000 regular readers, and hike the yield (price per page after agency commission) accordingly, the rewards would be exponential.

Alex brought Lucinda Chambers to the magazine as Fashion Director, and she fostered the roster of *Vogue* photographers, from Mario Testino and Nick Knight to Tim Walker and Patrick Demarchelier. The features content became sharper and more contemporary, with appeal well beyond fashionistas. The timing was good too. Fashion was widening its horizon from Bond Street to the high street, with the department stores grabbing their share of designer magic dust through diffusion lines and increasingly blatant rip-offs. Alex's *Vogue* harnessed this appetite, and circulation edged up.

Meanwhile, on *GQ*, we installed a loudmouth Chicagoan financial journalist, Michael VerMeulen, as Editor. When he arrived, he was thin as a broom, noisy but respectful. He would say, 'Okay, okay, I know what you want, Nicholas, and I'm giving it you in spades. I'm giving you women, I'm giving you sweet babes, I'm giving you investigative journalism, I'm giving you yuppie stuff, grooming, fashion, flash cars, sex. You're going to cream yourself, boss.'

He put a naked rear-view photograph of Naomi Campbell

on the front cover, and sales spiked by 60 per cent. He burst into my office. 'Okay, okay, so now we know what sells . . . its *black butt.*'

Each time I saw him, he'd put on more weight. In his first twenty months as Editor, he ballooned by seventy pounds. I signed off his expenses and they read like an episode of Man Versus Food – vast breakfasts, lunches, two dinners the same night in different places, all expensed. And booze, so much booze: Jack Daniel's Tennessee Whiskey, and Southern Comfort. And cocktails.

As a Christmas bonus, I ordered Michael a Savile Row suit with elasticated waistband, since he could no longer fasten up his old ones. We cautioned him about his health, but he replied, 'You ever seen me drunk, boss? I'm a working journalist, ergo I drink. You get that. I've got you Kevin Costner for the July cover, you'll see it tomorrow. You're going to cream yourself.'

Our second son, Frederick Timothy Coleridge, was born at St Mary's, Paddington, on 14 January 1993; Georgia insisted this second birth should take place in a birthing pool, a newly fashionable practice designed to create a more relaxed, laid-back experience. It was an early example of Georgia's lifelong fascination with alternative therapies, and a somewhat functional plastic tub was set up in her hospital room. What no one had explained was that a water birth dramatically slows down the action, with the unborn child soothed into reassuring slumber. Freddie's birth was the longest ever known. He eventually emerged, a round, scowling figure, skin wrinkled by hours in warm water. He grew up to be our tallest child at six feet and five inches.

We had moved from the wild Fulham frontier to Notting Hill, to a white stucco house at 29 Chepstow Crescent. There we were joined by the first in a series of energetic Australian nannies, Janene from Perth, followed by Jodi from Sydney. We glazed the drawing-room walls in Colefax yellow, and hung our growing collection of Indian miniatures in a pyramid shape above the fireplace. This has remained a design habit ever since.

One August, on the final evening of a holiday in the Orkney Islands, on the tiny isle of Rousay where we'd borrowed a croft from the architect Christopher Bowerbank, I received a telephone call from Stephen Quinn.

'I've got terrible news, Nicholas. The police just contacted me. Michael VerMeulen is dead.'

'Christ . . . what happened?' I was horrified.

'They don't know yet. But a blood sample indicates a great deal of whisky.'

'Jesus . . .'

'I'm afraid it's a bit worse than that. They've found traces of illegal drugs in his blood too.'

'Oh, no.'

'I'm afraid it gets worse. He was in bed with an Eastern European hooker . . .'

Through the window of the croft, I could see a raging sea towards the Broch of Gurness. We were in about as remote a place as it was possible to be, at least twenty-four hours' travelling time to London. The press would be all over it, once this got out, the story had everything. There was only one thing for it: the great British cover-up.

'Who knows?' I asked Stephen.

'Almost nobody. Kimberly does [Kimberly Fortier, our Communications Chief, later Mrs Quinn]. And the police . . .'

'Listen, I'll get the first ferry off Rousay, catch the car ferry from Stromness to Scrabster, then drive south. Georgia and the boys can stay somewhere overnight. I should hit London late tomorrow if I drive non-stop. Think we can keep the lid on it till then? I'd like to be there when we break it to the team. I should tell Jonathan too.'

We crossed at dawn to the mainland, and drove across the vast, empty prairies of Caithness at breakneck speed. The roads in this part of Scotland are dead straight, you can see several miles ahead, the scenery a blend of heather, bog and dramatic hills. Pre-mobile phones, communication meant stopping at red telephone boxes in lay-bys.

We were passing Berriedale Water when, half a mile ahead, we spotted two men crossing the road, weighed down with fishing rods and angling equipment. The first was wiry and stooped, and turned out to be a gillie; the second, abnormally tall, was increasingly familiar. It was Max Hastings, Editor of the *Daily Telegraph*.

We slowed down on the empty road. 'Max? Is that really you?'

'God, it's you, Coleridge.' He peered through the car window. 'Bloody bad luck about your Editor. I hear he was having a whale of a time.'

'Ah, you've heard.'

'Just went out on the wires, ten minutes ago. I was checking the news back at the lodge.'

'Well, I'm sure it won't be something for the *Telegraph*,' I said. 'Very tabloid.'

'Not at all, old boy. We're going big with it tomorrow. It's August. Nothing happening, no other news.'

We weathered the maelstrom of hideous publicity that followed, and gave Michael a serious memorial service at St George's, Hanover Square, packed to the rafters with writers, cocktail barmen and beautiful sobbing women in veiled hats. Michael was thirty-eight. I felt guilty afterwards, wondering what else I might have done to help him. His death was a blow to GQ too, which didn't recover its mojo until three Editors later, when we hired Dylan Jones.

On other floors of Vogue House, there was constant activity. We had launched *Vanity Fair* in Britain with a simultaneous printing of the American edition, but with different advertising, sold separately, and a multimillion-pound launch budget. Annie Holcroft, Publisher of *Tatler*, took on *Vanity Fair* as well. Media analysts cautioned that *Tatler* would be cannibalized by *Vanity Fair*, or vice versa, but this never happened, and both magazines grew in circulation and revenue, finding parallel audiences, both rich. Tina Brown, my old *Tatler* boss who had moved to New York to the relaunched *Vanity Fair*, quit for *The New Yorker*, and it was a joy when Graydon Carter, our old friend from *Spy*, was appointed her successor. Henry Porter joined soon afterwards as London Editor.

Along the corridor, in the soft furnishings department, Robert Harling finally retired from *House & Garden*, aged eighty-four. He had spent the final phase of his career squabbling with eighty-year-old Peter Coates ('Petticoats'), the discreetly camp Gardens Editor who was close to the Queen Mother and went to Royal Lodge for lunch, so was deemed unsackable. Robert and Petticoats communicated exclusively by memo, despite occupying adjacent offices. These carping notes ostensibly concerned the worthiness or otherwise of Gloucestershire and Wiltshire gardens, and how many pages they should be allocated in the next issue; but, in truth, they were proxies for deeper animosities.

I persuaded Sue Crewe to become Editor, which was regarded as a slight risk at the time, but turned out not to be, because she remained gloriously in post for twenty-three years. *House & Garden* is a very particular magazine. It is a vital piece of kit for that great swathe of interior decorators, professional and amateur, which inhabits every part of the country – fabric lovers, people with swagged curtain pelmets and fabric valances around their beds, people who love needlepoint cushions, silk lampshades and expensive wallpapers. The readership inhabits Old Rectories and Glebe Houses in every English village. If you choose a village at random – let's say Aston-under-Wold or Brassington Magna – you can be 90 per cent sure that the largest three houses in the village – Manor, Old Rectory and Glebe – all take *House & Garden* on subscription, with a couple more copies going to weekenders.

It was striking, when interviewing possible Editors, how many wanted to change *House & Garden* into a version of hard-nosed urban *Elle Decoration*. These were credible, qualified candidates, but they inhabited another, different universe, with little overlap to the world of *H&G*.

I devised a killer question to sort the sheep from the goats: 'Where do you stand on padded headboards?'

Elle Deco people despise them. They replied, 'They're seriously uncool. I like headboards on beds made of African Izombe wood or beaten corrugated metal.'

True *House & Garden* people reply: 'I adore padded headboards. You want them made quite high, so you can lean against them, covered with fabric. Colefax & Fowler or Osborne & Little or Pierre Frey.'

Sue passed the headboard test with flying colours. She had rather an interesting aristocracy-meets-boho background, honed by good taste, hard work and a penchant for clever husbands. It was a lucky day for us when she joined.

It was a bonus to work in an organization where an overwhelming proportion of staff were female. At one point, it reached 86 per cent. Stephen Quinn and I and a few other male

publishers, then nine-hundred or so ambitious, highly compe-
tent women, then fifty more men running the mail room, IT
and office supplies. I felt I was lucky to work amongst multiple
women, especially having had no sisters. Inevitably, large numbers of our staff were off on maternity leave at any one time. I
once complained about this to Barbara Tims, our veteran Personnel Director, thinking she would sympathize.

'I'm sorry, Nicholas,' she said tartly, 'I don't sympathize with
you at all. If you will insist on hiring all these attractive, desir-
able, blonde women to work here, you can hardly be surprised
if their husbands or partners wish to make love to them from
time to time.'

I joined the Council of the Royal College of Art, my first taste
of a public board. The process of becoming a Trustee was much
less complicated back then, largely consisting of having lunch
with the Chairman, Sir Michael Butler, a cadaverous former dip-
lomat and collector of seventeenth-century Chinese porcelain.
He spoke in very precise, posh tones, and struggled to keep the
Council under control in the face of perpetual provocation.

The cocktail of RCA Council members in the mid-nineties,
ostensibly supervising Britain's most progressive art school, was
pyrotechnic and, to me at least, gripping. Lord Snowdon, Lord
Saatchi, Lord Douro, Sir Terence Conran, Sir Alan Bowness
(the Tate Director), Sir Christopher Frayling (Pro-Rector), Dr
Alan Borg (V&A Director) were all on the board. Many were
quarrelsome, belligerent, fractious. It didn't help that Council
meetings were held straight after lunch. At any moment, one
Trustee or another would explode with fury, veering off at a
tangent or amplifying some private peccadillo. The board
seethed with prima donnas. At the end of every Council meeting you felt jittery with the sheer emotion of it all.

Fortunately I made some calmer friends on the board, who were sweetly welcoming. Helen Hamlyn* was one, Amabel Lindsay† and Caromy Hoare‡ were beacons of sanity, and I got to know the legendary former Editor of *Vogue*, Beatrix Miller, who puffed on cigarettes through every Council meeting, and narrowed her eyes when the divas struck up. Afterwards, we all had tea in the Senior Common Room, surrounded by works by Peter Blake, David Hockney, Henry Moore and Lucian Freud.

My father, seemingly overnight, had become front-page news. Lloyd's of London, as he had predicted, was facing two consecutive down years, and dozens of syndicates across the market announced colossal losses, requiring their 'names' (investors) to post big cheques to Lloyd's rather than receiving one every year, which had been the attractive tradition. Following decades of annual profits, which names had come to rely upon, it was understandably harrowing to have to stump up, even though, in theory, this was a possibility they warned you about. Suddenly, having seldom been mentioned in newspapers at all, we read about David Coleridge, Chairman of Lloyd's, every day. One woke up to him on Radio 4's *Today* programme and went to sleep with him on *Newsnight*. It was anxiety-inducing.

Lynch mobs of aggrieved Lloyd's names were set up, employing expensive QCs to search for any pretext in the small print not to pay their bills. Some of the hardest hit incubated conspiracy theories, meeting in Norfolk pubs to goad each other on. A Member of Parliament accused Lloyd's of London of

* Arts and education philanthropist. Widow of Octopus publisher Paul Hamlyn.
† Lady Amabel Lindsay, widow of Patrick Lindsay, swashbuckling Christie's auctioneer.
‡ Of Stourhead, Wiltshire.

being little more than 'a den of thieves', but had to apologize to the House shortly afterwards for the slur.

The newspapers began to refer to my father as 'the beleaguered Chairman of Lloyd's'. City Editors predicted that Lloyd's could not survive.

When we went home to Sussex for weekends, my father was miraculously unrattled by it all, and appeared as calm as always. He only mentioned the crisis if someone else did first; otherwise it never came up. My mother was irritated when a photographer from *The Times* turned up one Sunday, unannounced, to take a portrait of the beleaguered Chairman, who was inspecting his azaleas in the garden at the time.

The AGM in Richard Rogers' Lloyd's Building was filled to capacity (normally only a handful of retired names turned up, for the free biscuits, but this time there were thousands), and I watched my father take questions for six hours without once sitting down, and without once losing his cool, his thread, or his natural good manners. It was a brilliant and heroic performance, which probably saved Lloyd's; it made us all very proud, and taught me a life lesson. When the pressure mounts, and critics attempt to taunt or undermine you with carping points of process, or poorly understood matters of fact, or simple ill will, or lack of common sense, it is important to smile, remain utterly polite, be empathetic, and move on. I'm not sure I always manage it myself, but it is something to aim for.

Lloyd's of London survived, of course, and recovered full profitability with time.

15

The lifts in Vogue House were notoriously unreliable, one or other of them semi-permanently 'out of service', occasionally both. Installed in the 1950s to a quickly redundant pattern and dimension, no service company dealt with them or kept spare parts. The weird rectangular shape of the shafts meant they couldn't be replaced without dismantling the entire building. As Managing Director, I felt simultaneously responsible but wholly powerless where the elevators were concerned.

When the lift doors opened (if they did) it could be anyone inside. The Princess of Wales came in and out of Vogue House all the time in the early nineties to borrow clothes. Kate Moss, Linda Evangelista, processions of male models on their way to castings at *GQ*, interns collecting coffees, posh totty walking dogs, interior designers delivering lampshades to *House & Garden* or plaster frescoes to Min Hogg on *The World of Interiors* . . . this was the daily traffic of the Vogue House lifts.

In these early years at Condé Nast, my life was punctuated by certain regular fixtures. There were London meetings every couple of months when I met with Jonathan Newhouse, our Chairman, for three or four hours to riff the British business; I would prepare long lists of issues, both serious and trivial, for discussion. Should we launch a travel magazine? Dare we launch *Glamour*? How worried are we that *GQ* (our upmarket men's title) had been overtaken in circulation by *FHM* and *Loaded* (downmarket); should we ignore it, or adjust our own editorial recipe to compete more vigorously with cruder front covers?

Jonathan had a razor-sharp mathematical brain, and a taste for rolling the dice, boldly or recklessly, depending on how you viewed it. He also had a notably short attention span (shorter even than my own) so I would plant a nugget of gossip every sixth or seventh item, to perk him up. Just as we became weary of reviewing subscription renewal data, I would say, 'Oh, rather a good story from the *Vogue* Steven Meisel shoot last week . . .' or, 'GQ has appointed a new sex columnist, hotter stuff than the previous one.' And Jonathan would brighten up, and we would discuss the boundaries of taste for a GQ sex column (oral sex, yes; anal, probably not; S&M, maybe, but no imagery involving blood).

Then, annually in May, there was the yet-more-gruelling visit by Si Newhouse, when he flew by private jet around Europe, reviewing his continental outposts. These visits followed an unchanging pattern: Paris (which he liked), Munich (didn't like), Milan (loved), Madrid ('Can someone remind me why we have a business in Spain?'), London (dinner at the Connaught, lunch at Wilton's). I crammed for these visits like a university viva: mugging up on every nuance of circulation and trends, and exploring the most obscure appendices in the monthly accounts. And yet, each time, Si would pose a question I didn't know the answer to. One was: 'Er, Nicholas, I see the postal and carriage costs for the subscription copies of *Brides & Setting Up Home* magazine have risen by 2 per cent, but on *Vogue*, which carries a greater volume of pages, they have risen by 1.8 per cent. Er, do we know why?' I don't believe he was actively trying to catch me out, he simply had a photographic memory for figures and a driving curiosity for unexplained minutiae.

Si's visits frequently coincided with viewing a painting he was considering buying; he would slope off from Wilton's unaccompanied (he never used bodyguards, despite being the fourth richest man in New York) to view a Lucian Freud or Jackson Pollock.

'Did you like it?' I would enquire afterwards.

He shrugged, and sighed. 'I think so. It's, er, it's . . . a *powerful* piece.'

His parallel preoccupation was the British royal family, and part of my role was to feed him morsels of choice gossip about them (he wasn't fussy, though the Queen interested him the most). I would make sure I had a couple of stories to hand, each time he was due in London. His face lit up with pleasure. The Newhouses were the royal family of the publishing world, and Si the reigning hereditary monarch, so he felt a special affinity towards Britain's head of state.

Graydon Carter came to London regularly to visit the British Edition of *Vanity Fair*, and we put on lunches and parties for him. Graydon had become a big figure in every sense. Already the sharpest, most glamorous Editor in New York, he became the toast of Hollywood with his annual Oscars parties. He was a first-rate journalist with a flair for retro typography. His hair grew wilder and madder the longer he was Editor, until he resembled Ludwig van Beethoven, and his Anderson & Sheppard suits became more flamboyant. When he was in town, I would lure a mix of actors and actresses, journalists, politicians and novelists to amuse him and rustle up a bit of publicity.

We were short of one woman for a boardroom lunch at Vogue House, and I thought we might invite Princess Diana as a last-minute addition; she had recently separated from the Prince of Wales, and was living alone in Kensington Palace. My driver, Brian Greenaway,* dropped a letter to the Palace, handing

---

* Former Fulham Football Club winger turned chauffeur.

it in at the sentry box by the gate; within minutes, Diana was on the line saying she'd love to come.

The following day, a large photograph of her appeared on the front page of the *Daily Mirror*, showing her sunbathing topless on a balcony in Spain. The picture was so blurred and pixelated, you couldn't see much at all; but it caused a scandal and raised intrusion issues, and every columnist piled in. I thought: damn it, she's sure to cancel. The lunch was tomorrow.

Her Private Secretary rang to say she was still coming, but there could be no publicity, nothing. I must ring every guest personally and swear them to secrecy.

The Princess arrived and looked fabulous. Looking at the photographs today, her blue suit with gold buttons has something of an Aeroflot air stewardess about it; but, at the time, it seemed perfection.

She sat between Graydon and me at lunch, and was very tactile. It was unexpected. You can be seated next to a thousand women at lunch, and not one touches you physically. But Diana touched your elbow, your arm, covered your hand with hers, it was alluring. And she was disarmingly confiding, speaking without filter.

She said, 'Nicholas, can I ask you something? Please be truthful. Did you see the photograph of me in the *Daily Mirror*? The topless one?'

'Um, Your Royal Highness, yes, we get all the newspapers in my office. I think I did glance at it . . . not that it was very clear.'

'William rang me from Eton. Poor boy, he's only fourteen. He was upset. He said some of the other boys were teasing him, saying my tits are too small.' She held on to my elbow. 'Nicholas, please be frank, I want to know your real view. Are my breasts too small, do you think?'

I became breathless, I needed oxygen. I went as red as a

guardsman's tunic. I stuttered 'Er, Your Royal Highness, in as much as I can see under your suit, they seem, um . . . perfect to me. I wouldn't worry.'

'Thank you, Nicholas. I knew you'd tell me the truth. Thank you, I feel better now.'

At the end of the lunch, I walked her to her car, which was waiting outside Vogue House. Suddenly, four paparazzi sprang forward, taking a thousand snaps. In the pictures, Diana looks radiant, I look like her bodyguard or stalker.

Afterwards, I rang a newspaper friend, to see if he could find out who'd leaked her visit. He rang back in five minutes. 'I just spoke to our picture desk. Diana rang herself from her car, on the way to lunch. She often tips them off about where she'll be.'

My days in the office assumed a fixed routine. I arrived early at Vogue House, generally around 7.45 a.m., much helped by Brian Greenaway, who arrived outside our house from 7.30 a.m. to drive me in. Brian was to drive me for twenty-seven years; I spent more time in his company than with anyone else, probably including Georgia. He is a handsome former professional footballer, who played for Fulham at Craven Cottage. It was a lucky day when he entered our lives. There is nothing he doesn't know about me.

En route to Vogue House, I made lists of the twenty or so things I needed to accomplish that day: people to see, calls to make, reports to read. My office had three large windows overlooking St George Street, with a glass Le Corbusier desk, sleek modern sofas, a couple of hundred magazines on shelves, and a pair of Andy Warhol Chairman Mao prints, intended to imply ruthlessness. I tried to do everything dull in the first four hours of the day, so it was out of the way. After that, we chose front covers, discussed advertising problems, or invented ways to do-down our competitors. Lunch was at Le Caprice or the Wolseley or in the Sakura sushi bar next to the office, where sumo wrestling was broadcast on TV with the volume down. In the afternoons, I liked to drop in randomly on the magazines, to hear about articles in progress or exchange gossip. I enjoyed roaming the corridors. Nothing gives me more pleasure than a half-formed future issue pinned up on the boards, and reviewing the running order. I enjoyed messing with the sequence of articles and fashion shoots, which can make a significant difference to reader reaction. It is a similar skill to fixing the running order of tracks on a rock album.

I am allergic to long meetings. Some people see meetings as the highpoint of their day, settling down around a conference table with a plate of Bourbon biscuits and custard creams, the tea ceremony, the agenda, everyone having their say, very often formulating their opinions as they go along, or repeating what has already been said. I find meetings lasting longer than ninety minutes a form of torture; long presentations worse (Slide 1: 'Good morning', Slide 45: 'Thank you'). I can never resist turning straight to Slide 44 and reading the conclusion. I discouraged long meetings at Condé Nast. Almost everything can be resolved in forty minutes, by properly prepared people.

I started going to a tailor at 95 Mount Street to have suits made. Doug Hayward was not only an excellent tailor, but the model for John le Carré's Harry Pendel, *The Tailor of Panama*. His premises were filled with his celebrity customers, who sat in a row on a sagging sofa at the front of the shop, drinking coffee served by his manageress Audie Charles: Michael Caine, Roger Moore, Michael Parkinson, the photographer Terry O'Neill, Johnny Gold the owner of Tramp nightclub, and the Mayfair hair-loss expert Philip Kingsley. They used Doug's shop as a meeting place-cum-club. They would sit there half the morning, then move on to Harry's Bar next door for lunch.

Michael Caine and Doug had almost identical accents, you couldn't tell them apart. Rather weirdly, Ralph Lauren was another customer who you sometimes saw slinking in and out. Doug held strong opinions on tailoring. It irritated him that I carry a wallet in the inside pocket of my suit jacket, which he said spoilt the line of the cut: 'You don't need a wallet, Nick. What d'ya need a fucking wallet for anyway? Maybe one credit card – the rest is rubbish.'

Jane Procter had been Editor of *Tatler* for ten years. She had been a resounding success – though, over time, the magazine felt unstable. She was brittle, with something of the little girl lost about her. Staff departed on bad terms with the Editor, and there was an air of suppressed hysteria. There were diva issues too, occupational hazards on *Tatler*. To people who don't read it, no magazine in the Condé Nast stable is more trivial than *Tatler*. But to its circle of devotees, it is a magazine of almost totemic prestige; it can confer legitimacy on social climbers, endorse new social stars, and withhold status too. It is a special peril for *Tatler* staff to confuse their own status with that of the magazine, and to forget they are merely reporting on this glamorous world of the super-rich, and not actually part of it themselves. It is a magazine which thrives on illusion and provokes delusion.

On the rare occasions I needed to change an Editor, I always tried to do so with maximum dignity. I would have these conversations privately in my office. I would say we needed a change, offer a generous settlement and ask for their resignation. The press release, *Pravda*-style, would present it as the Editor's own choice to move on.

I rang Jane and asked for a meeting. I explained our decision. Jane stared with wild eyes, like Bambi's mother in the Disney film during the forest fire scene.

'You-can't-sack-ME,' she declared, in a scary, quavering voice. 'I-AM-*Tatler*.' She stood up, and threw open my fourth-floor office window onto St George's Street. 'If I can't edit *Tatler* . . .'

I think it was a gesture as much as a real threat. She smouldered in a chair. She produced a mobile phone and dialled her husband. He must already have been lurking somewhere in the building, because he turned up moments later. We were suddenly quite a party.

'Jane won't sign any gagging order,' he announced. 'Read my lips. We're going down to *Tatler* right now to tell the staff exactly what's happened. You're going to regret this.'

The assembled staff of *Tatler* heard the news in surprise, but not dismay. Within minutes, the whole building knew, then the world.

On Sunday, an article of unparalleled ghastliness appeared in the *Mail on Sunday*, titled 'Who killed The Purley Queen?', a reference to Jane's childhood home in that suburb of London. Every disgruntled staff member had weighed in, dissing their old Editor in unkind terms. Jane sued the *Mail on Sunday*. The case rattled on between lawyers for many months, each side gathering witness statements and evidence, before petering out with a token settlement.

I conducted a worldwide search for a new *Tatler* Editor but couldn't identify the perfect person. I had interviewed at least fifteen candidates when, one Sunday afternoon, glancing out of the window of our Notting Hill house, I spotted Geordie Greig★ of the *Sunday Times* in the communal garden, reading a newspaper and holding a glass of wine. I thought, 'I just wonder . . .'

★ Editor, *Evening Standard* (2009–12), *Mail on Sunday* (2012–18), *Daily Mail* (2018–). Author, *Breakfast with Lucian* (2013).

A reporter by training, Geordie soon brought his hard news skills to the frontline of society, as well as signing up David Hockney and Lucian Freud as *Tatler* contributors.

The highlight of his Editorship was a glamorously incongruous annual fund-raiser he founded, held at Althorp House, the Spencers' stately home in Northamptonshire, co-hosted by Geordie and President Mikhail Gorbachev* of Russia. The Geordie and Gorby Ball was an event you could not possibly have invented, even after the Berlin Wall came down, packed with British and Russian socialites, vodka and Caspian caviar. There are moments when you recognize how far the world has moved on in your lifetime, and this was one of them: seeing the ex-President of the Soviet Union, with his distinctive red-wine birthmark on his bald head, standing cheek-by-jowl with Geordie, Editor of *Tatler*, both in white tie and tails, joyfully greeting guests at the door of Princess Diana's old house.

Geordie produced an excellent magazine for the next ten years, and never fell victim to the lurking hubris of Posh Publishing. He would become one of my closest friends in the media and beyond.

Geordie had hired Isabella Blow as *Tatler*'s new Fashion Director, with the intention of groovying up the fashion pages. I had known Issie from years before, when she was a daffy boarding school pupil at Heathfield, who wore pie-crust frill blouses like Princess Diana and was a constant presence at Hampshire teenage parties. Over the intervening years, she had reimagined herself as an edgy fashionista, muse to the milliner Philip Treacy and to Alexander McQueen, and a key voyager in the darker

* General Secretary of the Communist Party, Soviet Union (1985–91). Referenced in Leonard Cohen track 'First We Take Manhattan'.

fens of fashion. She frequently wore a hat with a giant pink lobster on top, a corset or medieval armour.

I think that, even before Issie arrived at *Tatler*, it was understood she would need careful supervision. Her genius was driven by abrupt enthusiasms and impulse passions, and she viewed any attempt to rein in her spending as a challenge to her creativity. In her first week, she took a black cab from Liverpool to London, having hailed it in the street, later explaining she hadn't realized there was a railway station in Liverpool.

Issie was both fearless and fearful. Fearless in her approach to photographers and models, when she brought big names to the magazine. Her Gothic shoots with McQueen and the photographer David LaChapelle are among my favourite fashion shoots ever, also her Naomi Campbell butterfly hat front cover, which everyone loved, but didn't sell well. Issie was perpetually fearful of the world, plagued by breakers of depression. She worried about money, considering herself underpaid (she wasn't).

One evening, she had a drink in my office with Geordie and me, to make her case for a spectacular pay rise. This mostly consisted of a list of beautiful, expensive things she wished to buy, but couldn't currently afford on her salary. She stated that, being men, we had no idea of the cost of running two houses, including Hilles House near Stroud, her Arts and Crafts Cotswold mansion, and buying couture and paintings. We eventually awarded her a token pay rise and she left looking happy enough.

The next morning, I happened to pass Issie in her office. She was sitting at her desk, which was covered with fabulous pieces of antique jewellery. A salesman from S. J. Phillips of Bond Street was displaying emerald and diamond necklaces on a baize tray.

'Are these for a shoot?' I asked.

'For me, actually,' replied Issie. 'I'm spending my pay rise in advance.'

I was seated next to Issie at a fashion dinner at the Natural History Museum, and she had arrived wearing a full black burqa, with a veiled slit for her eyes, and a pair of stag's antlers on top. It made it impossible for her to speak a word, you heard only muffled sounds from inside. A posse of paparazzi permanently circled our table, taking pictures – which was, I suppose, the whole point.

I asked, 'Issie, are you going to be able to eat anything under that?' Waiters were arriving with the first course.

'I'm not here to eat,' she replied. 'That is not something I'm the least bit concerned about . . .'

Every month, some new saga erupted: her trip to Delhi when she booked herself into a suite at the Imperial hotel, with no means of settling the bill, and assuming Condé Nast would pay, even though it was a holiday; the love affair with a Venetian gondolier she'd met on the Grand Canal; her various, tragic attempts to commit suicide, by jumping off the Hammersmith flyover onto the road below, and asking her driver in Milan to take her to a Navigli canal to drown herself, late at night (but the driver couldn't, or wouldn't, find it). As a company, we paid for poor Issie to register into a succession of clinics and hospitals, some for months on end, but they did no good. The compulsion to kill herself was too strong inside her, and she eventually succeeded at Hilles with the aid of the weedkiller Paraquat.

Her memorial service at the Guards' Chapel was a full-blown fashion moment, with 2,000 mourners, led by Anna Wintour. Some commentators at the time blamed the savagery and malice of the fashion and magazine industries for her death, but I suspect the causes lay much deeper in childhood, and even in her DNA, and her many friends were powerless to change that.

★

I began visiting New York regularly for work, to catch up with the Condé Nast gossip and call on advertisers. Generally I had supper with Graydon Carter at his first restaurant, the Waverly Inn, next to his house on Bank Street in the West Village, and Tina Brown kindly threw dinners 'for' me in Sutton Place South, filled with film stars and socialites, writers like Dominick Dunne and Fran Lebowitz, and activist curios like Bianca Jagger and Gloria Steinem.

Often I would visit my friend Cristina Monet Zilkha at 125 East 74th Street. I had first met Cristina when she was a cult rock star, married to the pop mogul Michael Zilkha, and her album *Sleep It Off* on ZE Records was riding high. Over time, she had morphed into a souped-up Madame de Pompadour figure, inhabiting an apartment filled with English Regency furniture, Charles X chandeliers, Empress Josephine cabinets and a prevailing spirit of the grande horizontale. On each visit to the city, I would take her out to dinner at some fashionable restaurant where it would be impossibly hard to secure a table. 'Don't be late,' I would plead, knowing she would be. She always was, causing unbearable anguish, as I waited and waited and head waiters menacingly enquired, 'Do you still wish to hold the table, sir?' longing for me to relinquish it. Eventually Cristina would appear, and it was worth it, just. She is never dull. She is part of my New York.

Back in London, an Editor named James Brown was appointed to GQ; we had lured him from *Loaded*, then at the height of its reputation, a lads' magazine full of energy, vulgarity and wit. It was another risk, since James wasn't house-trained and had an alluring hellraiser reputation, but it was hoped he might bring a bit of pizzazz to our men's title, which had been looking too safe lately. James was the Damien Hirst of magazines, or possibly the Banksy, and it felt pleasingly iconoclastic to shoe-horn him into *GQ*. This is the sort of thing magazine executives do from time to time: the reckless gamble which proves we still have it.

James was short and adolescent, with a disarming smile and long, curly, footballer's hair. It was impossible not to like him. He was intriguingly unsophisticated, and everything was new to him.

'Have you ever read the *Daily Telegraph*?' he asked me one day. 'I found one on my seat on a train, I'd never opened one before. It's quite good, you know.'

He seemed particularly delighted to be issued with a company American Express card, which was to see much action in the vodka bars of Soho.

I think we realized early on that a terrible mistake had been made, but these things need to run their course. Each week, some further rock star-style outrage was reported to me.

The curtain fell on James soon afterwards. He was fun while he lasted.

Georgia, the children and I were staying one weekend in Sussex with Dominic and Rosa Lawson. Dominic edited the *Sunday Telegraph*, Rosa ran Tiffany & Co., the Bond Street jeweller. They had also invited William and Ffion Hague – William was Leader of the Opposition – and the Irish rock star Bob Geldof with his girlfriend Jeanne Marine and his daughter Peaches.

We were an incongruous party, thrown together at the Lawsons' mill house in a bucolic East Sussex valley. The Coleridges, Lawsons and Geldofs all had young children, so were up and about by 6.30 a.m. each morning, making breakfast in the kitchen. Across a stable yard was the Hagues' bedroom, above the garages. The curtains remained defiantly drawn.

Geldof, who turned out to be a Tory voter, gazed across the

yard. 'I hope to *fok* he's *fokking* her,' he declared. 'If they don't produce a sprog before the General Election, we're *fokking* finished mate, it's *fokking* essential.'

We ate breakfast, waiting for the curtains to twitch. Hours passed. At last the curtains opened, followed by the door.

'Look out for high colour, the *fokking flush*,' said Geldof.

William and Ffion wore matching baseball caps. William was carrying a hardback biography of Lord Salisbury, with a bookmark stuck halfway through. 'Morning all,' he said in his broad Yorkshire voice. 'Sorry we're late, I've been reading this fascinating life of the third Marquess of Salisbury.'

'We've only *fokking lost*,' groaned Geldof.

Not long afterwards, I was commissioned by Dylan Jones to profile Hague for *GQ*. I only occasionally wrote for our own magazines; it worried me that, if the Editor didn't like the article, it could cause them embarrassment to reject it. This time I said yes, and headed to the Houses of Parliament.

The first ninety minutes of the interview were unremarkable. It is hard to get anything fresh from an MP, and the Hague story was well trodden. But then he began reminiscing about his teenage years in Yorkshire, in Richmond, where he delivered barrels of beer to pubs from a dray.

'It was hard physical work,' he said. 'But at least they gave you a pint of ale in each pub, when you'd finished the delivery.'

'So how many pubs would you deliver to in a day?' I asked.

'Oh, it would have to have been twelve, sometimes fourteen. It varied.'

I felt the electric current down my spine, when you know you've struck gold.

'So you might easily have drunk fourteen pints in a day.'

'On a hot day, yes, it would have been,' replied Hague. 'You sweated it out.'

The interview, when published, made the front pages of every national newspaper: 'Fourteen pints a day was normal – Hague'. The story ran for days. 'I was Britain's Biggest Boozer' – *Daily Mirror*. Some commentators suggested it was a PR plant, designed to hot-up Hague's good boy image, but I don't think it was. I think it was exactly as he told it.

The Labour party produced special commemorative William Hague beer mats ('Tory froth'), which were distributed to hundreds of pubs. They were intended to undermine him, but probably had the opposite effect.

16

We used to take the children camping at our friends John and Lea Hoerner's house, Cornwell Glebe, near Chipping Norton. The tents were pitched on the lawn, yards from the back door, since the seven-year-old campers seldom made it through the night, retreating to their bedrooms well before dawn. But we loved our weekends at Cornwell Glebe.

John was the big boss of Harvey Nichols, Debenhams, Topshop and most other high street fashion chains – the most powerful man in British fashion – and also Chairman of Battersea Dogs Home; their house was overrun with abandoned mutts they had rescued, seldom fewer than ten, sprawling in the kitchen and racing joyfully round the garden in packs. American-born Anglophiles, John and Lea's Cotswold manor house was a hymn to Englishness and English style, but always with the latest gadgets and state-of-cool barbecues and waffle-makers. John was stocky and powerful, very slightly resembling in his appearance John W. Pepper, the Louisiana sheriff from the 1973 Bond movie *Live and Let Die*; he would appear in the kitchen each morning in stripy chill-proof pyjamas to prepare waffles drenched in maple syrup, piled high on a platter.

He was also Chairman of the British Fashion Council and wanted to stop; being Chairman of the BFC is one of those thankless pro bono positions that you aren't allowed to relinquish until you find a gullible successor prepared to take it on. One weekend, over lunch, John craftily seated me between two flattering, persuasive fashionistas, and before I knew it, I'd agreed to do it. Little did I know what lay ahead.

The offices of the British Fashion Council at 5 Portland Place were peculiarly shared with several other fashion bodies and associations, including the Knitting & Clothing Export Council and the National Union of Tailors and Garment Workers. The Fashion Council represented the glamorous, glitzy wing of the industry, responsible for staging biannual London Fashion Weeks and the British Fashion Awards, as well as promoting young talent and British designers. Alexander McQueen, Stella McCartney, Paul Smith and Burberry were the star attractions, padded out with fifty more British designers of sundry talent and fame, all of whom put on catwalk shows. The Chairman was expected to attend every last one of them, fifty shows a season, twice a year.

Council meetings were held in a draughty, spartan boardroom with twenty-five or so fashion big shots ranged around the table: a disparate group of mulish, carping blowhards, each with a private agenda and emphatic opinions. Department store chiefs and designers ran perpetual low-level skirmishes with fashion college professors and Cypriot garment manufacturers. We were a 'big tent organization', which meant everyone felt free to blurt out whatever they liked, as it entered their heads. After each meeting, I felt bludgeoned and drained, and it took guile and effort to keep things on track.

I suggested we spruce up the boardroom with framed photographs of the top 100 British designers, like photos of celebrity customers in an Italian restaurant. It would remind us who we were there to help. But the BFC Chief Executive said, 'Technically, Chair, only two of the four walls belongs to the British Fashion Council. If we were to hang photographs of Sir Paul

Smith and Alexander McQueen on your two walls, we would need to do the same for union officials on the other two . . .'

But I came to love London Fashion Weeks. There would be ten fashion shows a day, held as inconveniently far from one another as possible. Half were staged in the official tented catwalk village, pitched on the Duke of York playing fields on the King's Road, where I had once played sport as a Hill House pupil, or outside the Natural History Museum; the remaining shows were held in mind-numbingly edgy venues across East London, in skating rinks, former abattoirs, disused tube stations, decrepit Hoxton lofts or underground car parks. I would ricochet from one to another, ploughing through gridlocked traffic, minded by Fashion Week's communications chiefs, Jane Boardman and Claudia Crow. I was devoted to them. Each day, some fresh PR horror erupted in the *Daily Mail*: this show was obscene, that one featured size zero anorexic models, another was a health and safety hazard; or else some government minister wished to attend a show and the designer didn't want him on the premises. We lurched from crisis to crisis.

The *Sunday Times* fielded a camp old fashion reporter named Colin McDowell, who seldom enjoyed much in Fashion Week, and reminded us of Statler and Waldorf, the cantankerous grumps in *The Muppet Show*. What do you think of it so far, Colin? 'Rubbish!'

To attend every show, unfiltered, was disorientating: the brilliant and the dire, innovative and pedestrian, celebrity-slick and grimly depressing, randomly juxtaposed. McQueen's macabre line of beauty, Julien Macdonald's high-glamour pageants with soap stars like Martine McCutcheon seated front row, the rebirth of Burberry with miles of check plaid, the chilly modernity of Nicole Farhi in the Banqueting House, Whitehall. And then there were the nearly-famous designers, perpetually on the brink of breakthrough, the great white hopes of British fashion: the geostrophic Turkish designer Hussein Chalayan and the Polish Arkadius, whose seminal shows 'Le cock' and 'Virgin Mary wears the trousers' I was proud to witness. London in the early 2000s was a fashion capital of shooting stars, exploding brightly in the firmament before crashing to earth in a lingering smell of sulphur.

There were designers with genuine businesses – Jasper Conran, Matthew Williamson, Caroline Charles and Pringle – and charming veterans like Paul Costelloe and Ronit Zilkha, who somehow endured from season to season.

The British fashion industry was still notionally overseen, governmentally, by the Department of Trade and Industry, though they were more comfortable engaging with the motor and steel industries than fashion. Patricia Hewitt was Secretary of State, and I visited her twice a year at the DTI's brutalist headquarters in Victoria: my job was to make sure the grants and funding for Fashion Week didn't stop flowing, and to persuade the DTI to subsidize the air travel and hotel bills of key American and Japanese department store fashion buyers, whose million-dollar orders were crucial to the health of British designers.

Each time I met with her, Patricia Hewitt was cloistered in a conference room with an array of spads and civil servants, none of them fashion folk. And, each time, they unveiled a new idea.

'Nicholas, we have a concept for an innovative digital hub, which could come with matched funding. Tell us what you think . . . The department sets up a governmental intranet site, which can be accessed only by registered fashion designers using a special code. It could be called "Inspiration-by-Design", that's our working title. Then, whenever a young British designer has a stroke of genius – some great new idea – they post it on the website, and share it with all the other British designers. Say, for example, Alexander McQueen has this brilliant concept for a new trouser cut, he would put it out there, for the benefit of the whole industry. What do you reckon?'

The assembled group of advisers leant forward, pens raised, pads flourished, for my verdict.

How to explain? This is possibly the worst idea on earth, and the very last one that could possibly work. Ever. Period.

I longed to be encouraging, but I dreaded the next idea.

Patricia Hewitt asked, 'Have your young designers considered incorporating the *pashmina* into their designs? Many of my friends are finding pashminas invaluable, to throw over an outfit on a chilly night.'

It was the Department of Trade and Industry which came up with the notion that Prince Andrew, Duke of York, could be a useful ambassador for British fashion, and I was instructed to introduce him to a selection of cool designers: 'the edgier the better' was the brief. A plan was hatched that I would take the Duke on a tour of design studios and showrooms from Chelsea to Hoxton, culminating in a boardroom lunch at Vogue House at which a dozen top fashion editors would be gathered, to explain the inner workings of the industry.

Things got off to a good start at Jasper Conran's studio. Jasper pranced about in an oatmeal-coloured suit, showing the prototypes for a new range of orange trousers, and made various suggestions on how government might better support the industry. The Duke listened intently, amiably peremptory. He reminded me of an army general 'taking complaints' during an annual barrack-block inspection. He assured Jasper that all his points would be duly reported back to the powers that be.

We were driven to Hoxton in a royal Daimler with six police motorcycle outriders, holding each set of traffic lights for maximum speed. Having done the journey in fifteen minutes, rather than the customary hour, and arrived way ahead of schedule, we pulled over onto a car lot, in which inner-city kids circled the royal limo on BMXs and skateboards, or pressed their faces to the car windows.

I asked the Prince how his makeover of Royal Lodge was going, the Windsor Great Park house he had recently inherited from the Queen Mother, and which he was currently renovating.

'There's a devil of a lot to do,' he said. 'Her Majesty Queen Elizabeth the Queen Mother hadn't paid much attention to wiring or plumbing for some considerable time, so we've had to fix that. And I'm stripping out the old rose garden [location for numerous Cecil Beaton royal portraits] and replacing it with a pitch and putt golf course. And installing a bowling alley . . .'

We trooped into a warehouse building, used by collectives of fashion designers, including Elspeth Gibson, the object of our visit. Protection officers strode ahead and behind, on full alert for imminent ambush. The metal lift reeked of marijuana. Elspeth, the delightful Nottingham-born designer, was showing the Prince her latest collection of lace, beading and embroidery, when an alarm sounded, followed by an urgent intercom announcement. 'There-has-been-a-major-incident-in-the-building. Do-not-repeat-do-not-leave-the-showrooms-and-lock-all-doors. Police-officers-have-been-alerted.'

We were in lockdown. The royal protection squad took up defensive positions by the door. Another officer moved closer to the Principal.

Several floors below we heard the sound of a gunshot. Eventually, a fresh posse of police stormed in, and escorted us from the premises, past yellow 'Police Incident Scene' tape. They seemed surprised to discover Prince Andrew in the building.

Lunch at Vogue House felt like a sanctuary. The boardroom

with its walls of black and white photographs by Snowdon, Bruce Weber, Albert Watson and Patrick Demarchelier looked film-star glamorous. Already grouped around the table were the Editors and fashion editors from *Vogue*, *Vanity Fair*, *Tatler* and *Glamour*, primed to decode British Fashion.

The Duke – fired up by the Hoxton shooting episode, and by the super-chic array of female editors – was in gung-ho mood.

'Let me ask you all a question,' he said. 'Because, looking around at you, I rather doubt you'll call this one right.' Turning to his Private Secretary, he said, 'Write down their answers, we'll see who comes closest . . .'

'Now,' continued the Duke, 'if you were steering an 8,000-ton Daring-class destroyer into harbour, how far in advance of reaching port would you shut down the engine? Now, come on ladies, don't be shy, I want you all to guess.'

The cream of British fashion editors exchanged uneasy glances. It would have been hard to assemble a less informed group on this topic.

Eventually, Alexandra Shulman, *Vogue* Editor, said, 'Okay, I'll have a guess. Five hundred yards?'

The Prince roared with laughter. 'Way off! Who's next? Come on, who's next?'

Lucinda Chambers, *Vogue* Fashion Director, said, 'Half a mile?'

Anna Harvey, *Vogue* Editorial Director of New Markets, said, 'A thousand yards?'

Kate Reardon of *Vanity Fair* hazarded, 'A mile?'

'Not bad,' said the Duke. 'Anyone else, ladies?'

They all guessed. I wish I could remember the answer (it was quite high, more than a mile, I think) but time had run out, and the motorcycle outriders were circling and revving.

The great fashion briefing was timed out.

★

Each November, we staged the British Fashion Awards, an evening outstripped in sheer length and celebrity heft only by the Oscars. Held in vast tents in London parks, or at the Old Billingsgate Fish Market, the awards evenings comprised at least 30 categories of winners, followed by dinner for 800 to 1,000 people, with every fashion house taking a table and boasting a democratic pick 'n' mix of celebrities from A-list Hollywood stars and supermodels to pop-up reality TV strivers.

For weeks beforehand, there would be disputes over the precise location of tables in relation to the top table, and designers saying they would only turn up if they could be guaranteed the top prize. Victoria Beckham made it a condition she would only attend if her whole family was invited along too – parents Tony and Jackie Adams, sister Louise, Louise's partner and more. It was my role as Chairman to chat up the Beckham family at dinner, whilst celebs and demi-slebs of the Pamela Anderson, Cat Deeley, Holly Valance and Holly Willoughby variety milled about, posing for pictures on all sides.

The extended Beckham and Adams family, encountered en masse, was intriguing; their entire lives revolved around the towering fame of son-in-law David and eldest daughter Posh, and the stress that brought with it. They relished it and resented it, but would consider no solutions to better manage it.

Jackie Adams told me that, every weekend, the family assembled at Victoria and David's country house in Hertfordshire, Rowneybury House ('Beckingham Palace') for lunch. But it was ruined each time by journalists from the Sunday tabloids turning up at the property and shouting questions through an intercom at the front gates. The intercom connected to the kitchen, where the Beckham family was eating. Every few minutes, a new voice would bawl, 'Ere, Doyvid, 'ow d'ya think yer gowing to do 'gainst Arsenal next game?' or, 'Oy, David,

Wally Skunk, *Sunday People* here, wots all this rumour 'bout you and this blonde bird? Anyfing in it?'

'What can we do?' fretted Jackie. 'It's so intrusive.'

'Have you considered switching off the intercom, or moving it to another room?'

'We can't!' wailed Jackie. 'What if an *invited guest* turned up and wanted letting in?'

Later, she complained that their family holidays were ruined by paparazzi, constantly stalking them and giving them no peace.

I said, 'Have you considered buying a house with a very long drive? Do what the royal family does at Balmoral and Sandringham. They don't get much disturbance. Miles from anywhere.'

'It's okay for them, the royals,' said Jackie. 'It's not the same thing at all. David and Victoria are *globally recognized*. Everyone wants a piece of them.'

Jackie told me she kept compendious cuttings books about her daughter and son-in-law, running to hundreds of volumes, and employed two girls from the village to stick everything in. They subscribed to international cuttings agencies to ensure they missed nothing. 'Even newspaper articles from Hungary, Poland, Cyprus, you name it. They all write about Victoria and David.'

Not long afterwards, the Rebecca Loos episode broke, with an alleged affair between David Beckham and his former personal assistant in Spain. How, I wondered, did they cope with that? The Rebecca Loos cuttings would have filled a dozen volumes. Did the girls from the village have to glue them all in, in multiple languages?

The Prince of Wales attended the British Fashion Awards as guest of honour and was a big hit. He was trying to add careers in fashion for disadvantaged youths into his Prince's Trust programme, so was in fact-finding mode. My job was to escort him down a line of designers and introduce them to him, though as we got closer to the night, the Clarence House team became more jittery by the hour. The cast of characters was a minefield: Alexander McQueen had form for anti-royal outbursts (having famously sewn the words 'I am a cunt' into HRH's suit lining, while working at a Savile Row tailor), Stella McCartney was famously anti-foxhunting. ('Can you absolutely *guarantee* she won't make a scene?' I was asked by a courtier. No, I couldn't, not possibly.) Others might easily be drunk or coked-up.

The seating plan for dinner was virtually impossible to construct. In the event, it was sabotaged by Kate Moss and the actress Minnie Driver switching the place cards around at the last minute, so we needn't have vacillated for so long.

The awards were the first time I had witnessed the Prince of Wales in action in the field, so to speak. He is clever at it, and well briefed (the briefs laboriously prepared to a specific template, but he studies them carefully). It is absolutely not the case that he asks, 'Have you travelled far to be here?' which is the royal cliché. He must have a strong short-term memory, because he retrieves nuggets of biography on cue, which can only have come from the briefings. It is flattering to people. And he lingers when he finds a conversation rewarding, and he is serious.

I've noticed he has developed a neat way of disengaging from a conversation group, when it is time to move on. He makes a final point, laughs, shrugs, looks regretful, allows himself to be moved on, but then, as he walks off, turns again, back towards the group he's just left, and laughs again, sometimes pointing his finger in a jocular manner, as if to say, 'You!' The impression is that he is still enjoying the previous conversation, still engaged by it, and it gave him pleasure. It provides elegant closure.

It was not long afterwards that I became involved in the most complicated, stressful, unbearable and ultimately most rewarding fashion event of my life. It was entirely my own fault, there is no one else to blame. As he departed the Fashion Awards at midnight, heading for the royal train, the Prince had said, 'Perhaps you can dream up something to raise funds for my Prince's Trust, some kind of performance?'

Rashly, I heard myself replying, 'I'm sure I can think of something, sir.'

The idea we came up with was Fashion Rocks, and it seemed simple enough: seventeen world-famous rock stars would perform one track each, while seventeen international fashion brands put on catwalk shows simultaneously. We would hire the Albert Hall, sell tickets and raise a million pounds for the charity. As the months rolled by, the concept grew bigger and bigger, until it involved 165 models, 10 supermodels, 72 hairdressers, 62 make-up artists, 100 dressers from 17 different designer houses, 17 rock and roll artists, 116 band members and backing singers, 1,900 backstage passes (140 of these for personal bodyguards), and TV crews for more than a hundred overseas broadcast syndicate deals. Nobody involved in this perilous, unnerving enterprise has ever fully recovered.

Like all these things, it began gently enough. I persuaded various serial philanthropists like Lily Safra★ and the car parks tycoon Sir Donald Gosling† to put in £100,000 each to get the party started, and then we began the endless job of coaxing fashion houses to take part. We aimed high: Dior, Chanel, Gucci, Dolce & Gabbana, Armani, Yves Saint Laurent, Prada and Versace were the first eight approached, but none would commit until (a) all

★ Brazilian-born philanthropist, socialite, four times married. Owns Villa Leopolda, French Riviera.
† Chairman, National Car Parks. Benefactor, naval and royal charities.

the others had already done so, (b) their own rock act was clearly better than the others, and (c) they had been promised the best models, preferably exclusively, so the other designers couldn't use them too. I travelled to Paris, Milan and New York nine times, and wished I'd never had the damned idea. Meanwhile, other designers committed – Ralph Lauren, Tommy Hilfiger, Alexander McQueen, Stella McCartney, Burberry, Donna Karan. The Americans were in if the Italians were in; the Italians looked to the French. The Brits were game, so long as it was cool.

The rock stars were worse. Robbie Williams was in, then out, then in again. Beyoncé was a breakthrough. Bryan Ferry said yes exactly when most needed, but YSL's Tom Ford forgot to thank him, so he was nearly out again in a huff. Duran Duran were in, out, in. Sheryl Crow was a yes maybe. All night, for months, the ping of texts and the flashing red light of incoming emails ruined my sleep (I slept next to my BlackBerry). Björk was a yes for McQueen, and Grace Jones for Stella. The fight for supermodels intensified. Unless Versace got all six they'd requested, they were out. If we lost Versace, we'd lose Robbie. If we lost Robbie, we'd lose Beyoncé, who'd only agreed because he was doing it. If we lost Versace, we also risked losing Prada. Kate Moss, Karolína Kurková, Naomi Campbell, Karen Elson, Stella Tennant, Eva Herzigová, Jodie Kidd . . . they all wanted them. *Vogue*'s Charlotte Stockdale agreed to be Fashion Creative Director; her happy, glamorous, can-do face raised my spirits. Sam Gainsbury joined as Fashion Show Producer, Sally Atkins and Graham Pullen as Show Producers for Clear Channel, Malcolm Gerrie as TV Producer. It was a crack squad.

Chanel agreed to be in it. Armani threatened to pull out when they thought they'd lost Beyoncé. Dior would only be in it if they opened the show. ('Dior cannot be anywhere except first. It is a corporate requirement of the brand.')

The top designers had never been part of a joint show before. Never. Not once. It was impossible: so they reminded us, day after day.

Their requests grew longer and more emphatic: in the Albert Hall, their box must be closest to the Royal Box. Who was closer? How could that be, when Burberry is not in the same league as Armani? Which designer will first be introduced to the Prince of Wales? Which designer will close the show? There were raging bouts of model envy, rock star envy, dressing room envy, running order envy, billing envy.

I have perfected the knack, when things are teetering on the edge of disaster, of appearing supremely calm. It is an act, nothing more. Inside, I was dying of fear.

The only certainty was that, in less than two months' time, the Prince of Wales and Duchess of Cornwall would be sitting there, in the Royal Box, and the lights would dim . . . and I wasn't sure there'd be anything for them to see at all.

One evening I lay on my bed and declared, 'If I could sell our house and give all the proceeds to the Prince's Trust, and not have to go through with this show, I would.' That was the low point.

With five weeks to go, we were five acts short, and the remaining available ones were unacceptable to the unteamed designers. 'How could we accept your suggestion [an Alpha Minus chart topper] when Armani has Beyoncé and Dior has Joaquín Cortés, the flamenco star?'

The 6,000 tickets sold out in 36 hours. We had decided to make it black tie, which I'd had reservations about, but I was wrong because it added to the spectacle. I found it impossible to imagine the event ever happening . . . there were too many hurdles still to overcome; even to visualize a happy outcome might jinx it. I couldn't sleep. It could all collapse at any moment. We now had all 17 fashion houses in place and 16 rock artists, plus a specially recorded finale video from David Bowie singing 'Fashion', with all 175 models parading.

Clarence House asked for briefing notes on the designers and musicians, for presentations during the intervals. We told half the designers, 'You're being prioritized and introduced first.' We told the others, 'The most important designers will meet HRH during the second interval.' It worked.

There was a week to go. I was driven to Somerset to the Babington House hotel, where our soon-to-launch magazine *Glamour* was holding a sales conference. About sixty *Glamour* staff were staying overnight, my role was simply to thank them and make a suitably motivating speech at the end of dinner. All the way down the motorway, worrying pieces of Fashion Rocks news kept arriving. Sheryl Crow had been signed to perform during the Ralph Lauren segment, but she'd run into Tommy Hilfiger at a party in New York and now wanted to switch horses. Furthermore, she was insisting she 'only wanted to sing for Tommy, he's a personal friend'. Ralph Lauren went ballistic. It was World War Three. 'If we don't get Sheryl, we're out,' said the Lauren people. 'And we'll cancel all Ralph Lauren advertising in Condé Nast magazines . . . worldwide.' (Bang goes a couple of hundred million dollars and my job.)

I went to bed with the drama still raging. At 2 a.m. there was a furious hammering on the hotel door, and cries of 'fire, fire, evacuate'. I drew back the bedroom curtains. Outside, yards away, was an immense blaze, the hotel swimming pool and spa complex engulfed by flames. The electricity was cut, corridors plunged into darkness.

Outside on the lawn, sixty *Glamour* girls in nighties and dressing gowns milled about, saying, 'OMG, I just hate you seeing me without make-up, Nicholas!' or, 'Would this be a good time to talk about me maybe having an assistant?'

Babington House staff circulated with coffee, while thirty fire engines roared up the drive. The heat from the blaze scalded our faces.

The only other hotel residents were an elderly French couple. He complained, 'Somebody should 'ave told us this was going to 'appen. This fire. Nobody warned us about it. It is unprofessional.'

As the dawn light rose over the embers, a text pinged onto my phone. 'Everything resolved. Ralph Lauren has agreed to Andrea Bocelli as their act instead. Love Claudia.' Claudia Crow had talked them down. I don't know how she did it. It took all night. I still owe her.

The dreaded evening of Fashion Rocks arrived. With a sense of hideous foreboding, and anxiety cramps in my stomach, I got changed into black tie and we set off to the Albert Hall. Georgia looked gorgeous in a floor-length red dress. Kensington Gore was criss-crossed with red carpets, lasers and 'step-and-repeat' boards emblazoned with sponsors' logos. The first guests were already starting to arrive. Two hundred paparazzi had requested pitches in the roped VIP arrival zone. Tom Ford and Giorgio Armani were checking the proximity of their boxes to the Royal Box. John Galliano had arrived in London from Paris but promptly gone missing, having slipped his minders at St Pancras station; his PR team looked harassed.

Grace Jones was holed up at the Dorchester, allegedly refusing to perform unless given more free clothes by Stella McCartney. Bryan Ferry, surfacing from backstage, said he hadn't seen so many beautiful women in one place in ages – 170 models were getting changed in the corridor outside his dressing room. Harvey Weinstein★ loomed on the Grand Tier, ogling Karolína Kurková.

★ Film producer. Founder Miramax, Weinstein Company. Massage enthusiast. Sparked the #MeToo social media campaign.

Elizabeth Hurley, who was presenting Fashion Rocks, had nineteen changes of outfit in her dressing room, one by each designer in the show, and two changes for the finale. She wore them all. She was wonderfully game throughout, and never a diva. I loved her for that; she is a Real Person, as well as a star. Circling the corridors, seeking their boxes, were the improbable foursome of Dame Joan Collins, Sir Philip Green,* Richard Gere and the Swedish footballer-turned-Calvin-Klein-underwear-model Freddie Ljungberg. The Royal Box was being swept for bombs by the palace protection squad with sniffer dogs.

The Prince of Wales and Duchess of Cornwall arrived – first motorbike, second motorbike, third motorbike, they're here – and we trooped up to the box. It was one of their first public outings as a couple. Camilla was notably easy and fun. The faces of a dozen famous fashion designers peered towards the Royal Box, perhaps registering for the first time their respective proximities. Down below, in the stalls, a sea of dinner jackets and shimmering evening dresses. The National Anthem was sung, house lights dimmed. We weren't one second late starting, unheard of at a fashion event. The Prince of Wales inserted cotton wool ear plugs from a monogrammed silver box. He removed them only once, for Andrea Bocelli, the blind tenor.

Joaquín Cortés was dazzling, ringed by parading Dior couture models. But the show took off with Beyoncé, up second, performing 'Crazy in Love'. There is a section in that track when it goes 'Uh oh, uh oh, uh oh' and then 'I look and stare so deep in your eyes / I touch on you more and more every time' et cetera, and the chorus swells ('So crazy right now'), when the whole audience erupted, and the Albert Hall lit up. It was a moment of

---

* Too-flash fashion retailer. Topshop, BHS. Owner of super-bling super-yacht *Lionheart*.

pure relief, and release and joy for me, because I knew then Fashion Rocks was going to be a success, even a triumph.

The event from here on became a blur. I remember Robbie Williams performing 'Feel', with the supermodels Eva Herzigová, Yasmin Le Bon and Karen Elson fawning all over him. He was mesmerizing in a black Versace suit and silver trainers. 'I scare myself to death / That's why I keep on running / Before I've arrived / I can feel myself coming . . .' he sang. Then added, 'On *you*,' leering at the models with a very dirty expression.

I remember Duran Duran and Bryan Adams, and then in no time it was the first interval.

The royal receptions during the intervals were the most surreal thing. Georgia escorted the Duchess of Cornwall down one line of celebrities, while I accompanied the Prince of Wales. 'Sir, may I present Miss Grace Jones and Ms Stella McCartney?'

'Sir, may I present Mr Domenico Dolce and Mr Stefano Gabbana and, er, the boy band Blue?'

'Sir, may I present Miss Donatella Versace and Mr Robbie Williams?'

'Sir, may I present Mr Alexander McQueen and Miss Björk from Iceland?'

And so on. It was magnificently incongruous.

Beyoncé was so small and frail, you worried she might snap in half. Tommy Hilfiger, who had the record number of personal bodyguards (six), was carefree. Mario Testino took pap-snaps of Naomi Campbell and Paris *Vogue* Editor Carine Roitfeld, so close to the royal progress it felt like photobombing.

Philip Green lumbered up, asking how much I'd paid the acts; he had a big birthday looming and fancied hiring several of them himself, he said. Jay Kay in a pale blue Burberry House check coat hobnobbed with Jade Jagger. Kelis and Sharleen Spiteri high-fived at the bar.

The McQueen segment with Björk performing 'Bachelorette' – her most beautiful, haunting song – her face appliquéd
with thousands of Swarovski crystals, was a highlight. Bryan
Ferry's 'Let's Stick Together' for YSL was another. The *Daily
Telegraph* reported it was 'the biggest night of fashion, rock and
royalty ever seen, anywhere in the world'.

We made our £1 million on the night, and eventually £3
million when all was said and done. Fashion Rocks was over,
and with it my fleeting career as an impresario.

17

If any reader has formed the impression that the fancy cast of characters in the previous chapter comprises my circle of personal friends, they are mistaken. The fashion and celebrity crowd which provided the backdrop for my working life has little overlap with my actual friends, who have hardly changed in forty years. Few people enjoy a celebrity encounter more than I do, but I seldom took them home. Our inner circle, consisting of perhaps twenty couples, plus an outer layer of fifty more, is the group I mind about, and consider real, legitimate friends. The rest are glorious birds of paradise, flitting across the scene for an issue or an event, before disappearing back to their own habitat.

Our family was expanding fast. Sophie Cecily Coleridge had been born on 14 March 1996, back at St Mary's, Paddington; in a hospital bed this time, not a birthing pool. We loved having a daughter, it was a novelty. Sophie's middle name was intended to be Cicely, after my beloved Girl Guide grandmother, but I got confused at the christening at St George's, Hanover Square.

Our fourth and final child was born on 21 December 1998. Thomas Maximilian Coleridge. Four being the maximum number of children you can fit in a car, without the indignity of a people carrier, we declared our family complete.

We moved home in Notting Hill to a tall white house, 39 Kensington Park Gardens, which backed onto a communal garden, as seen in the film *Notting Hill*. There were a couple of acres of shared lawns and shrubberies, and a children's playground with bark chips and a garden committee chaired by television boss Peter Bazal-gette★ and Geordie Greig. Everyone said, 'How wonderful being on a communal garden, they are just the best,' but I never embraced it. I felt perpetually on show, incessantly intruded upon by neighbours. No sooner were you reading the newspaper in a deckchair than an eager-eyed American wife in a baseball cap would hove into view, chirruping, 'How are you folks doing today? We'd love to get you guys over for a cook-out one day.' Lurking behind her would be a stroppy, exhausted investment banker husband, jet-lagged from a week of M&A activity in Seattle. Communal gardens didn't do it for me. In the *Sunday Times* property section, I spotted a house for sale in Caithness with a sixteen-mile-long drive. I concede it looked a bit gloomy, with its towers and crenellations, but the location excited me; no neighbours to hound us there. Georgia took one look at the brochure and vetoed it outright. She was right, of course.

Alexander and Freddie went to a charming nursery school round the corner, named The Acorn, filled with the children of film producers and hedge funders; it was the full-on Notting Hill experience. At weekends, we trudged round the Serpentine or went to a play centre called Bramley's, with brightly coloured plastic slides and rope netting, guaranteed to induce an instant headache.

My Cambridge Jade Garden set still formed the nucleus of my friendship group. For some unexplained reason, most of us had four children each. I don't think it was competitiveness, though Nick and Sarah Allan knocked out their four in record time, lapping us at the third. With Nick, I embarked upon the first of

---

★ Sir Peter Bazalgette, founder Endemol. Chair, Arts Council England (2012–16), Chair ITV (2016–).

a series of joint India jaunts, and later, with Kit Hunter Gordon and some of our respective sons, walked the thirteen-mile walls of Kumbhalgarh Fort in Rajasthan between jungle and steep cliffs, with golden eagles hovering overhead. Kumbhalgarh remains one of my favourite places in all India, rural and blessed; few foreign visitors spend enough time there to walk the walls of the fort, few Indians would see the point. With Georgia and friends, we discovered the Landmark Trust, and started renting follies and gatehouses all over the country for weekends and holidays.

We began staying with James Stourton at his house, Marcus, near Forfar in Angus, north of Dundee. This soon became an annual August fixture, which the whole family looked forward to, swimming in the icy-cold North Sea at Lunan Bay and tramping Glen Clova and Glen Muick. Every summer, I offered £5 to the first child to fully submerge themselves in the sea. Money talked: they sprinted across the sand, undressing as they went, and into the polar-temperature surf.

Angus is a peculiar part of Scotland since every village and hamlet, however small, has a resident earl and countess installed in a large castle at the end of a long, long drive. James took his guests for tea with a different one each day.

I asked James, 'Do you think they mind these daily intrusions by strangers? Piling into their houses, eating their cake and then leaving?'

'Oh Lord, no,' said James, 'they love it. They wait *all year round* for some amusing visitors. You have *no idea* how boring it is up here, nothing to do at all. They're desperate, crying out for stimulation.'

I doubt they really are, but it was fun for all of us.

James wasn't yet Chairman of Sotheby's, but heading that way. Of all my friends, he could be the most charming, but also mischievous and reckless. Once, after we had left Cambridge, we were driving south from Scotland, a carload of friends, when James said, 'Oh, by the way, I need to stop in Derbyshire for half an hour to value some pictures. Some clients want me to look at them. It won't take long.'

We arrived at a large, Jacobean-looking house. 'We'll wait in the car,' we said.

'Oh no,' said James. 'I'll say you all work for Sotheby's, then we can all go in and look around.'

The front door was opened by a serious-looking young man, about our own age, and his pretty wife.

'I'm James Stourton . . . and this is Nick Coleridge, he's head of our Sotheby's vintage agricultural machinery department, so if you have any old tractors that need valuing, he's your man. And this is Lucy Acland, she's our expert on fireplaces and andirons . . .' and so forth. We were all assigned a spurious expertise.

We were taken to inspect a giant pair of oil paintings of highland cattle wallowing in bog, which James rapidly valued. Then we left.

It was bad luck that neither of us had recognized the client as a Cambridge contemporary, who had immediately identified most of the party as imposters. He complained to Sotheby's and sent his paintings to Christie's instead. James found it hilarious.

It was through Victoria Mather that we met another couple central to our friendship group: Johnnie and Sarah Standing.* Johnnie is an actor in the Noel Coward meets David Niven tradition, and a painter; Sarah is the beautiful daughter of the film director Bryan

---

* Sir John Leon Bt: veteran British actor. Sarah Standing: style journalist, shopkeeper.

Forbes and the actress Nanette Newman. They live in a converted coach house in Pimlico, and we bonded at once.

Victoria was Travel Editor of *Tatler*, later *Vanity Fair*; when on form, the sharpest, most astute travel editor in the world. General Managers of grand hotels to this day quake at mention of her name; she did not hesitate to berate any concierge or room butler who failed to meet her unfeasibly high standards, and she saw it as her responsibility to patrol the world, always in First Class, and seize upon any lapse or corner-cutting at an Oberoi or Ritz-Carlton.

At a dinner at Christie's in King Street we met the tall, beanpole-thin Robin Wight and his equally tall wife Anastasia. We liked them at once, perhaps because Robin's lime-green and bright violet Ozwald Boateng suits were the opposite of any-thing I'd have worn myself. Robin was a celebrity advertising man, the name above the door at the Wight Collins Rutherford Scott agency, and a would-be politician. He had stood as a Con-servative candidate at the 1987 General Election in the strongly Labour constituency of Bishop Auckland in County Durham; his campaign slogan was 'It'll be all Wight on the night', though sadly, when they counted the votes, it wasn't.

We didn't yet realize that Robin is a serial husband, marrying over and over again. As I write this, I'm amazed we didn't intro-duce him to Tessa Dahl. At his fourth wedding, virtually all his previous wives sat happily together in the front pew, as well as his legion of children and stepchildren.

Every four years, Charles Moore gave a birthday party at their house in Islington for his wife Caroline; she was born in a leap year on 29 February, so technically, at the age of thirty, Caroline was only seven-and-a half. These parties were full of friends, journalists and politicians and, owing to the character of the hosts, had a particularly happy atmosphere.

One year, I was gossiping with the *Spectator* columnist Taki Theodoracopulos when Margaret Thatcher loomed up, Prime Minister no longer, and living the life of a semi-recluse in Chester Square. She was a staunch critic of the new National Lottery, which she disapproved of on moral grounds, as an encouragement to the poor to gamble.

She told us that, earlier that very day, she had been buying a newspaper in her local newsagents when she had spotted an elderly lady purchasing a lottery ticket.

'I approached her at once,' said Lady Thatcher, 'and urged her not to waste her precious coin. I said, "Don't waste it, dear, you should *invest* that pound instead. Invest it in *the future of British manufacturing and industry*. Watch your savings grow, dear. That's the way to become comfortable."'

She must have been a terrifying spectacle to the poor old lady, who was only trying to buy herself a little hope, and dreaming of Caribbean cruises.

Lady Thatcher now wagged her finger at Taki and me, in a scary way. 'I hope neither of *you* will *ever* contemplate buying a lottery ticket? It's not a game, it's a *racket*.'

My non-fiction book *The Fashion Conspiracy* had surprised everyone by selling quite well, and publishers started suggesting other non-fiction ideas. *The Fashion Conspiracy* has been translated into multiple languages, though not in the end into Japanese, since the elderly Japanese translator had suffered a massive heart attack halfway through his efforts and slumped down dead on top of my manuscript, and was not discovered for a month (he lived alone).

I was invited by the publisher, Lord Weidenfeld, to have breakfast with him at his flat on the Chelsea Embankment, scene of a thousand book launches and filled with Pope portraits by

Francis Bacon. George Weidenfeld said he had 'the perfect next subject for you. Come for breakfast at eight thirty.'

I rolled up. The great publisher was still in bed, but heading for the shower, according to his Hungarian manservant. I gazed out of the vast bay windows onto the Thames, and the Buddhist pagoda across the river in Battersea Park.

Weidenfeld eventually appeared, wearing a very short black towelling bathrobe, which barely covered his thighs. He sat himself down in a high-backed armchair, like a throne, and motioned me to sit on a low, leather stool in front of him. The Hungarian manservant brought coffee and a plate of chocolate croissants.

From my low vantage point, my field of vision was dominated by only one thing: Lord Weidenfeld's testicles, enormous and swollen, resting on the chair seat. They were barely a yard from my face.

Weidenfeld was saying, 'There has never been a good book about the international arms dealers. I envisage you interviewing all of them, Nicholas . . . in the States, in Egypt, Malaysia, Israel, the Sudan, Lebanon, the Congo and Rwanda of course . . . this book has global reach. I can help you meet them. Some of the Africans are perhaps not entirely respectable, but . . .'

As he shifted about on the chair, reaching forwards for his demitasse, the robe fell further open, now showcasing the full tackle.

In these situations, ought one to say something? Probably yes, but I missed my moment, it would now have been too late. So I tried to keep my eyes locked on his face, while the celebrated gonads occupied the foreground.

Eventually, the Hungarian manservant stepped forward with a linen napkin which he deftly unfurled across Lord Weidenfeld's lap.

★

Alexander and then Freddie headed to Summer Fields, a prep boarding school in Oxford, at the age of eight. We had intended sending them to London day schools, but the ones we visited felt cramped and closed in, and it didn't help that we were shown round by lacklustre, stooping teachers on grey, overcast days. We visited Summer Fields in a blazing heatwave, with small boys running carefree on the lawns, and were shown round by a ginger-haired eleven-year-old pupil from Wandsworth, delightfully smiley and well adjusted. If he was the role model, then we wanted in. Some of our American friends were astounded by our decision to send eight-year-olds away to boarding school, and disapproved. But I explained it is an Old English tradition, unlike in the United States where they send children away for the entire summer to camp.

Each time I visited Summer Fields, I half expected the sinister old team from Ashdown House to have infiltrated the place, and I kept a sharp eye open. But modern prep school headmasters have morphed into marketing directors, chiefly concerned with ensuring that all children and parents are 100 per cent happy at all times, and never utter a bad word against the school in case it goes viral; and prep school assistant masters in blazers have young, open-faced wives in tow. And every dormitory has anti-bullying codes pinned to the walls, and safeguarding policies and whistle-blowing procedures. That, at least, is the impression they like to give.

It was unfortunate that our son Freddie, aged nine, locked Rowan Atkinson's son Benedict into a steel locker in the changing rooms. It caused a frightful fracas at the time, including Georgia feeling compelled to apologize to the then Mrs Bean on Sports Day. But it blew over.

Our sons claim to have enjoyed Summer Fields very much indeed.

18

The night Princess Diana died in the Pont de l'Alma tunnel in Paris, the Coleridge family was at an Enid Blyton fancy-dress party in Norfolk, given by the camp cabaret artist Kit Hesketh-Harvey,* my Cambridge contemporary, and his actress wife, Katie.

No sooner had we left the barn where the party was still swinging, with men in shorts dressed as Julian and Dick from the Famous Five, and women in gingham smocks as Anne and Aunt Fanny, than news of the tragedy began filtering through. By morning, it was confirmed, and the world's television stations had an unquenchable need for 'talking heads' to milk every aspect of the unfolding drama.

Each time I switched TV channels, there was another Condé Nast staffer sounding off. There must have been ten on air at any one time. We were fielding experts on Diana's fashion, her marriage, her family, her sons. A Style Editor from *GQ* was broadcasting about the Prince of Wales's suits, a Travel Editor opining on the best suites at the Paris Ritz. It felt desperately undignified.

I sent out a directive there should be no more Vogue House experts speculating about Princess Diana, and it played badly. I soon got a telephone call from *Tatler*'s Social Editor, Ewa Lewis.

---

* Camp musical performer, Kit and The Widow. Brother of *Today* programme editor Sarah Sands. Married to actress Katie Rabett.

'Nicholas, this ridiculous fatwa on doing TV interviews, it doesn't apply to me, does it?'

'I'm afraid it does, Ewa.' I explained my thinking.

'Well,' she said, 'you are creating a big expensive problem for me. I've been offered six grand to do a half-hour Japanese TV slot about her, and the same from Korea. And the thing is; I've got some very expensive cosmetic dentistry coming up, and twelve grand would come in handy just now.'

'But you didn't know Princess Diana would be killed in a car crash when you booked your dentist. So it is hardly my fault.'

'Yes, but these opportunities don't come along that often . . . I'll be expecting a good pay rise to compensate.'

We spent hours at Vogue House trying to crack the enigma of which front covers sold best. A good cover makes a 15 to 20 per cent difference to sales at news-stand, and you felt there should be a formula, an algorithm, to get it right every time. The people in the circulation department had a stack of old wives' tales, passed down the generations, on what did and didn't sell. These included: blonde models outsell brunettes, smiley faces outsell frowns, green covers never sell, models must have direct eye contact with the reader, grey is a bad background colour, red and fluorescent orange are the strongest logo colours . . . the list went on. Unless the cover had an ultra-bright image of a blonde, grinning Claudia Schiffer staring directly out, with a cherry-red logo (not in any way obscured by the model's head) then the circulation team was full of foreboding, shaking their heads in dismay.

We held monthly Cover Meetings in my office, with the various Editors displaying their wares to an audience of Creative Directors, Publishers, marketing and circulation geeks. The cover options would be propped up along the sofa, and we would chew over them.

With magazines like *House & Garden*, *The World of Interiors* and *Condé Nast Traveller*, there could be as many as ten choices: farmhouse kitchens, Knightsbridge drawing rooms, riads in Tangiers, Caribbean beaches. The options were infinite.

Circulation, at this point, would make one of two possible observations. They would say, 'Whenever we feature a four-poster bed on the cover, we see a ten per cent spike.' Or else, 'My vote goes for the sandy beach with the palm trees. But can we "push" the blue of the sea a bit? Make it look more turquoise and inviting? And boost the sunshine?'

With *Vogue*, *Tatler*, *Vanity Fair*, *Glamour* and *GQ*, all of which rely on celebrity covers or supermodels, the choice was limited: generally only one subject, but several different crops (a close-up face, a full-length shot or an arty blurred version). Once again, everyone at the Cover Meeting conformed to stereotype.

Circulation said, 'I'm a bit dubious about the choice of personality. I mean, have readers heard of Anne Hathaway? She's not exactly a household name.' (Unless the front cover had David Beckham, Kate Moss, Kate Middleton or Daniel Craig on it, Circulation was dubious.)

The Publisher then said, 'I'm firmly in favour of the full-length shot. It's got to be. She's wearing Prada, and they need a cover.'

The Editor then said, 'All my staff prefer the edgy, arty image. We held an office poll and it was overwhelming.'

Circulation then said, 'It's blurred. So we'd need to factor a thirty per cent fall at news-stand.'

The Editor then said, 'I think I prefer the full-face image myself,' and so it was chosen. But the fact was, we hardly knew what sold, even after years of practice.

Until Princess Diana died, she was a banker as a cover star, a 25 per cent uplift in sales every time. But celebrities would work for five, six, seven front covers in a row, then suddenly lose their magic, readers became inured. Jennifer Aniston was a banker for five years, until she wasn't. So was Angelina Jolie and Cameron Diaz. Catherine Zeta-Jones worked on *Glamour*. Victoria Beckham was hit and miss (good on a *Vogue* cover, hot on *Glamour*, a flop on *Tatler*). Cheryl Cole had her moment. So did Jennifer Lopez. Naomi Campbell could go either way. Scarlett Johansson was a 'difficult get' (months, years spent trying to secure her) but readers didn't know that and she sold averagely. Salma Hayek and Gwyneth Paltrow disappointed. Kylie Minogue did the business.

Sometimes several of our magazines were stalking the same cover celebrities simultaneously, and that was awkward for me. Alexandra Shulman might say, 'We've got Keira Knightley lined up for August, Nick,' and I'd know Geordie Greig had her on his July cover of *Tatler*, and Jo Elvin had her for August *Glamour* as well. Meanwhile at GQ, Dylan Jones was trying for a semi-naked Keira sprawled across a fur rug for a GQ cover.

As the only person who knew about the impending multiple pile-up of Keiras, I had to box clever. I could ask one magazine to back off, or postpone, but it was complicated. Invariably the smaller magazines had worked longer and harder to secure the celebrity, so felt fiercely entitled to their scoop. But the celebrity's publicist valued a *Vogue* cover above all others.

There were other lessons too, painfully learnt. Covers with male celebrities, on a women's magazine, never sell. No exceptions. Even double-covers – a man and a woman together – seldom perform. We expected a Robbie Williams and Gisele duo on *Vogue* to fly off the shelves, but it didn't. Same thing with a brilliant Elton John and Elizabeth Hurley cover (bling Elton in red frock coat, straddled by Hurley with plunging neckline and gleaming white teeth), which we all adored at the Cover Meeting, but which underperformed. Johnny Borrell from

Razorlight with Russian supermodel Natalia Vodianova did fine, but didn't soar.

Readers, if asked their opinion, said, 'Why are all cover models so *young*? It's ridiculous. Why not put some older women – role models who have actually achieved something in their lives – on the front cover? I mean, I'm forty-five and I'm your typical reader, and I'd like to see women I can relate to.'

But whenever we tested the theory, they flopped. The covers that actually sold showed skinny, gorgeous, young superstars.

We were launching new magazines at a rate of knots. *Condé Nast Traveller*, edited by Sarah Miller, later by Melinda Stevens, was a succès d'estime, and sometimes turned a profit too.

The riskier venture was *Glamour*, launched against *Cosmopolitan* and *Marie Claire*, which had led the market for decades. *Cosmo* had been the highest-selling women's monthly since the 1970s, shifting half a million copies; it felt unassailable. There was something wonderfully audacious about challenging it, and perilous too, a £40 million punt which could easily go disastrously wrong. Condé Nast was on a winning streak, but seen as a bit posh and la-di-da for its own good, and our three big, muscular competitors (Hearst, IPC and EMAP) would have crowed if we fell flat on our faces.

I hired an editor, Jo Elvin, over breakfast in Belgravia at the Halkin hotel. It is a singular art, hiring editors: two-parts gut instinct, one-part analysis of their track record. I had interviewed Vere Rothermere, owner of the *Daily Mail*, for my book *Paper Tigers* and asked him how he chose editors.

He replied, 'It's difficult, because you can never be certain until you see the person in action. You see, in this business, people have a sort of literary persona, which is distinct from their everyday persona. It comes through not only in the articles they write themselves, but it comes through into the whole newspaper. This is very important because it's this charm, and you can't know whether someone has that ability until they are actually doing the job. Sometimes you'll find this able and intelligent and charming man, but what he produces is something entirely lacking in charm. So it's totally unknown, it's a guess. You have to wait and see.'

Rothermere was right, you can never be sure. But with Jo Elvin, I was pretty certain. I'd seen a dozen candidates, but she got my attention: a feisty Australian, focused and funny, with a quirky wit. She loved the idea of launching *Glamour* in Britain, she was fearless. She also bought into our secret plan: to launch as a 'handbag-sized' magazine and price it at £2 (half the price of *Cosmo*), which we could afford to do, because the smaller page size meant a saving in paper. Then we would blanket-promote on TV and try and buy our way into the market.

'All you have to do,' I told Jo, 'is produce a sassy, breezy, glamorous, celebrity-powered, widely appealing, non-smutty magazine which will sell in Manchester, Birmingham, Liverpool, Hull, London, everywhere.'

'Okay, boss, no pressure then,' said Jo. 'Clear brief.'

We hired away the Publisher of *Cosmopolitan*, Simon Kippin, who knew the secrets, and assembled a crack team. As the launch date crept nearer, tension mounted. We printed 700,000 copies and booked the first TV slot in every Saturday prime-time ad break. Our game-changing 'handbag size' and take-no-prisoners price strategy remained largely a secret. Kate Winslet was the cover star, fresh out of *Titanic*. Would we hit an iceberg ourselves? we wondered.

On launch day, I toured the supermarkets with Simon Kippin and Jonathan Newhouse, our Chairman, inspecting the displays. We had paid a fortune for in-your-face promotions in every big newsagent and supermarket, and we wanted to see the impact. It was unfortunate that, at our very first stop, Sainsbury's on the Cromwell Road, not a single copy of *Glamour* was anywhere to be found, let alone the giant cardboard 'gondola ends' and 'shelf talkers' we had anticipated.

A gormless retail assistant said, '*Glamour*? I haven't heard of that one. Is it an "adult magazine" at all? Have you searched on the top shelf?'

'No, it's a new young women's magazine. You may have seen some of our TV ads on Saturday night?'

'No, *sorree* . . .' She tossed her hair. 'I do watch the telly, but usually put the kettle on during the adverts.'

Our tour, intended to show the Condé Nast heir our dramatic £10 million promotional campaign, was not going well.

'Tell you what,' said the gormless assistant, 'we do have other women's titles available. *Cosmopolitan* and *Marie Claire* . . .'

Eventually we discovered several thousand *Glamours* piled up in the stockroom, and Jonathan and I lugged them to the shelves ourselves.

After this inauspicious start, matters perked up. The first week's sales figures were so impossibly strong, we disbelieved them. The second week's figures were even stronger. We felt like a political party on Election Night when an exit poll forecasts an unanticipated 200-seat overall majority: too good to be real. Each evening, from across the country, fresh dispatches came through: *Glamour* is outselling *Cosmopolitan* two-to-one in Coventry, Canterbury, Reading, Sheffield, Farnborough. *Glamour* is outselling *Marie Claire* four-to-one in Exeter, Gloucester, Middlesbrough, Stoke-on-Trent and across the East Midlands. We knew we were winning when the *Cosmo* team moved into panic rebuttal mode, accusing *Glamour* of being a 'pygmy' magazine of little appeal.

When the first set of official six-month circulation figures was released, *Glamour* had come from nowhere to become the best-selling women's monthly in Britain. After a year, it became the best-selling in Europe, with an audited sale of 680,000 copies. There was something very sweet, for a luxury publishing house like Condé Nast, to have invented and launched the mid-market leader. Jo Elvin deservedly scooped every Editor's prize going, and Simon Kippin won every Publisher's prize. It was, as they say, a good gig.

Morale at Vogue House had hit a high. It felt like a golden place in which to work, in these years of plenty at the start of the new millennium. I think it is unusual, in any workplace, to find oneself part of a group which, irrespective of work, would be your friends. But so it was, and I was blessed.

I recently found an old photograph of the British team, the fifty or so key Editors, Publishers and executives lined up like a school group, some sitting cross-legged on the floor at the front. Alexandra, Dylan, Jo, Sue, Geordie, Sarah Miller, Rupert Thomas of *The World of Interiors*. There, too, are Peter Stuart, Publisher of *GQ*, Helen Fifield, Publisher of *House & Garden*, Emma Redmayne, Publisher of *Interiors*, Jamie Bill, Publisher of *Condé Nast Traveller*, Claire German, Publisher of *Brides*, Kate Slesinger of *Vogue*, Patricia Stevenson of *Tatler*, Simon Leadsford of *House & Garden*. And people like our Marketing whizz, Jean Faulkner, Nicky Eaton of Press and PR, Sarah Jensen, Production Director, Sue Douglas, Customer Publishing for clients.

All ten of our British magazines were climbing in sales and advertising, and we were working on three more launches at least. Staff numbers grew from 250 to 925 in London; profits hit new highs. And it was fun. My friend Annie Holcroft, the *Vanity Fair* Publisher, was the company prankster. Somehow, she had got hold of a rubber stamp of my signature.

The first indication was a memo to All Staff, ostensibly com- ing from me. It read: 'For economy reasons to save on electricity, staff are no longer permitted to use the lifts unless there are a minimum of five passengers wishing to go up or down. Please form a queue in the lobby, or on your respective floors, until five or more staff members have assembled. At this point, you may press the button to summon a lift.'

Embarrassingly, at least thirty staff believed it.

Following a London visit by Si Newhouse, Annie faked another memo. This time, Stephen Quinn, the *Vogue* Publisher, was the object of the spoof. It read: 'Following the recent visit from our New York proprietor, S. I. Newhouse Jr, it has been decided to rename Vogue House as Tatler House. This is for legal and tax reasons, enabling a write-off of accumulated investment and goodwill in the *Tatler* brand against the purchase price of the building. Please ensure all writing paper, business cards, invoices etc. are updated accordingly.'

The first I knew about it was Stephen bursting into my office, eyes blazing. 'Have you completely forgotten that *Vogue* makes half the damned profit of this *entire company*? It would be humili- ating for *Vogue* to work in Tatler House . . .'

I stared at him. 'I don't know what on earth you're talking about.'

He sighed and looked thoughtful. Then said, 'Annie Hol- croft, curse her.'

I had now been Managing Director of Condé Nast in Britain for ten years, and Jonathan Newhouse and his wife Ronnie Cooke Newhouse, the Creative Director, gave a big party to celebrate in the Ballroom at Claridge's. I don't suppose any of us realized I was only at the one-third mark of my eventual time at Condé Nast. Looking back at the party photographs, we all seem absurdly young, which indeed we were – between the

200 guests, we were 4,000 years younger than we are today: Maurice Saatchi, Tony Snowdon, Terence Conran, Martin Sorrell, Joan Collins and Vivienne Westwood, Mario Testino and John Galliano, Isabella Blow, John Morgan, Nigella Lawson, Nicky Haslam . . . There is something almost macabre about the photographs, knowing now what we couldn't have predicted: the sadnesses and early deaths, scandals and divorces that lay ahead for so many (but not all).

Si Newhouse was still making annual inspections of the European company. Even Jonathan prepared carefully for these visits, which were seen as something to 'get through' without tripping up, or triggering unsolicited advice on how to run our business. But they were interesting; away from Manhattan, ensconced in the Connaught, Si was habitually indiscreet on the subject of magazines he was stalking to purchase (Hearst was generally the competitor) and Editors-in-Chief he hoped to lure or intended to fire. Often he bought his fiercely intellectual wife, Victoria, with him, and sometimes his daughter Pam and her husband.

Georgia asked the younger Newhouses over dinner at the Connaught, 'Do you read a lot of the Condé Nast magazines yourself?'

'We don't take *any* of them,' Pam replied. 'We don't approve of them. They are too materialistic and showy.'

'What about *House & Garden*? That's pretty inoffensive.'

'That one is the *worst*.'

Si liked to eat early at 7 p.m. Each restaurant we went to, he asked, 'Er, Nicholas, it doesn't seem to be very *full* here. Is it no longer *fashionable*?' He looked crestfallen.

'Don't worry, this is still quite early for London. It'll fill up later.' Which it did, but there was always an anxious period of just us in a deserted, echoing dining room.

★

Each morning, I received stacks of post from readers, favour-requests and complaints. These fell into three categories.

The first were letters begging for work experience, several of these a day. They would begin, 'Dear Mr Coleridge. You don't know me from Adam, but I met your godmother at a dinner party in Wiltshire and she said you wouldn't mind me writing. My daughter, Annabel, is fourteen and a pupil at St Mary's, Calne. She is passionate about English (she is forecast an A grade at GCSE) and art. She would love to do a month's work experience in July (we fly to Corfu on the 26th). Please don't feel you have to reply, you must be so busy, I won't be the least bit offended.'

The second lot were letters from mad people, often com-plaining about *Tatler* employing Tom and Emma Parker Bowles as food and motoring correspondents. They had it in for Camilla and sent poison-pen letters in biro and block capitals, heavily underscored. Sometimes (bizarrely) they put their addresses at the top, and we would Google Street View them – finding a neglected bungalow on an edge-of-town Hartlepool road.

The third lot came from rich, grand widows in Cadogan Square. They wrote, 'I was most upset to find a "special offer" for a *House & Garden* subscription, offering the magazine for £21 for twelve issues. I have been a loyal subscriber for thirty years, and my most recent renewal price was £24.50. Why am I being *penalized* for my loyalty? I await your explanation with interest.'

The richer people are, the more ready to complain. At din-ners, I became used to the wives of millionaires declaring, 'I can't believe *Vogue* costs four pounds. *Four pounds!* And it is full of advertising! Ridiculously overpriced.'

I replied, 'Four pounds is what it costs to dry-clean one leg of a pair of chinos.'

'Well, that is perfectly ridiculous too. I grant you that.'

★

My Number One hero, David Bowie, was on tour at Wembley Arena, and I took three other diehard Bowie fans: Alexandra Shulman, Dylan Jones and *Vogue* Creative Director, Robin Derrick. We were driven to the venue by Brian Greenaway.

On the way, Dylan announced, 'I've organized for us to go backstage after the show to meet Bowie.'

Alexandra and I were full of misgivings. We felt anxious about meeting our hero, in case it broke the spell.

The show was brilliant, he played all the classic tracks. As the audience filed out, we walked down half a mile of concrete backstage corridors and arrived outside the star's dressing room.

Only one other person was waiting to be introduced. It was Charles Kennedy, chubby-faced Leader of the Liberal Democrats. He had flown down from his Scottish constituency for the concert, straight from judging an agricultural show. He wore a hairy three-piece tweed suit.

The door to the dressing room opened and we formed a greeting line, like at a royal reception. Bowie was pin-thin. He approached down the line.

'And this is Nicholas Coleridge,' he was told.

'Not the same Nicholas Coleridge who writes books?' he said. 'Iman and I really enjoyed your last three novels.'

Your last three novels . . .

It was the crowning moment of my life. I was unable to speak. I grinned inanely.

All the way home in the car, Alex and Dylan confirmed, 'He really did say it, Nick. It isn't a dream.'

I made a point of meeting would-be journalists because you never knew when you'd strike gold. One day, my old friend Edward Stourton rang me. He said, 'Nick, I know this is a pain, but could you possibly see an ex-girlfriend of my son? She wants to write. I'd be so grateful if you could. She stayed with us in Greece this summer, and swam stark naked in the pool every day. I was trying to read my book, and she paraded up and down in the nude.'

'Happy to help,' I said. 'Ideally, can she come to my office at eight thirty a.m.? The diary's pretty full at the moment, it would be easier if she could arrive early.'

Not long afterwards, the young female writer appeared. From first impressions, I marked her down as a *Vogue* or *Tatler* sort of girl.

We talked about journalism, and I asked, 'Which of our titles are you most interested in contributing to?'

'*GQ*,' she replied, not missing a beat. 'I want to be your sex columnist.'

'And, er, are you a particular expert?'

'Yes, I've had a lot of experience – and not just vanilla sex. In fact, I find I can't come properly unless I'm tied up in Lycra rope.'

It was 8.40 a.m., I was holding a cup of coffee. The cup started to rattle in the saucer, coffee slopping over the rim.

'Let me ring Dylan Jones,' I said. 'He's the Editor. He tends to get in early. I think you two should meet at once.'

Two hours later, Dylan rang me. 'God,' he said, 'if you get any more like that, send them straight down. Unbelievable. I've no idea if she can write or not, but I've commissioned three pieces.'

She remained *GQ*'s red-hot sex columnist for the next four years, until she married and felt obliged to resign.

19.

I had developed a routine for writing my books around my job, which enabled me to publish a novel or non-fiction book every eighteen months. On Saturday and Sunday mornings I retreated to the end of the garden (I prefer writing outdoors), began work at 7 a.m. and never went on much beyond 11 a.m. Four hours: if I wrote 250 words an hour (which isn't a lot) that amounts to 2,000 words per weekend, 10,000 a month, 120,000 a year = a 350-page book. Keep your foot on the pedal a bit longer, and it's 500 pages.

I wrote for very particular reasons: because I enjoyed it – the craft and planning and structure it imposed on the weekend. I don't play golf or shoot, and the growing shelf of novels was testament to the passage of time. And I relished the control of the author over his characters, conforming to my absolute will (you sometimes hear distinguished novelists saying, 'I never know what a character will think or do next,' but I always knew). It was the polar opposite to my magazine day job, where decisions are consensual, the product of large teams and creative compromises and the talent of others. A bid for the permanence of hard covers in an ephemeral world. And a chance to process and refashion the vagaries of real life into a shape with a beginning, middle and end.

I write longhand with green Pentel pens on yellow American legal pads. I find the process of writing by hand more satisfying, without the intrusion of tech, glare of screen, battery fatigue, cutting and pasting.

Friends sometimes tried to guilt-trip me by saying, 'I'm surprised you have time to write anything at weekends. What
about your poor children?'

But when they were small our children happily messed about
for hours in their pyjamas, slopping cereal and watching telly;
and when they became teenagers, they were asleep until after
my day's writing was done. New books took them by surprise.
'When did you write that, Dad?'

'While you were still asleep.'

And, after I'd reached my daily word count, I overcompensated; cajoling them into long walks, which luckily they have
developed a taste for.

I had written a non-fiction book, *Paper Tigers*, ludicrously fat
at 600 pages, about the world's 30 top newspaper proprietors.
This necessitated multiple trips to New York to interview the
super-civilized Sulzbergers of the *New York Times*, Washington
for the celebrity Grahams of the *Washington Post*, Los Angeles
for gunslinger-eyed Rupert Murdoch and geeky Otis Chandler
of the *Los Angeles Times*, Mumbai and Delhi for the great Indian
owners and, one by one, stalking and bagging all the British
ones from patrician Vere Rothermere to bombastic Robert
Maxwell.

Normally I tape-recorded these interviews, which were
three hours in length. But, for some reason, Rothermere of the
Daily Mail sent word that I could only take notes, not subject
him to a tape recorder. (Presumably for deniability later on, if
required.)

My shorthand is quick, but I wanted to catch every nuance of
speech, which is tricky when you are writing notes and trying
to sound intelligent at the same time.

There was a shop I passed each day on South Audley Street
called The Counter Spy Shop, which sold surveillance equipment

to amateur detectives and snoops. It had always intrigued me, it was probably run by 'Q' from James Bond as a side venture.

Inside, at considerable expense, I bought a fountain pen with a recording device concealed in the nib, which I was advised to place on the table between me and my 'target' for crystal-clear results.

For three hours, the clandestine pen whirred and vibrated on the coffee table between me and Lord Rothermere, making me increasingly anxious. I was afraid that, at any moment, it would reach the end of the tape and noisily rewind, exposing my sneakiness.

The interview concluded and, on a park bench in Kensington Gardens, I played back the tape. All you could hear was the rattling of coffee cups on saucers and a distant, incomprehensible drone of voices.

Conrad Black was my favourite proprietor. I found him mesmerizing, his voice, his looming physical presence and tycoon posturing. And the way that his sentences – often paragraphs long – were formed like Russian dolls, each containing a sub-clause or parenthesis, and then another one inside that, and then another. Transcribing a taped interview, some sentences ran to several pages, as complicated to unravel as tangled headphone cable. And his declarations rattled with arbitrary prejudices, feuds, accusations, insights, erudition and mogul-class name-dropping.

Georgia and I were at a charity event at Buckingham Palace, guests of the advertising tycoon Maurice Saatchi, and found ourselves standing in line with Conrad to be presented to the Princess Royal, Princess Anne.

As the royal presence approached, Lord Black of Crossharbour began to preen.

'Your Royal Highness,' he declared in booming, senatorial

tones. 'May I commend you on the magnificence of your paintings here in the Picture Gallery. They are considerably more
impressive than those at the White House in Washington, where
I was privileged to be dining with the President earlier this week.'

Princess Anne stared at him, nonplussed. 'Oh, really? Well,
one seldom notices the pictures here oneself, having known
them for so long.'

And then she moved on.

I wrote two novels set in the magazine industry, both edited by
Rosie Cheetham. She is a famously astute book editor, and I
learnt a lot from her, about structure above all. And she had a
way of quizzing you about your characters, probing you on
motivation and foibles, that obliged you to consider them more
deeply.

I refined the plot of *Godchildren* with Rosie at The Ivy restaurant in Soho, and later at her kitchen table in Gloucestershire.
The premise of my fattest, 711-page novel was rather neat: mys-
terious tycoon has six godchildren – rich, poor, pretty, plain,
posh, insecure. As the story unfolds, the godfather's life becomes
ever-more intertwined with his godchildren – as boss, benefactor, lover and object of fascination. The godchildren's lives also
become enmeshed, cemented by godfatherly trips to the South
of France and the Bahamas, and rides on his private jet. The
character of the godfather, Marcus Brand, drew on at least six
role models from different parts of my life: Jocelyn Stevens and
James Goldsmith, with a twist of Robert Maxwell and a nod to
Conrad Black; there might be a dash of the banker Evelyn de
Rothschild in there too, and indeed Jacob Rothschild.

Godchildren enabled me to write about a whole sweep of time
from the fifties to the millennium, bringing it all in: school,
drugs, love, the Feathers Ball, Hong Kong, India, New York.

The longer I worked on it, the longer it grew. Soon the manuscript needed to be bound in two volumes, then three. I used to slip away for a week alone, usually to Morocco, to concentrate on it undisturbed. Another long chunk was written in a glass-sided bus shelter on a family holiday to the Isle of Bute, while Scottish rain battered against the cliffs.

Like *The Fashion Conspiracy* before it, *Godchildren* had one glorious week at the top of the charts, mostly read, as it had been written, on long-haul flights or poolside at hotels. A friend sent me a photograph of five different people reading copies on adjacent sunbeds at the La Mamounia hotel in Marrakech, and another group was spotted at the Amanpuri in Phuket. My kind of readers.

I had dedicated it to my own godchildren: to Helena, Edie, Ione, Ewan, Cara, Ned and Willa. They rather gamely assembled in a suite at Claridge's, to be photographed for the publicity campaign. Years later, a gossip columnist tried to imply that *Godchildren* was based on my godchildren's actual lives, and that Marcus Brand, the predatory tycoon, is based upon me (this was after Cara Delevingne and Edie Campbell had become supermodels). But they were all aged about eight when the novel was published, so it clearly wasn't.

My literary agent, by this point, was the great Ed Victor, the party-minded super-agent. Georgia and I had met him and his wife, Carol Ryan Victor, one Easter holiday at the Gazelle D'Or hotel in Taroudant. That year, the Moroccan hotel was filled to the brim with vaguely famous guests: Charles and Caroline Moore plus the ad-man Charles Saatchi, the Conservative Cabinet minister Michael Portillo and the photographer Terence Donovan, and their wives.

Under normal circumstances, being British, we would have kept ourselves to ourselves, fearful of intruding on holiday privacy. But

Ed, being Ed, had no inhibitions. Each morning, he patrolled the line of sunbeds.

'Carol and I have reserved the big table under the olive trees for lunch. Charles and Kay are joining us, so are Michael and Carolyn . . .' and so on. We were all drawn into Ed's gregarious orbit.

After lunch, he organized cut-throat Monopoly tournaments. Portillo, then Chief Secretary to the Treasury, always came second. Saatchi always won, with hotels on every property on the board.

Ed became my agent before the end of the week.

It was a thrill when *Godchildren* was shortlisted for the naffest-named literary award in publishing: the WH Smith Thumping Good Read Award. But not quite thumping enough to win.

Every other year, another fat multi-character novel appeared: *A Much Married Man*, *Deadly Sins*, *The Adventuress*. I think I've written fourteen. I could never have lived on the proceeds of my books, let alone supported a wife, four children, school fees, holidays and the rest, despite the foreign editions.

The mechanics of plotting a story absorbed me, moving characters like chess pieces: knight to f4 to trap bishop, queen counters and takes rook. Or, in my case: Marcus to Tetbury to trap Saffron, Jamie counters in Annabel's to take Abigail. I have always found it easy to empathize with other people's points of view, even when my own are emphatically different, so multi-character sagas suit me.

Ed Victor copy-tasted my books at the halfway point. That was our system.

Georgia read them thoroughly first, then Ed who could gut a manuscript over a weekend. Then he'd call: 'Nick, you know, I *like* this. I really do. I can *sell* this for you. But there's one thing you've got to change first, I insist.'

'What's that, Ed?'

'In chapter fourteen, the character Hannah, the girl he meets on the flight from Jakarta and has sex with in the hotel. You've given her ginger-coloured hair. It doesn't work. Better if you make her blonde or brunette.'

'Sure, Ed. I'll change it.'

Then he would talk for an hour or two about his more famous clients, and the megadeals he'd pulled off for them. 'I spent Saturday night with Keith Richards and Eric Clapton, both my clients, and then lunch on Sunday with Tina [Brown] and Harry [Evans] in Quogue. Her new book deal is *fabulous*, Nick.'

When my own were published, Ed took me to lunch at The Ivy Club. He could be wonderfully warm. He would say kind things, then couldn't resist: 'You know, Nick, it was *very fortunate* I caught that detail about Hannah's hair colouring. It didn't work. You remember I told you to change it?'

He used to say, 'I think you've made a pact with the devil, Nick, to get twenty-five hours out of every twenty-four-hour day.' It was flattering, until I discovered he used exactly the same line on Nigella Lawson, Dylan Jones and Geordie Greig.

He was in all respects a super-agent.

20

Vanity Fair published a landmark profile of the Egyptian-born tycoon Mohamed Al-Fayed in September 1995. It was written by the American journalist Maureen Orth and, in comparison with later articles about the controversial owner of Harrods and the Paris Ritz, it was unexpectedly restrained. On a scale of one to ten, with one as a 'puff piece' and ten as a 'total hatchet job', this was a six. Maureen was sympathetic towards Fayed's campaign to get a British passport, but hinted at episodes of alleged sexual harassment. I remember reading it and thinking, 'Skilfully done. She hasn't dodged the issues, but we probably won't lose the multimillion-pound Harrods advertising account either . . .'

How wrong I was.

Less than a week later, there arrived at Condé Nast the most aggressive, rapacious and bellicose legal letter ever received. It had been composed by Schillings of Bedford Square and you had to hand it to them: it was a humdinger. As is customary in such letters, it ran to three pages of vehemently expressed indignation at how their saintly client had been traduced, and culminated in a demand for an abject apology and compensation of £100,000,000. At least I think it was a hundred million, there were so many noughts, you had to count them carefully. More alarming still, not only was Graydon Carter named personally in the suit as Editor-in-Chief, as well as Maureen Orth and Condé Nast, but so was I.

I always wonder, when firms of libel lawyers construct such

letters, especially when acting for people like Fayed, what is going through their minds. Presumably they don't believe a word they're writing, and are howling with laughter, holding their noses and thinking only of the fat fee. But, on the receiving end, I find legal letters rather unnerving, with their especially thick writing paper, sombre letterheads and fake outrage.

The Fayed opening salvo was a collector's item. It was the start of a two-year-long war, as dirty as they come, with a thrilling sequence of devious tricks and double-bluffs.

It was greatly to the Newhouses' credit that they never even considered caving in. Si Newhouse just shrugged and laughed, and so did Jonathan. As the stakes rose, they never once blinked.

Having agreed to fight it, we needed to defend our case. Maureen Orth's article had invoked sexual misconduct but given few specifics. It was clear we needed to find credible witnesses and sworn affidavits, but where to begin? *Vanity Fair*'s London Editor, Henry Porter, and I met with the magazine's London lawyer, David Hooper, and made plans. As the months passed, we became increasingly paranoid at our meetings, and communicated in quieter and quieter voices, until we were almost whispering. Henry felt we might be being bugged, and the Vogue House phones and meeting rooms were regularly swept.

Henry and I visited a firm of risk management experts (code for private detectives) at an office behind Buckingham Palace. The entrance was in a basement, with state-of-the-art security. We were ushered into a meeting room, where three executives were awaiting us. They resembled smooth, groomed actors from the TV show *Suits*.

We began outlining the legal challenge and our need to identify young women who claimed to have been harassed by Fayed; ideally four or five convincing witnesses prepared to testify.

Was this something they could help us with? The risk experts exchanged glances.

'Gentlemen, I'm going to stop you right there,' said the boss. 'Don't say another word. I have to inform you, we are already retained by the gentleman in question.'

The room suddenly turned chilly, the meeting ended abruptly. As the junior member of the team walked us to the door, he said, 'I think you'll find most of our competitors work for him too. Just to warn you.'

Henry and I stood at the top of the area steps, in mild shock and rolling our eyes. This was going to be interesting.

Henry received an overture, out of the blue, from a man purporting to be a disgruntled former Fayed security man, with important information to impart. After some due diligence (including confirming we couldn't pay him for any information), Henry met him in a pub in the East End, in a run-down neighbourhood of boxing clubs and seamen's missions.

The disgruntled security guy said he had been unfairly fired by Fayed, and wanted to get even. He hinted at a trove of explosive material he was eager to share, but constantly reverted to the prospect of being paid. 'Even a couple of grand would help.' The meeting ended inconclusively.

The following weekend, a story appeared in a Sunday tabloid, stating that enemies of Mr Al-Fayed had been caught in a honey trap, attempting to buy dodgy information to discredit him. The security man had been a plant, wired for covert recording. The article reported that a complaint had been made to the Crown Prosecution Service, the tape submitted as evidence of an attempt to pervert the course of justice.

This was a problem for several months, until it could be demonstrated that the tape had been spliced and edited, by a person or persons unknown.

I had met Mohamed Al-Fayed regularly in my working life. Sometimes I accompanied our Publishers on forays to sell advertising to Harrods, which meant calling on the Chairman, and being made to hang about for an hour or more in a waiting room full of reproduction Regency furniture. This room was rumoured to be bugged; I have no idea whether or not it actually was.

Eventually Mohamed would appear: stocky, powerful and swearing. 'I hope you haven't been waiting fucking long time? They should have told me you were here, the cunts. Now we talk. You giving me fucking special deal, yes? Otherwise fuck off.' He brimmed with similar banter.

It amused him I was losing my hair, as he was himself; it was a bond. 'You like me, no fucking hair. That's because we always fucking, all the time fucking. *Hah!* How many girlfriends you have? Your cock big, yes?' Then he pointed to the Harrods Managing Director, hovering in his slipstream. 'That man has too much hair. No fucking! He is not like us, always fucking sweet pussy. Am I right, my friend?'

There were generally four bodyguards in attendance, scowling bruisers with fat necks and earpieces. They accompanied him everywhere. It was never clear why the Harrods owner needed a personal security team, when the owners of Harvey Nichols and Selfridges had none.

The fight got dirtier. Fayed's Director of Public Affairs, Michael Cole,★ a tall, claret-faced courtier in a Turnbull & Asser suit, was instructed to contact Harrods' suppliers (the fashion brands, jewellers, luxury companies) and deter them

★ Former BBC television news reporter and royal correspondent. Gave evidence at the inquests of Diana, Princess of Wales and Dodi Fayed. Gifted his collection of Savile Row suits and ties to the Victoria and Albert Museum.

from advertising in Condé Nast titles. Had this strategy worked, it would have cost us several hundred million pounds. Every week, we received phone calls from fashion companies in Milan, Paris and New York, or from jewellers with concessions in Harrods. 'We have been told not to advertise with you any more. What should we do?'

Fortunately, the Condé Nast relationships ran deeper than their fear of Fayed, and only one Italian lingerie brand was sufficiently intimidated to ditch us. The two hundred others held their ground.

Slowly, very slowly, we were building our defence. A perfect witness was found, a young woman who had been plucked from the shop floor to work for the Harrods Chairman. She had an astonishing story to tell, full of credible details about his Park Lane apartment and Scottish castle, Balnagown. But would she swear an affidavit, and be prepared to appear on the stand?

A date had been set at the Royal Courts of Justice, for a case expected to last three weeks. The Fayed side was marshalling its own witnesses, including children's charities, to testify to his good character. Some of our own witnesses were nervous, fearing reprisals. I called on the boss of another department store, who insisted we speak up on the roof in case we were under surveillance.

For the fashion shows in Paris, I customarily stayed at the Ritz. This was another Fayed trophy-asset, and it felt like madness to continue, but some recklessness made me. It was a stupid decision, I was perpetually on edge. I felt the receptionist giving me a strange look, before disappearing too long to an inner office . . . to do what, to tell whom? The Assistant Manager who showed me to my room said, 'We have put you in a special suite this visit, Monsieur Coleridge.' It overlooked the Rue Cambon.

The human mind plays tricks. Did I imagine it, or were there strange clicks on the telephone? There was a big gilt mirror, mounted on the wall at a peculiar angle opposite my bed; was I being watched? Perhaps a bunch of goons were sitting behind a two-way mirror. I undressed in the bathroom.

Adjoining my suite was a 'service area', permanently locked, which fed the paranoia. The smoke detectors in the suite appeared abnormally large, almost like CCTV cameras. The trundle of a room-service trolley, passing along the corridor, made me start. And when I checked out, I carefully repacked my suitcase, to ensure nobody had fitted me up with a pilfered bathrobe or Ritz soap.

The court case was barely eight weeks away. We had somehow found four strong witnesses and a host of lesser ones; the files ran to several hundred pages of statements. The impending showdown promised extensive press coverage. Teams of QCs were retained by both sides.

We reached the moment of disclosure: the exchange of documents, when each side can see for the first time what the other side has. We wondered what they'd make of our roster of red-hot affidavits.

Shortly afterwards, Leonard Lauder of the cosmetics conglomerate rang me at home. He was one of our largest advertisers, and a key supplier to Harrods. He was in peacemaker mode. 'If you hear anything from Harrods, any overture, you should seize it. We want you to make peace . . . that is, *I* want you to.'

The next morning, I took a call from Michael Cole. His voice was wonderfully inveigling, you could hear the treacle. 'And how is the lovely Georgina? And the children?'

'Georgia and the children are great, thank you.'

'Nicholas, it would be useful for us to meet up. To talk about this distressing situation.'

'Sure. I must run it past the lawyers, but I don't see why not. Where? A restaurant? My office? And when?'

'Why don't we meet today in the steam room at the Bath & Racquets?' he said. 'It's discreet. And if we meet there, we will know neither of us is wired . . .'

The Bath & Racquets Club, in a mews behind Claridge's, is an exclusive men-only gym. It had been started by Mark Birley, the nightclub king, several years earlier: it looks exactly like Anna-bel's, with oil paintings and Turkish rugs, but with Cybex exercise machines instead of a dance floor. Half the members are Greek shipping billionaires ('Good morning, Mr Embiricos. Good morning, Mr Goulandris. Good morning, Mr Niarchos,' says the glamorous receptionist). The rest are hedge fund mana-gers. And it has the best Turkish bath, lined with Carrara marble.

I shuffled into the swirling mist, towel wrapped around my waist. Michael Cole, defiantly naked, lolled on a marble slab. The steam was so dense, we could scarcely see.

'Nicholas,' Michael began, in philosophical mode. 'You and I, we are very similar. We both work for great men, immensely rich men. They are stubborn, and always have to win, is that not so?'

I nodded along.

'It is left to people like ourselves, Nicholas, to sort these mat-ters out for our principals. To save them from themselves, if you will.'

I continued nodding. Here comes the deal . . .

'We shouldn't be at war. We should be working together, not against each other. Condé Nast is the greatest magazine pub-lisher in the world, Harrods is the greatest department store. Mohamed is a man of honour, I can personally attest to that. And he wants to advertise with you again, to increase it in fact . . .'

The case was quietly dropped. Condé Nast asked for nothing in return and we made no deal, but we agreed not to disclose our affidavits, and never have.

Condé Nast was expanding around the world at dizzying speed. Jonathan Newhouse had a new company mantra, which he regularly proclaimed: 'More magazines, more money.' We were launching brands like *Vogue*, *Glamour*, *Architectural Digest* and *GQ* in new markets at the rate of 20 a year. In a heartbeat, we were big in Japan, big in Korea, in China, Brazil, Greece and across Eastern Europe. Now there were 18 editions of *Glamour*, 20 *Vogues*. And the newer brands were rolling out too: multiple *Condé Nast Travellers*, multiple *Wireds*, multiple *Vanity Fairs*.

As a company, Condé Nast sometimes felt like a precarious place to work, though I worked hard to keep the British part stable. I have a theory that, providing they don't become bored, experienced Editors and managers do a better job than a perpetual churn of replacements. Many of our top team worked twenty-five to thirty years in Vogue House, and knew every nuance, expectation and client intimately. And Editors produce their best work from their thirty-seventh issue onwards, once they've learnt by trial and error what works and what doesn't.

Did I ever worry about my own tenure at Condé Nast? Tina Brown once told me she never took Si Newhouse for granted, and I did the same for his cousin, Jonathan. He rang repeatedly at weekends – sixteen times was the record – to get my take on this or that, important or trivial. Whenever Jonathan had good suggestions to make, and they often were, I embraced them at once; when they were bad, I played for time until they withered on the vine. I am a believer in 'owner's privilege' to play freely with their own toy, but also in the duty of the Managing Director to call it right, and to manage the cat's cradle of relationships and consequences which characterize the inner workings of any organization. I considered myself lucky in our owners, and lucky to be working for a private company.

A small international board, known as the Executive Committee, met every couple of months to plan and review our world domination. Four or five of us assembled from around the globe, numb with jet lag, for meetings lasting eight or more hours in a sealed conference room. It is a truism about all boards that members always gravitate to the same seats, in the same configuration, and frequently say the same things too. So it was at Condé Nast. There was a brilliant Italian named Dr Giampaolo Grandi, who ran Condé Nast in Milan. He was an unexpectedly professorial figure at the epicentre of the fashion industry, with his wool V-neck jerseys and dusty tweed jackets like an English prep school geography master. But he was always worth listening to, and I greatly admired him. After lunch, with a flash of anger, he would exclaim, 'If I may be a little *provocative*, what you are speaking is complete rubbish, I am sorry to say this but you clearly know *nothing* about reality, and *nothing* about publishing.' We looked forward to his outbursts.

Then there was James Woolhouse, a super-polite and reserved Englishman based in Hong Kong, who oversaw our Asia Pacific titles. In an earlier age, under the British Empire, he would have been Chief Collector for the State of Maharashtra. From time to time, he would say, 'Being brutally frank, that magazine will never make money.' Being brutally frank was James's stock-in-trade.

And there was Bernd Runge from East Germany, who brought an enticing note of John Le Carré to the group. He ran our Russian and German operations, as well as overseeing the Eastern Bloc. He was a dashing, duplicitous, rather handsome figure who had been educated at Moscow State University, spoke multiple languages and was hard to pin down. His fellow board members were instinctively suspicious but couldn't quite explain why. It was unfortunate when Bernd was exposed in *Der Spiegel*, the weekly German news magazine, as a former Stasi informant who had spied on his own sister under the Honecker regime. It caused quite a brouhaha at the time. With almost incredible magnanimity, he was allowed to stay on at Condé Nast. But it all went wrong in the end.

During this period, almost all focus was on print; the agenda at our board meetings was filled with careful analysis of this magazine or that, and its DNA, and which markets were ready for an edition next. (Although we had launched vogue.co.uk, our first website, in 1992, six years before the 1998 launch of Google and twelve years before the 2004 launch of Facebook, digital still remained a tiny enterprise within Condé Nast, next to the profits of print.) Or we discussed photographers: how to hold on to Mario Testino, Patrick Demarchelier, Bruce Weber, Craig McDean. The annual retainers offered to work exclusively for Condé Nast became larger and larger, running to multimillions of dollars. Photographers were key components in fashion's febrile microculture. Celebrity photographers work with celebrity stylists, which guarantees celebrity models, which in turn invested our magazines with an aura which made them irresistible to advertisers, and made Condé Nast rich.

Despite heavy investment in new launches, annual profits for the international division were spiralling towards $200 million. There was a glorious confidence and optimism. Almost anything felt possible, everything an opportunity. We launched a dozen *Vogue* restaurants and *GQ* bars around the world, *Vogue* luxury conferences, a Condé Nast fashion and design college in Soho, with Susie Forbes as headmistress, and another in China.

As well as peddling our own brands, we tried to acquire new

ones. I devoted much time to trying to buy *The Spectator* for
Condé Nast, when Conrad Black was selling it, but in the end
Lazard's couldn't separate it from the Telegraph Media Group.
And we had a twenty-year ambition to buy *Country Life*, but
neither IPC nor Time Inc. would let it go. (This was hardly
surprising: *Country Life* has a near-perfect business model, made
a ton of money, and furthermore stands at the fulcrum of a
clearly defined world where estate agents in wellington boots
meet scholarly architectural historians.) Each time a new CEO
was appointed at IPC, I wrote again offering ever larger sums
for *Country Life*. One of them (rather rudely) simply returned
my own letter with the message 'Not in a million years, mate'
scrawled across it.

I was fast approaching forty, and an idea was hatched for a big
joint-fortieth birthday party with the old Cambridge gang:
Nick Allan, Kit Hunter Gordon, two Stourtons – James and
Edward – and Peter Pleydell-Bouverie. Numerous meetings
were held to review possible locations for the great event, which
grew larger and more ambitious each time. We discussed guests
ad infinitum, quickly regressing to old jokes, already twenty-
years stale, about university contemporaries who definitely
should or shouldn't be there.

We worked out that half our potential guests were held in
common, half were 'exclusive'. So a complicated system like a
single transferable vote was devised, administered by Jane
Pleydell-Bouverie, identified as the most efficient wife. Under
this scheme, if a guest was nominated by three or more hosts,
they didn't count against anyone's personal allocation. Then the
remainder of spaces were distributed equally. It was decided we
would invite 800 people to a giant Battersea warehouse overlooking the Thames named Adrenalin Village (since bulldozed

to make way for Norman Foster apartments). It amused us, when inspecting the Gents lavatories at Adrenalin Village, to find a contraceptive vending machine on the wall offering curry-flavoured rubber johnnies.

Scenery and sets were borrowed from an opera company, dim sum in Chinese baskets catered by Christopher Gilmour, the restaurateur brother of Jane. Nick supplied the play-list. James oversaw the printing of the invitations.

By now, several months had been spent negotiating the guest list. The invitations were minutely supervised by Jane, with all the precision of a polling officer at a general election.

The party was an uproarious success. The theme was 'The Emperor's New Clothes' and many guests turned up virtually naked, wrapped only in cling film. Some came as Roman emperors, others as Chinese emperors, Ottoman pashas and Rajput maharajas. Georgia wore a Vivienne Westwood bodysuit and came as Eve from the Garden of Eden. The cocktails were knock-out.

Halfway through the party, there was a surprise influx of unidentified extra girls, who had featured on nobody's list, and never undergone Jane's meticulous scrutiny. Who on earth were they? They seemed loucher, chavvier and more exotic than the rest, in basques and bras.

They turned out to be special additions by James, who had simply handed out a stash of spare invitations at some nightclub he frequented, to jolly things along.

I was friends at Condé Nast with John Morgan, a man of charm and good manners, who was the Style Editor at *GQ*. We had sushi lunches together, where he talked about British tailoring, etiquette (he wrote a column on this topic for *The Times*) and being gay. (He teetered on the brink of coming out, but never quite took the plunge. He developed crushes on grand, straight young men, which would never come to anything, and made him unhappy.) I found his life intriguing: he subsisted largely on canapés at drinks parties which he attended for the purpose, and prioritized good Savile Row suits above all else. He lived in Albany on Piccadilly, in a tiny top-floor room hardly bigger than a cupboard, which would once have been a manservant's lodging. It was Jeeves's room, exquisitely decorated, with his enormous suit collection overflowing from the wardrobe. He did all his food shopping at Fortnum & Mason across the road.

He was absurdly extravagant, and often sought my advice on his finances, which he never then took. I recommended he stopped ordering bespoke suits, he had at least forty, it felt like plenty. But he loved the interaction with tailors: discussing horn buttons and turn-ups. He could spend an entire morning at Huntsman or Henry Poole, deciding whether or not to have a ticket pocket in his next suit.

His last words to me were, 'You're so wise, Nicholas. I've taken your advice and cancelled four new suits. Well, postponed them. But you're going to be cross with me – I've commissioned a full-length portrait of myself in oils, wearing my silk opera cloak in the courtyard of Albany . . .'

Shortly afterwards, John killed himself one lonely Sunday afternoon. He had clambered through the tiny bathroom window of his flat and plunged down into the internal well. I believe he had chosen the internal well, rather than the courtyard, so as not to disturb other Albany residents. It was characteristically polite of him.

Early on Monday morning, two police officers turned up at Vogue House, and were sent up to see me. They explained a body, presumed to be John's, had been recovered, and could I please identify it in the morgue on Horseferry Road. Although badly cut and bruised, I identified him at once, and indeed the Huntsman suit.

Condé Nast gave him a magnificent send-off at St George's, Hanover Square, which 800 people attended, including half the tailors of Savile Row. I tried hard to persuade John's parents to come down – they lived in a bungalow on the outskirts of Perth – but they didn't feel able to. I wish they had, to see how well loved and respected their son was. I often think how different it might have been, had one person rung him on that fateful Sunday afternoon and invited him over for tea.

John was civilized and a gentleman, in the best sense, and I missed him.

I was still arriving at Vogue House each morning before 8 a.m., and was lucky to have PAs prepared to do likewise, though later my PAs had assistants to cover the early shift. During my thirty Condé Nast years I had six PAs,* who did an average of five years each; most eventually left to get married. At least two of them had long-term boyfriends who never popped the question. My job, in these situations, was to corner them and ask, 'Well, what are your intentions towards my PA? It's been six years . . . it's no business of mine, but I think she'd appreciate it.' Both times, they were engaged within a month.

Si Newhouse returned to London, this time with a problem he hoped I might solve.

His beloved pug dog, Nero, had recently died, and Si and Victoria were heartbroken. I knew how much they had loved Nero: when they flew from New York to Paris on Concorde, Nero had

* The roll call of honour (maiden names) went Julia Elliot, Henrietta Holroyde, Charlotte Allan, Lisa Murray, Katharine Barton, Emma Brown (understudied by Georgina Middleton).

his own seat. In fact, they booked four seats, with the fourth one for Si's briefcase.

'What I need you to establish,' said Si, 'is whether Nero's air miles can be transferred to our new pug, Cicero? Nero built up quite a stock of these air miles, and I wonder, with your connections, whether you could, er, facilitate this?'

I asked, 'You don't think you could simply substitute Cicero for Nero? I mean, the people at the check-in desk might not be able . . .' my voice trailed away. This was playing badly.

'You mean, they might confuse Cicero with Nero? But they look quite distinct. There's no resemblance between the two dogs.'

I rang Rod Eddington, Chief Executive of British Airways, and explained the conundrum. He was sympathetic, but obdurate: no pug-to-pug air miles transfer was possible. But, out of respect for Mr Newhouse, some bonus air miles could be awarded to the billionaire Condé Nast proprietor.

21.

One hot Thursday afternoon when I had recently turned forty, we bought a farmhouse in Oxfordshire, not far from Chipping Norton. It was built of the local honey-coloured stone from the quarry in Great Tew, and sat in the middle of a hundred acres of gently undulating hills and fields. It had plenty of space, with a tennis court and swimming pool; there was nothing not to like about Rignell Farm.

I disliked the place the minute we moved in, and it changed our life in quite an unexpected way.

I feel the need to point out that we moved to Chipping Norton several years before the invention of the 'Chipping Norton set', that largely illusory power axis of David and Samantha Cameron, the Jeremy Clarksons and various Murdoch offspring and News International executives, which was briefly believed to run the nation from the East Cotswolds.

In fact, I had spotted an aerial photograph of the farm in *Country Life*, and seen in it a means of escape from the encroaching claustrophobia of the Notting Hill communal garden. I sensed that fresh country air and rolling acres would soothe my over-revved brain, and provide punctuation to the ceaseless round of work and parties. So we downsized in London, and became country weekenders again.

There are multiple things to like about this corner of Oxfordshire: the colour of the stone in the market squares, the hedges laid with hazel and willow, and Banbury Cross. We lived on a hill above the villages of Barford St Michael and Barford St

John, and would walk the four miles to The Falkland Arms pub in Great Tew, through empty countryside, past tumbledown barns and ancient circles of standing stones. Soho Farmhouse had not yet opened on the route, bringing with it the Beckhams and half the staff of Condé Nast. My fondness for walking deepened on those ancient footpaths.

We made the house pretty and the children took to it. Tommy was not even two years old when we arrived, and our sweet Sophie only five. She dressed herself in a series of pink and sparkly outfits, though in contemporaneous photographs with her girlfriends, I see her making Girl Power salutes. As the only girl with three brothers, she needed to. Alexander and Freddie came home to the farm at weekends from Summer Fields, and we walked through canyons of mustard-yellow oilseed rape to the shop in the village.

Socially, Oxfordshire is full-on. Our new neighbours were vehemently hospitable, and soon signed us up for successions of Saturday night dinner parties. To Londoners, forgetful of country ways, they seemed very formal: dinner jackets, long dresses. And often, women leaving the men alone to their port after dinner and to their man-talk of politics and the economy. Tony Blair was Prime Minister with a fresh 179-seat overall majority, but our Tory neighbours were undeterred. 'I canvassed the village recently, and they're already fed up with Labour. We've got Blair on the run now, no question about it.'

A neighbour kindly rang to invite us to dinner. 'It's *literally* going to be kitchen supper, totally informal,' she said. 'The men will all be wearing velvet smoking jackets, white shirts but no ties, ironed jeans and monogrammed velvet slippers.'

Or they would ring in April saying, 'Now then, diaries out. How are your Saturdays in October, November and December looking?'

Sometimes, at weekends, we drove to visit my brother Tim and his wife Daria, just over the border in Northamptonshire; they lived on a farm in Little Preston with my nephews, Edward and William, and a herd of Aberdeen Angus and Charolais cattle. Tim would shortly become Mayor of Kensington and Chelsea, and is still regarded by many as the best Mayor the borough ever had. And we became friends in Oxfordshire with the political éminences grises Peter and Lucy Chadlington,* who lived in the prettiest of set-ups at Dean Manor near Chipping Norton, and where at Sunday lunches they entertained half the Conservative front bench.

I felt uncomfortable at Rignell Farm from the start. It was odd and disconcerting, I hadn't experienced anything like it before. The drawing room harboured a strange smell, sweet like honey with a dash of patchouli oil, particularly pungent in an area around one of the windows. We did everything to clear it, but without success. We thought it might be a plant outside in a flower bed, but the smell grew stronger in winter. We tried every kind of cleaning product, but still it lingered. The smell made me nauseous, and we avoided using the room.

There was an atmosphere about the house which was oppressive and unresolved, like the aftermath of a quarrel. It affected me more badly than anyone else in the family, though Georgia felt it too, and she became interested in it as a phenomenon.

One of Georgia's newly discovered psychic friends, named Amaryllis Fraser, felt the presence of a young ghost-like man, hovering by the window. She said he had committed suicide six months earlier by jumping off a tall building. This was

---

* Lord Chadlington of Dean. Public relations adviser. Founder Shandwick, Chairman Huntsworth, Chairman Royal Opera House (1996–7), Witney Conservative Association, Tory donor.

confirmed by a local builder, who lived in Barford St Michael, who said, 'You know a young lad who lived here killed himself not long ago? Threw himself off the roof of a car park in Banbury.'

Georgia organized an exorcism in the drawing room, conducted by the local vicar with prayers of banishment and a holy chalice; the atmosphere lightened for a while afterwards, though later it returned.

She persevered. She became interested in land clearance, past lives, ley lines, nature spirits, kinesiology, chakras, reiki and much more besides, and enrolled in courses at the Centre for Psychic Studies in South Kensington, opposite the French Lycée. Various psychic experts and gurus arrived at the house, poring over Ordnance Survey maps and tracking ley lines with crystals and dowsing rods. A wartime airfield, not far from the farm, at which numerous trainee pilots had crashed, was held to be significant. Our shelves filled with books about old souls, kinetic energy and auras.

The honey smell was connected by another expert to a whole tribe of ghosts: the young man, the wartime airmen, a family of farmers who died in a flu epidemic, plus some spirits from an Iron Age barrow in an adjacent field. All were resisting their final resting place in the afterlife. Their wretchedness hung about the house.

Much of Georgia's latent interest in healing and alternative medicine flowed from the Mystery of the Strange Smell at Rignell Farm, and her efforts to alleviate it. Although I am by nature more sceptical than Georgia, I concede that she made the atmosphere at the farm consistently less sinister, and the unpleasant smell all but disappeared. But, by then, I had mentally moved on, and Rignell Farm was on the way out.

I sometimes wonder whether our time in Oxfordshire was

'meant', with the higher purpose of introducing Georgia to the world she has embraced, and in which she excels. It certainly introduced us to a tribe of psychic experts, who taught her the skills she uses in her healing practice.

My favourite of these experts is a soul rescuer and land healer named Terry O'Sullivan. His theory (quite plausibly true) is that certain human souls have returned many times to this earth, in different human forms, with a hazy imprint of their earlier lives influencing their present characters. These past lives can be probed and revealed by experts, who inform you that you were once an Assyrian slave in Nineveh, a nun in a tenth-century Cistercian monastery or a Victorian flower seller, and so forth. Sometimes these prior lives account for psychological or even physical traits in living people. That, anyway, is the theory.

Personally, I buy the concept of 'old' souls and 'new' ones. There are plenty of very new souls in Britain, mostly hanging out at motorway service stations and in supermarket car parks.

Georgia likes to keep her healing world separate from family life. In London, where she practises, she goes to great lengths to keep the identity of her clients secret, and we are never told who they are, let alone why they are undergoing treatment. Occasionally, some rather prominent person approaches me at an event and tells me that Georgia is 'an absolute genius who cured my back/insomnia/hereditary problems with my mother' or whatever. She is very good at it, by all accounts.

On one occasion, Terry the healer found me reading on the sofa. He was instantly transfixed. 'This is fascinating,' he said, peering closely at my face.

'What have you seen?' I asked. 'What's so fascinating?'

'Your past life. You have been here several times before, you know, a very old soul indeed. But one especially interesting thing – in a former life you were Admiral Horatio Lord Nelson.'

I admit it was gratifying. Ever since, I have felt a special bond with the hero of Trafalgar and Cape St Vincent. I cannot drive round Trafalgar Square without looking up at his statue.

'It's Dad's statue,' say the children, smirking, knowing it annoys their mother.

We continued visiting India regularly, even when the children were very young. Counterintuitively, India is an easy country to travel around with children. No matter where you are, you can find boiled eggs, toast, custard cream biscuits and chicken. I love Indian food, the spicier the better, but you can always slip backstage in an Indian kitchen and request plain roast chicken, without a trace of spice or chilli.

And India works in other ways too: the fabulous weather, the particular light of India, at dawn and dusk especially, the hardly considered, hardly visited, hardly surveyed forts and temples in the middle of nowhere. We criss-crossed the country as a family in Ambassador cars, and later in jeeps, and those holidays were among our very happiest and most bonding.

But in case you think our poor, deprived children never experienced a proper British holiday like their friends, let me reassure you that Cornwall, Paxos and Kefalonia all played their part too.

And even the dreaded Corfiot Kassiopi, and its teenage foam discotheque, was not denied them.

22

There are two big annual awards jamborees in the magazine calendar, black-tie ceremonies held in glitzy hotel ballrooms with ankle-deep patterned carpets. All the big publishers take tables, generally several tables, and you know when you arrive that you will likely still be there, trapped in your seat, in six or seven hours' time.

When you eventually emerge, shortly before dawn, anything at all could have happened in the world outside: a change of government, atomic war. You have been sealed in the basement ballroom of the Grosvenor House hotel, watching thirty prize categories being awarded, from hundreds of shortlisted contenders.

You never knew there were so many magazines, or so random. 'In this hotly contested category for Best Magazine Front Cover, the shortlisted titles are *Coarse Fishing*, *Practical Caravan*, *Vogue*, *Auto Express* and *Home & Antiques* . . .'

The *Vogue* table sat up a little straighter in anticipation.

'And the winner is . . . *Practical Caravan*.'

The Editor of *Practical Caravan* would then high-five his way to the stage, in a blizzard of applause, and make a long speech before receiving his trophy. Later, the entire staff of *Loaded* or *Woman's Weekly* would conga up to the stage in a blaze of glory and pose for selfies with a *Big Brother* celebrity.

In the years that Condé Nast titles didn't win multiple awards, we became sullen and mulish, and condemned the whole thing as an obvious fix.

The years we won, we headed on to Annabel's, to celebrate victory with champagne.

I was a judge once or twice at these events, and sat on the selection panel. The process of choosing winners was gloriously daft. One judge declared, 'I don't think we should hand the prize to *The World of Interiors* because they use all these really good, expensive photographers, and employ all the best stylists, and have really good quality paper and printing . . . so have an unfair advantage. My vote goes to *The Big Issue*.'

I used to sit at the awards ceremony dinner with a notepad, totting up our wins and those of our competitors. A satisfying result was Condé Nast: 9, IPC: 3, EMAP: 3, Hearst: 2. I was insanely competitive.

The largest awards ceremony is organized by the Periodical Publishers Association – PPA – the industry's trade body, then headquartered in Holborn. When I joined its board, I was the youngest member; twenty-five years later when I left, I was the oldest. As a lover of short meetings, I found its four-hour marathon sessions headache-inducing, with much of the agenda spoken in coded acronyms.

One publisher would declare, 'I see there's an upcoming NRS meeting to discuss TGI. Will this impact on ABC and will AOP have a voice on the subcommittee?'

Another would reply, 'If I may interject – through the Chair, of course – I think you will find that the IPA and NPA have views on this too, and both PamCo and GA are consulting on the new AMP.'

(Translation: National Readership Survey, Target Group Index, Audit Bureau of Circulation, Association of Online Publishers, Institute of Practitioners in Advertising, News Publishers Association, Publishers Audience Measurement Company, Google

Analytics, Audience Measurement Platform. Just in case you were wondering.)

All the big cheeses from Hearst, Time, Future, Haymarket, Hachette and EMAP would roll up at board meetings, as well as representatives of the smaller publishers. The smaller the publisher, the bigger the briefcase, I noticed; they arrived with giant, faux-crocodile attaché cases, and made a big show of flicking open the brass catches, with loud look-at-me clunks. Inside, was the agenda and a KitKat.

At meetings, we were collegiate but watchful of one another. Throughout the nineties and the first decade of the new century, when magazine companies were inventing new titles at the rate of several hundred a year, we were perpetually alert to espionage. Would EMAP dare launch a competitor against *Vogue*? Would Hachette move into the *GQ* space? Every victory for a rival was a personal reproach; every success by us – a disruptive launch – could only be fully savoured if the pain showed on a competitor's face.

During this period, which will be seen by historians as the apogee of print magazine ambition, we vied for talent, for prizes, for kudos. Sly Bailey, Chief Executive of IPC, arrived at meetings in a floor-length mink coat. My old boss Terry Mansfield of Hearst took every opportunity to draw attention to himself and his magazines, presenting at conferences in a wizard's hat ('Magazines are magic, ladies and gentlemen').

We had dinner together as a group several times a year, at which we discussed exciting issues of the day, such as Tesco and Aldi pushing too aggressively on margin, and how best to lobby government on resisting VAT on magazines. (Our argument against VAT was that magazines are educational, which they surely are, and encourage children to read, which perhaps they do. It was easier to make the case for *The Economist* and *New Scientist* than for *FHM* and *Viz* comic.)

These conspiratorial meals were held in fancy French restaurants, and ran to numerous fancy courses, with the chef appearing in his whites and toque to present special *amuse-bouches*. It must have been someone's idea of what the Boss Class appreciates.

Tension rose before the new circulation figures were due for release. By tradition, all the magazine companies posted their circulation figures simultaneously, which were then analysed and reported by the media press, while teams of public relations executives spun the narratives we wanted them to write. So if (say) we hit a rough patch on *Vanity Fair*, down a couple of thousand copies, our team would move into divert-and-distract mode: 'The big story, of course, is Hearst's *Esquire* dropping 5,000 news-stand copies. Apparently it's full-on panic stations over there.'

Afterwards, of course, we denied saying a thing.

I was asked to be the magazine industry's representative on PressBoF, parent organization of the Press Complaints Commission, and reluctantly agreed. 'It literally takes two hours a year,' I was assured. 'There are only two meetings, sometimes they don't even last as long as an hour.'

All the key newspaper honchos were on it – Paul Dacre of the *Daily Mail* representing Associated Newspapers, Rebekah Brooks of News International, Murdoch MacLennan and Guy Black for Telegraph Media. It seemed churlish to say no.

Five minutes after I joined, the phone hacking scandal broke, and all hell broke loose.

Lord Leveson set up his star chamber to take evidence, and every TV celebrity, footballer and starlet piled in, claiming their mobile had been hacked. Our sinecure committee met in emergency session over and over again. There were meetings in newspaper offices, secret dinners in private rooms at Mark's Club. Max Mosley (the uncle of my old Venice friend Rupert Forbes Adam) emerged as the scourge of the press, goaded by a *News of the World* exposé of his role-playing sessions with five willing escorts. Hugh Grant waded in too, pushing for draconian press supervision. Politicians of every party competed with each other in their condemnation of the media. Suddenly, our little committee found itself the last bulwark of a free press.

It was engrossing to watch the big beasts in action. Paul Dacre, quietly spoken, inherently powerful, king buffalo of the herd, dominated the room. Guy Black, by now Baron Black of Brentwood, was fixer-in-chief, who determined every outcome with pre-meetings, and pre-meetings to the pre-meetings. While Rebekah Brooks, finding herself in the eye of the tornado, felt compelled to take a break from press regulation.

Max Mosley proposed a government-endorsed press regulator named Impress, which he subsidized himself, while the newspaper owners wanted an independent regulator overseen by a judge: the Independent Press Standards Organization, acronym IPSO. As the Leveson fallout became daily more rancorous, both sides raced to sign up as many national, regional and local newspapers to their side as possible, as well as Britain's 8,000 magazines.

Normally, magazines are remote from issues of press regulation and political manoeuvring. The only time politicians think of women's magazines is in the run-up to general elections, when someone at party headquarters remembers the female vote. *Vogue* and *Glamour* are then badgered for soft profiles of the party leaders, usually conducted on an InterCity train. *GQ* was generally permitted something more robust, when

David Cameron or even Jeremy Corbyn would be paraded in a Hugo Boss suit and grilled by Alastair Campbell or Matthew d'Ancona.

Post-Leveson, the sheer volume of the magazine industry made it significant in the Impress versus IPSO war of attrition. Suddenly, I was the person who could 'deliver' magazines to one side or the other.

Paul and Kathy Dacre invited Georgia and me to Glyndebourne. The rest of the opera party comprised Guy Black and his partner Mark Bolland, and the columnist Simon Heffer* and his wife Diana. As we perched on the Glyndebourne lawn eating poached salmon, various friends at adjacent picnics made horrified faces, spotting us with the Populist Right.

We were filing into the auditorium to take our seats, when a disastrous thing happened. I should explain I had grabbed my dinner jacket in a hurry and forgotten to bring braces for my trousers. By tightening the side-vents, the trousers just about stayed up. But as we shuffled along the row to our places, the trousers suddenly dropped to my ankles, while several hundred opera lovers filed past. I spent the remainder of the night with one hand in my waistband, hoisting them up.

Back in London, Hugh Grant took me to lunch at a sushi restaurant named Chisou, to pitch the case for fiercer privacy laws. Chisou is around the corner from Vogue House and at lunchtime filled with Condé Nast staffers. I must have eaten there more than a hundred times. Japanese waitresses in kimonos shyly deliver the *tempura* and *ikura*. Like most Japanese places, the staff never recognize you, regardless of how regularly you eat there.

---

* Carrot-headed political commentator. *Daily Telegraph, Daily Mail. A Life of Thomas Carlyle* (1995).

Arriving with Hugh Grant was a revelation. One by one, the shy waitresses approached our table. With schoolgirl giggles, they blurted 'Bridget Jones' or 'Notting Hill'.

Another waitress arrived with a complimentary green tea ice cream for the movie star. Not once in my hundred visits had I received so much as a bonus *maki*.

We caught up on what had happened in our lives, since Hugh plus Elizabeth Hurley had joined Georgia and me at our engagement dinner at the Tollygunge Club in Calcutta. He was as dry and charming as ever.

Hugh was disappointed when the magazine industry signed up en masse to IPSO. But it felt like the right call for freedom.

23

Condé Nast had grown very big in China. Profits from the Chinese magazines had overtaken those of Britain and Italy, previously the two biggest, and our board meetings increasingly focused on keeping the Chinese government happy.

Delegations of Chinese publishers and officials were invited to London and New York, to cement relations and keep the revenue flowing. These visits largely consisted of tours of the offices, extravagant toasts and a chance to visit Burberry.

Usually I hosted a lunch for the visitors and their interpreters, which the British Editors were summoned to attend. There were many exchanges of pleasantries: 'Mr Lin say he is honoured to visit ancient culture of United Kingdom. Mr Lin says China also very ancient culture. We have terracotta warriors.' And so forth.

Sometimes the conversation became more testing: 'Mr Zhao asks are all Editors at Condé Nast magazines paid same amount of money?'

Around the table, everyone perked up. Alexandra Shulman of *Vogue*, Dylan Jones of *GQ*, Jo Elvin of *Glamour*, Kate Reardon of *Tatler*, Sue Crewe of *House & Garden*, Sarah Miller of *Condé Nast Traveller* . . . all leaning in.

'Please tell Mr Zhao, no, all Editors are paid different amounts, depending on how long they have worked for Condé Nast and how large and profitable their magazine is.'

This was relayed by the translator.

Then, 'Mr Zhao asks which of ten Editors in room is paid most high money and which paid most low?'

'Ah, in England our tradition is not to say which person is paid most and least. All are lucky. All well paid.'

'Mr Zhao say he believes Editor of *Vogue* is paid most money, even though she is lady.'

Life in the goldfish bowl of Vogue House continued to intrigue. It was a rare edition of the *Evening Standard* which didn't carry a Condé Nast gossip story. A Londoner's Diary scribe, James Hughes-Onslow, must have had multiple hotlines into the building, because he knew everything.

He would send me emails as follows: 'The Editor of *Tatler* backed her black Amazon Land Cruiser into the Editor of *House & Garden*'s Golf GTI five minutes ago in the Vogue House car park. Your comment?'

It was *Tatler* which inspired the punchiest headline on any newspaper story ever.

The Editor of *Tatler*'s assistant owned a sweet little dachshund named Alan Plumptre, which she brought every day into the office and which dozed underneath her desk in a basket.

One lunchtime, she asked an intern to walk the dog around Hanover Square. As they returned to the office, a jogger who worked on *GQ* approached the revolving Vogue House doors and jogged on inside, spinning the door as he went.

Alan the dachshund bounded forwards, and was instantly squashed between the doors, one half of his long body in each section. Ten firemen dismantled the door, but to no avail. Poor Alan Plumptre was dead.

The story went viral. It made the front page of every newspaper. It was a between-the-bongs item on the television evening news. The *Daily Mail* splashed: 'Britain's poshest dog decapitated in *Vogue* revolving door'.

It was the perfect tabloid headline. It escalated the PA's dachshund to 'Britain's poshest dog' (by dint of the *Tatler* association), introduced the emotive word 'decapitated' and dragged *Vogue* into the story too. Genius really.

Our programme of new launches hadn't let up. Sixty magazines became 80, then 100, then 140. Our publications now had a monthly readership of 200 million. Each title, with its separate network of editors and writers, photographers and contributing editors, stood at the nexus of its local market: taste-making, discriminating, curating. In the fashion and decorating worlds especially, Condé Nast called the shots, anointing new talent as the Editors saw fit.

With the growth in the number of our magazines, so the volume of events and parties grew with it. It was a rare night now that I didn't go to four or five: fashion awards, decorating awards, travel and spa awards, *Tatler*'s Little Black Book parties, beauty awards, *Wired*'s technology conferences, bridal fairs, Arnaud Bamberger's Cartier dinners, menswear and grooming awards ('and the prize for best astringent aftershave goes to . . .'); many of these glitzy events, in theory at least, were profitable for Condé Nast and designed to consolidate our ownership of particular markets with advertisers and opinion formers. Georgia often accompanied me to the parties, which was sweetly supportive and helpful, because she has a gift for connecting with people.

Long before the acronym FOMO – Fear Of Missing Out – passed into the vernacular, I suffered from two rare sub-strains of the partygoer's disease: FOFS and FOLOPD. FOFS is Fear Of Falling Short (i.e. not showing up at events where perhaps you should, for work-related reasons). FOLOPD is Fear Of Letting Other People Down, which leads you to make speeches you never wished to make, or give work experience to teenagers because you feel some tenuous sense of obligation towards their parents.

I had become a serial speechifier, making speeches at far too many things. My inability to say no made me a natural victim. I gave speeches at schools (my own and other people's), speeches at media conferences, to groups in the House of Commons, at college Speech Days. I gave speeches in the gym at Tudor Hall, the girls' boarding school, where the rising smell of ripe plimsoll was overpowering, and where the pupils afterwards asked, 'Will you autograph my copy of *Tatler* and *House & Garden*? My aunt used to, like, work at Condé Nast.' I made speeches at Oxbridge societies, at luxury travel conferences, at the Headmasters' Conference, in regional museums and London fashion colleges. The more speeches I gave, the more I was asked to give. I gave eulogies at memorial services, at weddings, keynotes at fragrance conferences and book festivals. Every time a speech loomed, I complained, 'How the hell did I get roped into this?' But I never learnt.

Conversely, I am also prone to FOOW: Fear Of Outstaying Welcome. This one goes back to a holiday in Bembridge on the Isle of Wight. I was ten or eleven years old, a guest at the Bembridge Dinghy Club Ball, a disco event for ten-to-fourteen-year-olds. It must have been 1968 because they played 'Fire' by The Crazy World of Arthur Brown during the party. I was bopping about with a pretty girl with freckles. The track ended, another track began. I continued dancing.

The girl said, 'Don't you know anything? You're only supposed to dance *one song with each girl*. Then you change partners.'

I have never forgotten the sensation of outstaying my welcome.

It accounts for the slightly brisk way I operate at parties, having conversations of only one or two minutes' duration, before moving on. I like to 'buzz around'. Never lingering. Georgia is better than me at parties, being ready to have proper, in-depth talks. She consequently discovers far more than I ever do. But I cover more ground.

Meanwhile, new editions of *Glamour* were springing up in all the old Eastern Bloc countries, and we were making plans to open companies and expand joint ventures in India, Brazil and Thailand.

In London, we looked enviously at an edgy fashion biannual named *Pop*, edited by a hard-core fashionista, Katie Grand. It occupied a position on fashion's wild frontier, less established than *Vogue* but with access to many of the same models and stylists. We felt it would be a cool magazine to publish.

The only snag was, it belonged to Bauer, the German publishing conglomerate. We didn't believe Bauer got much pleasure out of owning *Pop* – they were happier with mass-circulation titles – but nor would they sell to Condé Nast. The very fact we wanted it, made them want to keep it.

Katie Grand got to hear of our manoeuvrings and asked to have lunch. We met at J Sheekey's, the fish restaurant off St Martin's Lane. I liked her at once. She was funny and smart, and a free spirit, and not at all a diva, as I had been warned. She said, 'I hear you want to buy us, and we want you to buy us. So why don't you just launch a rival to *Pop* and I'll join and bring the whole team with me.'

'Everyone?'

'Sure. They'd love that. I mean, Bauer versus Condé Nast? Hello! No contest.'

We spent a fortnight emailing each other, riffing possible names for the new magazine. I was in Bombay, Katie was in Lamu. *Heroine* was a contender at one point, as was *Heroin*. *Superglam* was another (terrible name). So was *Famous*. And *Plastic*. Altogether, we came up with 200 possibles. Magazine titles are tricky, all the ones you really like are already registered to someone else, often to scent companies: the same kind of generic names. In the end, we settled on *LOVE*. Four or five letters is ideal for a magazine logo. All the best ones are short.

We took offices for *LOVE* in Clerkenwell, to keep them separate from the corporate vibe and limo culture of Vogue House. True to her promise, Katie arrived with her team, every last one. The wholesale transfer of an entire magazine staff (more of a banking phenomenon than a publishing one) drew acres of publicity, and was seen as an audacious coup. The ripples lasted for months. It must have been intensely annoying for Bauer. And *LOVE* was a hit from the off, and instantly profitable. The same cover models appeared issue after issue – Cara, Edie, Margot Robbie, Lily-Rose Depp, Kylie Jenner, Miley Cyrus.

I used to visit their offices to review upcoming issues, pages pinned to boards on the wall: it was exciting to see thirty-page portfolios of work by Mert and Marcus, Craig McDean and Bruce Weber. But my main role was to keep a beady eye out for images which might be deemed pornographic, and thus be withdrawn from the shelves by WH Smith. There is often a paper-thin line in fashion between cultural edginess and seedy porn. Photographers sent borderline images they longed to see published, but which violated our 'no blood, no semi-erect dicks, no soft-paedo shots, no extreme BDSM images' rule. Katie seldom liked these shots herself, but it suited her for the Man from Headquarters to impose the judgement call.

There was a glorious Collections portfolio by David Sims of female models in designer clothes and, at the end of the shoot, a single, close-up photograph of a pair of men's chinos. Through the chinos you could see the clear outline of a half-cocked penis, and the penis was peeing down the inside of the trouser leg. The picture was titled 'Pissy Pants'.

Katie said, 'I'm almost sure you're not going to love this one.'

'I don't. It's gross.'

'David loves it.'

'Do you?'

She laughed. 'No! But I'm waiting for you to tell me not to use it. Then I'll tell David.'

Katie gave me a framed print of 'Pissy Pants' for Christmas, but it was an awkward image to hang, either at home or in the office.

When consultants visited Condé Nast (seldom in those magical days) they always asked the same question. They asked, 'Why do you bother having twenty different editions of *Vogue*? Why not have just one global issue, published out of New York, with translations for different overseas markets?' They became tremendously excited, sketching out potential savings in tens of millions of dollars, savings on photographers, on supermodels, on staff. Instead of 140 magazines, we could have 8!

Except that it wouldn't work.

The culture of each market is so different, and the way people dress. In Germany, women wear top-to-toe single designer looks: skirt by Dior, shoes by Dior, jacket by Dior, leather cap by Dior, sunglasses by Dior. In Britain, they mix it up: skirt by Dior, shirt from Zara, coat Prada; it is considered unsophisticated to wear a total designer look. Italians, Americans and Russians wear real fur, British don't. Japanese wear sugar pink. Chinese wear conspicuous in-your-face logos. And there are deeper cultural complexities. Spanish *GQ* publishes virtually no articles about sex. Germany prefers international celebrities to local ones ('We have no celebrities in Germany'). Korean *Vogue* favours smiling K-pop models, German *Vogue* favours glum ones, ideally with a Helmut Newton S&M vibe. Indian

Vogue favours Bollywood movie stars. Italian *Vogue* and Paris *Vogue* are chic and influential and sell relatively few copies; American *Vogue* is commercial and influential and sells 1.2 million copies a month.

That is why there could never be one *Vogue* for the world.

Dylan Jones had already turned the annual GQ Men of the Year Awards into the most celebrity-jammed extravaganza of the year. And Jo Elvin, at *Glamour*, started doing the same thing with her Women of the Year Awards. MOTY was held at the Royal Opera House, later Tate Modern, while the 'Glammies' were held in a tent in the middle of Berkeley Square. Both ceremonies took ten months of planning, with side deals struck to secure A-list celebs. At a typical MOTY, you got Keith Richards, Michael Caine, Tony Blair, Lewis Hamilton, Iggy Pop and Madonna, all on stage at once. WOTY gave you Olympian sports stars and never fewer than three Kardashians, two Spice Girls and an *X-Factor* judge.

My role was to entertain a cosmetics advertiser on one side at dinner, and a celebrity on the other. I kept notes on whom I found most and least alluring: Heidi Klum (unexpectedly amusing), Elle Macpherson (a bit flaky), Samantha Cameron (slight crush on her), Kim Kardashian (talked about how much in love she was with her fiancé; the marriage lasted two months), Cheryl Cole (tiny, not much small talk), Lara Stone (definitely sexy), Pippa Middleton (gorgeous), Jeremy Corbyn (we discussed Pink Floyd and the Corbyns' recent summer holiday to a Premier Inn hotel in Dundee).

It was my task, from time to time, to call on Sir Philip Green, the retail billionaire, at his Arcadia headquarters behind Oxford Street, on Berners Street. I was deployed when the Topshop advertising budget in *Vogue* was being challenged by Green, who always wanted an impossible deal, and negotiations had reached an impasse. The sum in dispute was generally something like a £100 discount on a double-page advertisement, about the price of twenty seconds of fuel on his superyacht, *Lionheart*.

As part of his negotiating technique, he always pretended not to rate *Vogue* ('It doesn't help me sell any fucking clothes right, nobody fucking reads it, right? Only c★★ts, right?') while the Condé Nast team tittered away, mouthing platitudes and refusing to budge.

With Philip Green, it is all about Philip Green. You felt he was playing to the room, relishing the attention.

He came to the celebrity dinners *Vogue* and *Vanity Fair* gave, invariably switching the placement about to get a better seat. Often I had him on my table. He had his mobile clamped to his ear half the time. At a *GQ* dinner, he took a sip of wine and grimaced. 'Are you trying to fucking poison me? This tastes like piss, right? I'm sorry, Nicholas, I don't mean to offend, but I can't drink this.' The claret, in all likelihood, was five up from the bottom of the restaurant's wine list. We were entertaining 200 guests. ''Ere, let me order some better wine,' he would continue. 'Don't worry, I'm paying, it won't be you.' He summoned the sommelier. 'Show me your best stuff.'

Then he would order a bottle of claret ('No, make that three bottles') of vintages priced at £2,700 or £3,000. The bottles would arrive, cold from the wine cellar, and be poured for the table. 'That's better, isn't it?' he'd declare, beaming. 'That's more like it. Isn't that better? You can taste the difference, right? Lucky I was here, right?'

On paper, Sir Philip Green was the most successful of tycoons, with his billions and his multiple fashion businesses and his $150 million yacht moored in Monaco. But I have never yet met anyone who wishes they *were* Philip Green.

★

Not everything we tried at Condé Nast worked out. We launched a men's fitness monthly named *GQ Active*, intended to break into the six-pack gym market. *Men's Health*, published by Rodale, was market leader. Every front cover looked exactly alike: a bloke in a wife-beater vest or Speedos, rippling with well-oiled muscles. Their cover lines promised complete body makeovers in suspiciously short periods of time, such as 'Build beach abs in only ten days' or '4-week fat shredder: a rock-solid bod in under a month'.

I was convinced our more sophisticated fitness offering, with the added bonus of the *GQ* brand, would disrupt the market. But it scarcely dented it. It turned out that readers were perfectly happy with *Men's Health* and its outlandish claims. They were, quite literally, buying a dream. I took to lurking at the magazine display at a Welcome Break on the M40, watching readers deciding between *GQ Active* and *Men's Health*. An obese truck driver waddled in – he must have weighed twenty stone. He picked up three pork pies and a giant packet of Quavers, then a copy of *Men's Health* from the shelf, and carried it to the till. The cover line said 'Lose Your Gut – instantly!' I knew then we were sunk. We closed *GQ Active* soon afterwards.

Twice a year, every year, I went to catwalk shows in Paris and Milan. I have never been a fashion expert in the context of real fashion experts, but you absorb some of it intravenously. It was fun to sit at a show, watching parades of models pass by. I would check out the silhouette, check out the shoes, then drift into reveries about what this model or that model might be like in real life. So many models on catwalks are droopy Lithuanians, looking like they've just been released from the back of a truck from the Baltic States. Do they have families, boyfriends? Are they doped? In another life, could I be happy living with her or with her? All these subversive thoughts floated through my head.

And I enjoyed the hierarchical way that fashion houses still organized the seating at their shows, with *Vogue* Editors and celebrities in the front row, *Elle* Editors in the second and so on back. My position at Condé Nast secured front row, but I always felt my chair could have been allocated more usefully. Almost nothing had altered in the fashion industry in the decades since I wrote *The Fashion Conspiracy*, other than the shows were several times larger, with up to 5,000 press and guests, and celebrities paid or bribed with clothes to attend.

Anna Wintour still sat in the front row in dark glasses, flanked by Grace Coddington, Suzy Menkes and Hamish Bowles. The British Company alone would deploy up to forty staff at the Collections, staying the full month at hotels in Paris, Milan and New York. If you weren't at the shows, you weren't in fashion.

My two supermodel god-daughters, Cara Delevingne and Edie Campbell, became more famous daily. Without the slightest help from me, they started appearing regularly on *Vogue* front covers. Edie dated rock stars and the sons of rock stars, Cara gathered 40 million Instagram followers and went global.

An article in the *Daily Mail* splashed that Cara had taken a girlfriend, and I skimmed the news in the bath. Shortly afterwards, Cara's father, Charles Delevingne, rang. 'Seen the article today about your god-daughter?'

'I did spot it.'

'I just rang her. I asked, "Hey, Cara, are you one?" She replied, "No, Dad, I'm trisexual. I try everything . . ."'

Charles roared with laughter.

Not long afterwards, there was another Cara story in the newspapers, this time with an alleged drugs angle. My fellow godparent, Annette 'Scruff' Howard, former chatelaine of Castle Howard in Yorkshire, rang me in the office at dawn. 'Seen the latest about Cara?'

'I did actually. Ah, well.'

'No, not "ah, well". Not at all. Charles and Pandora are away on holiday. They're in the South of France. It's up to *us* as responsible godparents. We've got to get to her right now and *stage an intervention*. Get Cara admitted to The Priory.'

'But we can't kidnap her! That surely isn't our role?'

'Well, I'm very disappointed in you, Nick. I hoped you'd back me up on this.'

It was during this period of magazine life that the multimillion-aire publisher Felix Dennis unleashed his series of apocalyptic speeches predicting the death of print media.

'You are all doomed,' he loved to declare at magazine conferences, licking his lips and relishing the drama. 'You are dead men walking.'

Felix was a peculiar man. He had risen to fame as one of the Editors of *Oz* magazine with Richard Neville and Jim Anderson. Their 'Schoolkids' issue, featuring a sexually explicit cartoon of Rupert Bear playing with himself, led to their arrest by Scotland Yard's Obscene Publications Squad, and a high profile trial. Felix was given the most lenient sentence since the judge considered him 'much less intelligent' than the others, and therefore less culpable.

He had since become vastly rich through publishing computer magazines, and devoted his time to writing poetry, living with many women simultaneously, and planting a 3,000-acre forest in Warwickshire: 'The Forest of Dennis'. He became a friend of mine for a while, and was needy for praise of his poetry. I think the Coleridge surname made him see me as a qualified poetry critic. He also published a very successful lads' magazine called *Maxim*, which competed with *GQ*, though more downmarket.

We sometimes met at Lazard's, who gave media dinners in their 'safe house' on Pont Street in Chelsea, hosted by Marcus Agius and Nick Shott. These dinners were highly formal, suit and tie events, full of investment bankers, with ten or so newspaper and digital bosses seated around the table. You knew not to be late.

Felix was always late. We were standing on the balcony above Pont Street, waiting for him to arrive, while Lazard's executives fretted and checked their watches.

At last, a bronze-coloured Rolls-Royce drew up at the kerb. A chauffeur in peaked cap with Ruritanian plume opened the back door. The tiny figure of Felix hauled himself out.

Spotting us on the balcony, he called up. 'Sorry to be late, folks. I've been presenting a personal cheque for a million quid to Tony Blair at 10 Downing Street.'

The Chief Executives of the *Financial Times* and *The Economist* sucked their teeth in disapproval.

Over dinner, Felix treated the table to his views. 'There won't be any newspapers left by the time I'm dead,' he said. 'So you guys' – he waved his arms at the newspaper chiefs – 'you guys need to think of something else to do. Pronto.'

Looking at me, he said, 'And don't imagine Condé Nast is going to escape either. It's all over for you dudes. Look at *GQ* in the States. What's it sell? 800,000 copies a month. *Maxim* in the States sells two million.

'Want to know why?' he went on. 'Want to know why my *Maxim* outsells *GQ* almost three copies to one?'

'Sure,' I said. 'Tell me.'

'Because *Maxim* is about sex, and *GQ* is about socks. That's the difference. Free insight from Felix. Do with it what you will.'

The American print edition of *Maxim* was shut down three

Graydon Carter, *Vanity Fair* Editor-in-Chief, NC and S.I. Newhouse Jr, Chairman and proprietor of Condé Nast Inc., photographed at a *Vanity Fair* party, Manhattan, 1992. NC had flown to New York that day on Concorde, it is 5 a.m. London time to him.

Georgia and NC dancing at a *Daily Mail* party, Grosvenor House hotel, 1993.

Top left: John Galliano and Jonathan Newhouse at the party JN and Ronnie Cooke Newhouse gave for NC's 10th anniversary at Condé Nast, Claridge's, 2001. *Top right:* With Dame Joan Collins and Dame Vivienne Westwood. By a strange algorithm of placement, NC often found himself seated next to Dame Joan at dinners. *Left:* With Lord Snowdon and Ed Victor, NC's then literary agent. Victor accused NC of making 'a pact with the devil' to gain 25 hours out of every 24-hour day.

Newspaper cartoon of NC and Michael Cole, naked in the steam room of The Bath & Racquets Club, Mayfair, resolving the bitter two-year legal wrangle with *Vanity Fair*.

Harrods owner Mohammed Al-Fayed with his Director of Public Affairs, Michael Cole.

The Princess of Wales departing Vogue House after a 1991 Condé Nast boardroom lunch. NC looks like a protection officer or a stalker, trailing her across the pavement. At lunch, Princess Diana had asked NC whether he thought her breasts were too small. She was mollified when he informed her they seemed perfect to him.

Editors, Publishers, Executives and managers of Condé Nast Britain, photographed school group-style in the late nineties. The 40 people in the picture served a total of a thousand years for the company.

David Coleridge, centre, with his two eldest grandchildren, Alexander and Freddie, heading to Goodwood Racecourse. Glorious Goodwood was an annual fixture.

Above: Alexander and Tommy Coleridge paddling on Saddell's Beach, Kintyre. Tommy is about two. *Left:* NC with Sophie Coleridge, aged one, photographed on the terrace at Overbury Court, Worcestershire. Sophie was learning to walk at the time.

The brothers: Christopher, NC and Tim Coleridge on safari, Lugards Falls, Galana river, Kenya.

Freddie, Sophie and Alexander Coleridge sightseeing at Ford Castle, near Berwick-upon-Tweed, Northumberland.

The Emperor's New Clothes: Joint 40th birthday. Kit and Georgina Hunter Gordon, Edward and Miff Stourton, Peter Pleydell-Bouverie, James Stourton, Georgia, Jane Pleydell-Bouverie, Nick and Sarah Allan, NC. Cultural appropriation was not yet a thing. Photograph by Antoinette Eugster.

Geordie Greig, Issie Blow, Jefferson Hack, Kate Moss, Mario Testino, Rose Marie Bravo at a Burberry Show, London Fashion Week.

Elizabeth Hurley, presenter of Fashion Rocks, and her nineteen quick-change designer outfits.

Left: Beyoncé and Giorgio Armani at Fashion Rocks. *Below:* Bryan Ferry performing 'Let's Stick Together,' while Karen Elson struts by.

British Style Awards dinner at the Raphael Gallery, V&A: Stephen Quinn, *Vogue* Publishing Director, the supermodel Lily Cole, Sir Stuart Rose, CEO of Marks & Spencer, NC.

British Fashion Awards in a Battersea Park tent: NC, HRH The Prince of Wales, Alexander McQueen, who was named Designer of the Year.

Fashion Rocks: Björk performs 'Bachelorette' in the Albert Hall. The show was described as 'the biggest night of fashion, rock and royalty ever seen, anywhere in the world'. Photograph by Mary McCartney.

NC got up as Aladdin Sane for a *GQ* Bowie special.

GQ Editor Dylan Jones, NC, David Bowie, *Vogue* Editor Alexandra Shulman and *Vogue* Creative Director Robin Derrick, backstage at Wembley Arena. The thirty-second conversation with Bowie was a highpoint of NC's life.

A shameless promotion for his 2002 novel *Godchildren*, NC is photographed in a suite in Claridge's, with five of his seven godchildren, and his own children. Front row: Cara Delevingne, Helena Allan, NC, Ione Hunter Gordon, Sophie and Tommy Coleridge. Back row: Alexander Coleridge, Ewan Wotherspoon, Freddie Coleridge, Ned Donovan. Photograph by David Ellis.

Susan, Sophie and Georgia Coleridge loyally displaying a copy of *Godchildren* on a beach in Antigua.

Geordie Greig and *Tatler* Publisher Patricia Stevenson on the Louis Vuitton private jet to Paris.

Unlikely line-up at the *GQ* Men of the Year Awards, Royal Opera House: Bob Geldof, Simon Le Bon of Duran Duran, Chancellor of the Exchequer George Osborne, NC.

Above: Sophie Hicks, Edie
Campbell in Pienza, Tuscany.
Left: Sophie Coleridge, Sarah
Allan, Georgia Coleridge,
incognito at Jameh mosque,
Isfahan, Iran.

Sotheby's Chairman James Stourton shakes the cocktails while Tommy and Alexander
Coleridge look on. Photographed in the gold drawing room, Marcus, By Forfar, Angus,
scene of much fun.

Wolverton Hall, near Pershore, Worcestershire, photographed in heavy snow. The house was built in 1709, architect unknown, with later additions.

Friends staying at Wolverton: Charles Hudson, Johnnie Standing, Melissa Knatchbull, Sarah Standing, Sarah Sands, Rachel Johnson. It is hoped that nobody will dare leave a 'comment' in the visitors' book.

Sheep steeplechase, Ascot Racecourse, sponsored by The Campaign for Wool. Tommy Coleridge, Peter Ackroyd, NC, Marshall Allender, The Prince of Wales, The Duchess of Cornwall, Sir Nicholas Soames.

At the top of Glen Clova and Glen Muick. Sophie, Tommy, Freddie and Alexander Coleridge, near Forfar, Angus. The walk to the summit was led by James Stourton.

John Travolta and NC at an Indian *GQ* Men of the Year Awards dinner, Bombay. Travolta flew himself to India in his personal 747, but his 'wig carrier' flew separately with the extensive collection of toupées.

Presidents, Publishers and Senior Executives of Condé Nast International, circa 2012. Photographed in the bar of the Connaught hotel, London. A conspicuously large proportion of men in suits, some might observe.

Georgia with Boris Johnson, Mayor of London, at the wedding of the Duke and Duchess of Cambridge, Westminster Abbey, 2011.

Above: NC, David Cameron, *GQ* Editor Dylan Jones, at a *GQ* cocktail party, Brown's hotel, Mayfair. *Left:* Sir Philip Green, billionaire retailer and philanthropist, imparts management wisdom to NC at a *Vogue* party, Claridge's, 2010. Photograph by Nicholas Harvey.

Above: Supermodel and film star Cara Delevingne with her godfather NC, who is probably about to slip her £20 for her birthday. At the British Style Awards, Savoy hotel. *Right:* Sophie, NC, Georgia at Le Bal, Palais de Chaillot, Paris. Sophie's dress is borrowed from Alexander McQueen. Photograph by Jonathan Becker.

At the *Vogue* Centenary Dinner, Kensington Gardens: Jonathan Newhouse, Tom Ford, NC. It is rare for a magazine to reach a hundred years old, and still be at the top of its game.

The Jade Garden set: Cambridge friends from the class of 1979. Nick Allan, Kit Hunter Gordon, Edward and James Stourton, Peter Pleydell-Bouverie. Biannual dim sum at the Jade Garden, Wardour Street, Soho.

Dr Martin Roth, Director of the V&A, Sonnet Stanfill, Curator, Alexandra Shulman, British *Vogue* Editor, NC, *Vogue Italia*'s Franca Sozzani and Italian Prime Minister Matteo Renzi, at the private view of the Glamour of Italian Fashion exhibition, V&A.

The Board of Trustees and senior executives of the Victoria and Albert Museum, photographed by Hugo Burnand in the Medieval-Renaissance Galleries, 2016. 'The museum is run by a board populated by alpha-males and alpha-females, almost all accustomed to having the last word in their day jobs.'

The Victoria and Albert Museum, South Kensington, photographed from a drone. The museum has seven miles of galleries and corridors, and 2.7 million treasures.

NC riffing Dundee, Pink Floyd and fair-trade coffee with Labour leader Jeremy Corbyn, *GQ* Men of the Year Awards, Tate Modern. Photograph by Richard Young.

The Duchess of Cambridge, the V&A's first Royal Patron since Queen Victoria, NC and V&A Director Tristram Hunt at the opening of the Exhibition Road Quarter.

Coleridge family group, taken before a 'Worcestershire Saucy' themed 21st birthday party at
Wolverton Hall, Worcestershire. NC, Alexander, Sophie, Tommy, Georgia, Freddie.
Photographed on a Rajasthani wedding vehicle – a chagda – bought by NC at an Elephant
Family charity auction. Picture by Hugo Burnand.

years later, having failed to secure sufficient advertising revenue. Felix himself died three years after that.

GQ continues to flourish. The newspaper industry outlived him. The Forest of Dennis's 1.3 million native English trees are growing apace, and will outlive us all.

At some point in the early millennium, the Hong Kong Chinese businessman and socialite David Tang entered my life. We met in the Bath & Racquets Club, where we were both members, but neither of us did any actual gym or went near the StairMasters or running machines. Instead, we put on towelling dressing gowns and sat on a sofa, eating smoked salmon and gossiping.

Over the years, David did countless kind things for the Coleridges. He was epically generous. He lent his driver to Freddie in Cuba during his gap year, invited Sophie to lunch at his weekend house in Hong Kong, and invited Alexander, Freddie and Tommy to shoot at the best duck shoot in England, Cockhaise in Sussex. The other guns that day were Sir Nicholas Soames MP and the groovy jazz pianist Jools Holland, and they shot 800 duck. I was picker-up. David was already becoming large and unwell, his shooting stick dug deeper and deeper into the mud under his weight, as the ducks circled overhead.

He invited me to the Hong Kong Book Fair to participate in an annual fixture: the Sir David Tang Lecture Series. Each July, he asked four Brits as his guests, to be harangued by the moderator – David himself – for a couple of hours, as part of a panel with 2,000 Chinese book lovers looking on. My year, the other panellists were the historian David Starkey, the critic A. A. Gill and the food writer Tom Parker Bowles. You could not have identified four people keener to have more than their 25 per cent share of airtime on stage.

Tang's interviewing technique was abrupt and gloriously

tactless. He would say 'Adrian – A. A., whatever you're fucking called – you wrote the worst novel ever published, *Sap Rising*. Everyone says it stinks. How does it feel knowing Nick Coleridge's novels sell more copies than yours?'

Or, 'Nick Coleridge, it must be humiliating for you selling fewer books than Tom Parker Bowles's cookery books.'

Or, 'Nick Coleridge, I quote from a reviewer here – your books are "beach reads". Well, that's not exactly literature, is it? Isn't that a bit disappointing for a descendant of Samuel Taylor Coleridge?'

The whole trip was uncompromisingly generous: suites at the Mandarin Oriental, First Class flights, back-to-back meals in the Hong Kong clubs and restaurants Tang owned or fronted, cruises on his thirties yacht, the *Aunt Dahlia*. After four days of it, everyone was half dead. One of the speaker's wives actually wept with exhaustion as we headed to the airport.

He emailed me randomly from the strangest places. One message began, 'I am on a jet, private thankfully, across Mongolia. Amazingly there is full internet service. Just Skyped a friend in Auckland over Ulaanbaatar . . .'

David's final big dinner for 800 friends at the Dorchester was remarkable: every celebrity, politician and socialite. He gave a speech in which he said how delighted he was that sixteen British royals were present at his party, which is the sort of thing many people might secretly think, but few would say out loud.

He died not long afterwards of excess fun, food, drink and long-haul flights.

24

I was summoned to a dinner at Clarence House by the Prince of Wales, its purpose shrouded in mystery. All I was told was that it was something to do with the countryside, and HRH was assembling a small group to discuss an issue he felt deeply about.

We were an intriguing party that gathered around the dining-room table, beneath the John Piper paintings and a glorious wartime portrait of the Queen Mother by Augustus John. There were shepherds and sheep farmers, a Savile Row tailor, three fashion designers, Australian and Kiwi wool executives, a Yorkshire mill owner, several Thomas Hardy-style wool merchants, and British Wool Board honchos from Bradford. Little did I know this disparate band would come to play such a part in my life, and for so long.

Nepalese Gurkhas, with Prince of Wales ostrich-feather buttons, served as waiters. The individual butter pats, set before each place, were embossed with the Prince's feathers. The main course was lamb, which should have been a clue to our purpose.

The Prince was sharing with me his despair at our throw-away society. 'Young women today, they buy some synthetic outfit or other from a high street chain . . . H&M or that other one, whatever it's called, owned by that . . . man [Topshop, Sir Philip Green] . . . and when they've only worn it once or twice, they throw it away without a second thought and it goes straight to landfill [he pronounced it *lendfill*], where for all we know it lingers for a thousand years. In *lendfill*! Never decomposing or biodegrading. Whereas in one's great-grandmother's day, women would wear a good dress for years, passing it down through the generations, mother to daughter, and it would be altered – lengthened or shortened – according to the fashion of the day.'

As he spoke about the young women of today, I realized he could easily mean Sophie Coleridge, who was culpable of all these crimes.

'And the young men are no better,' he went on. 'They buy some mobile telephone or other, and it's still working perfectly well, when Apple or some such invents a new type, which one's always assured is better, and the young throw away their old one and it goes to *lendfill*, where the batteries leak forevermore into the soil, contaminating the planet.'

This time it was Alexander, Freddie and Tommy Coleridge he must have had in mind.

The Prince addressed the table on the crisis in the wool industry. The wool price had slumped to its lowest level for decades, to the point where sheep farmers were giving up and quitting the land. Sheep numbers were tumbling. They had halved in Britain since the seventies, and it was a similar story in Australia, New Zealand and South Africa. The wool price was now so low it cost more to shear a ewe than the value of the wool. Scientists were working on new breeds of sheep without any wool at all, which the Prince considered appalling. Meanwhile, the march of oil-based synthetic fibres such as polypropylene seemed unstoppable. Ninety-seven per cent of the world's clothes were made from unnatural fibres, and this was increasing. Every one of these garments eventually ends up in landfill, forever. It was a similar story in the carpet world, with real wool carpets being thrashed by man-made ones. The Prince painted an apocalyptic vision of a future world without sheep, altering the landscape of Britain from the uplands of Cumbria to the moorlands of Exmoor.

Gesturing to the man on his right, an amiable Worcestershire countryman named John Thorley, he announced that John had agreed to launch the Prince of Wales's Wool Project, to fight the good fight. Turning to the man sitting on his left – me – he said he hoped I would support his idea and play a full part. Being British, I instantly agreed.

It should be unequivocally stated that I am an HRH fan. He has been shown to be right in almost all his views and campaigns: on heritage, on architecture, on literacy, on the Prince's Trust, on the environment, on soil, on plastic bags, on rainforests, on red squirrels, on faith. And he is right about wool. Quite how right, I would learn over time.

John Thorley and I met up frequently in a Worcestershire pub near Malvern, named The Swan Inn at Newland. The impetus of the Prince's dinner had encouraged the wool boards of Britain, Australia, New Zealand and South Africa to part-fund the project, and there was further support from the Norwegians and the Shetland Isles. We resolved to be a big tent organization, promoting the benefits of wool in all its forms: in fashion, interiors, carpets, insulation, and the built environment. And we dropped the worthy working title the Wool Project for the more aggressive Campaign for Wool. Rather a smart logo was designed, featuring a green sheep. John was the Founding Chairman, and I was his deputy. The Prince was our Patron. We were good to go.

The Campaign for Wool was officially launched in February 2009, in a tithe barn in Cambridgeshire at Wimpole Hall. The barn had been designed by Sir John Soane for the third Earl of Hardwicke, and was certainly the coldest barn in Britain. The breath of the guests on that frozen winter's morning rose in vaporous gusts. The Prince made a stirring speech amplifying the plight of the sheep farmer, and the environmental peril of synthetics. My own speech contained one good joke: 'All we are saying is give fleece a chance.'

The campaign gathered steam when we invented Wool Week. Beginning as a London-centric event, it soon became an annual fixture nationally, then internationally, with Wool Weeks running in fifteen cities from Hamburg to Tokyo.

John Thorley was a delightful colleague, seventy years old with a wide roster of interests. He was Chairman of numerous arcane organizations, encompassing Welsh footpaths, independent abattoirs, a British semen export company (cattle semen, not human), and another HRH initiative to promote the eating of mutton. He had recently become a father for the first time, which imbued him with a certain frisky bonhomie. We got on famously.

It is surprising how rapidly you can absorb an entirely new subject. Prior to the campaign, I would have struggled to identify a Bluefaced Leicester from a Leicester Longwool, but soon I was pontificating confidently on Swaledales, Gotlands and Greyface Dartmoors, particularly when speaking to non-experts. We spent time in Bradford, historic capital of the wool trade since medieval days, still headquarters of the British Wool Board, and surrounded by the warehouses of wool merchants, scourers, spinners and mills. My friend Peter Ackroyd,★ a third-generation woolman, introduced me to Shipley and the Victorian model village of Saltaire, with Salts Mill and the millworkers' cottages. In the evenings, we discussed wool at Akbar's, the great balti mega-restaurant on Bradford's 'Curry Mile'.

The precarious situation of wool can be grasped from this one statistic: before the Second World War, a sheep farmer made half his profit from the meat of his flock, half from the wool. By 2010, he made all his profit from meat and a mild loss on the wool. And yet there were still 60,000 people working in

★ Global Strategic Adviser, Woolmark Company. President, International Wool Textile Organisation. Deputy Lieutenant, West Yorkshire.

one part of the British wool trade or another, in the long supply chain which runs from farmer to wool board (which collects, classifies and auctions wool in greasy form), then to wool merchants who send it for scouring, casting and spinning, before it eventually becomes a tweed jacket or roll of carpet.

We set about talking up wool to fashion designers and department stores, high street chains and anyone who would listen. Many wouldn't. But Harvey Nichols and Selfridges got behind the project, as did a host of brands from Jigsaw and Brora to L. K. Bennett. A breakthrough came when first Marks and Spencer, then John Lewis pledged for wool, and almost fifty stores devoted shop windows to Wool Week. Furthermore, they started reintroducing wool into their suits, and John Lewis shifted wool carpets from the back to the front of their departments. It felt like a small triumph.

Not everything ran smoothly. A busload of Scottish sheep farmers travelled down from the Borders, to experience the wonders of the campaign. They were particularly impressed by a display of edgy wool outfits by young designers, at which free drinks were available.

The combination of alcohol and excitement at the campaign's super-attractive PR team went to the farmers' heads. Their conduct soon turned inappropriate, with many wandering hands, and they had to be firmly warned off. It was #MeEwe.

We put on wool fashion exhibitions in London, to which designers and fashion people showed up, from Christopher Bailey of Burberry to Paul Smith to Mario Testino. And, not long afterwards, we took over Somerset House for a wool interiors show. Our Patron opened both events, and this encouraged more designers to get behind the campaign. The London Design Centre at Chelsea Harbour staged annual wool installations, designed by my sister-in-law Becca Metcalfe. Several dozen fashion colleges embraced the campaign, and wool hit the curriculum for the first time.

We invented a string of wool stunts. There was the grassing-over of Savile Row, with half an acre of turf and a flock of fluffy Merinos grazing between tailor's shops. Another was the burying of two sweaters – one pure wool, the other synthetic – in a flower bed at Clarence House, to demonstrate how the wool one quickly and naturally decomposes in soil. The Prince performed the burying task with a silver shovel, and the two jerseys were left to fester for six months. As the day of the unburying drew nearer, I became nervous, in case the big reveal was an anticlimax, with the world's press looking on. The great day finally arrived. And, lo, the wool jersey had all but disappeared, with a few fat worms digesting the final strands. As predicted, the synthetic one was intact. You could have put it through the washing machine and worn it again.

We set fire to wool and synthetic clothes at Clarence House, to demonstrate the fire-resistant qualities of wool. The synthetic sweater went up in a blaze, while the wool one smouldered and never caught alight. Wool carpets were safely blasted by a flame thrower, synthetic ones erupted like Vesuvius.

I had become Chairman of the campaign, with the excellent Peter Ackroyd as COO. The various wool boards, accustomed to centuries of rivalry, maintained an uneasy truce, though skirmishes could break out at any moment. The Prince of Wales devoted a startling amount of time to his campaign, criss-crossing the country to visit hill farmers. He would arrive in Bradford on the royal train, then tour wool mills and scouring plants.

Peter and I were summoned to Birkhall in Scotland to receive our instructions from the Patron. A big black Land Cruiser met us at Aberdeen airport, for the drive to Ballater. It is possible we felt a bit smug, being whisked along in this tip-top royal vehicle.

Thirty miles from Aberdeen, the car drove over a rusty nail, blew a puncture and jolted to a halt. We climbed out and stood on a grass verge, while lorries thundered past. It began to rain. The driver attempted to change the tyre, but the armour-plated car was too heavy. He rang Birkhall, who said they would organize a local taxi to collect us.

It grew dark. The lorries drove closer to the verge. The rain intensified. We retreated backwards against a fence. As we stood there, a pony stuck its head over the gate and grabbed a mouthful of my suit.

The taxi appeared. It was battered and reeked of cigarette smoke. Across the windscreen was a 'Say Yes to Independence' sticker.

'Where to?' the cabbie asked in a broad Scottish accent.

'Er, Ballater?'

'Not to the royals', I hope?' He drove on in brooding disapproval.

We staged a Wool Conference at Dumfries House in Ayrshire, with several hundred international wool experts, environmentalists and retailers. A great charter was unveiled by the Prince – the Dumfries House Declaration – which established global standards of animal welfare and environmental best practice. By the end of 2017, it had been signed by more than 500 organizations representing half a million wool workers around the world.

Has the campaign made any difference? Most farmers think a big difference. Ten years in, the Australian and South African wool industry is booming as seldom before; in Britain and New Zealand, it remains a perpetual slog.

I have met people through the campaign I would never otherwise have met, and learnt things I would never otherwise have known. And, at the very least, I can distinguish the sheep from the goats.

25

After the debacle of Rignell Farm, Georgia was understandably dubious when I fell in love with another country house so quickly. She accused me of being 'on the rebound' and drawn to the first pretty facade that came along.

She also felt it was 'far too big' and too far from London, and I was demonstrating shameful symptoms of *folie de grandeur*.

Of course, Georgia had a point. But I had fallen head over heels for Wolverton Hall, near Pershore, Worcestershire – and this time it was for keeps.

A Queen Anne beauty with seven bays of sash windows, Wolverton had been built by the Acton family in 1709, architect unknown. It was precisely the kind of house I'd always wanted to live in, with high ceilings, Georgian cornices, and a neglected air of melancholy which has always appealed to me, right back to my West Sussex days of climbing into the secret garden at Woolbeding before it was restored by Simon Sainsbury and Stewart Grimshaw. There was a large overgrown walled garden, with knee-high nettles and pieces of old abandoned cars and tyre hubs. Across a field lay a lake encroached by bulrushes. There were multiple outbuildings, two cottages and a barn with a collapsing roof. A Project House.

Pevsner was typically sniffy about the place, describing Wolverton Hall as 'absolutely plain apart from stone quoins and keystones. The present entrance has a substantial Georgian doorway with Tuscan columns and open pediment . . . all later.'

No questions about it, Wolverton Hall by 2004 was distinctly on its uppers. The Acton family had occupied the place since 1585, originally inhabiting a beamed black and white manor house, traces of which survive in various outbuildings. In the early eighteenth century they had razed the Tudor house to the ground, replacing it with new, improved, all-mod-cons Wolverton. In the mid-nineteenth century, a Victorian wing was thrown up, providing further bedrooms. The Actons kept the house until the 1970s, before finally selling up, whereafter it rapidly changed hands several times. One previous owner ripped out the fireplaces, along with the panelling of a Roman Catholic chapel on the first floor, and sold them for peanuts. By the time the Coleridges arrived on the scene, Wolverton was being lived in by a feisty widow, Suzie Elliot, whose late husband had been a legendary shot and Olympic rower. There were gaping holes in the kitchen wall, which made the house perpetually freezing. It had very nearly been sold off as a care home for the elderly, but the deal fell through.

As it happened, it was Georgia who spotted the advertisement in *Country Life*. For economy reasons, the estate agents had booked a quarter-page black and white ad, at the back end of the property section, immediately before the advertisements for English oak dressers and Dover Street art galleries, and the girl-in-pearls frontispiece.

The 'selling line' above the photograph of Wolverton Hall was heroically unappealing. It announced '42.5 miles from Birmingham'. Not '20 miles from Moreton-in-Marsh', not '14 miles from Broadway', nor even '7 miles from Evesham'. Perhaps they imagined the Industrial Revolution was still in full swing, and dozens of blast furnace and steam engine tycoons were queuing up to buy the place.

I loved Wolverton at once. A house originally surrounded by a 1,500-acre estate, it was now down to its last 20 acres, which felt ideal. We had no need of land. The last remaining field was filled with Bluefaced Leicester sheep (easily identified by the Chairman of The Campaign for Wool) belonging to local farmers Paul and Hallie Jeavons. The drive, which is pleasingly long, protected us from the roaring traffic of the A44.

We soon discovered our new house lay on the wild frontier of the Cotswolds and the West Midlands. Turn left, and you find picture-postcard Cotswold cottages and dovecotes. Turn right, and it's the business parks and logistics sheds of Worcester, Droitwich, Redditch, Wolverhampton and the Black Country. Accents change accordingly, by the mile.

Worcestershire is one of those mystery counties which many people can't place geographically. Some think it is north of Yorkshire, others believe it is over beyond Leicestershire in the East Midlands. In fact, it is bordered by Gloucestershire, Warwickshire, Herefordshire, Staffordshire and Shropshire, some parts being defiantly countryish and unruined, other parts less so. It is known as a county of apple orchards and asparagus fields, for the magnificent medieval cathedral in Worcester with the tomb of Bad King John, for the Lea & Perrins Worcester Sauce factory with its orange gates, and as the birthplace of Sir Edward Elgar. Topographically, it is mostly rather flat, but dissected by two great ranges of hills: the Malvern Hills and Bredon Hill, both visible from Wolverton. Bredon Hill is a setting for A. E. Housman's late-nineteenth-century poem *A Shropshire Lad*, with its paeans to local beauty spots, the River Severn and the Teme Valley.

There are virtually no celebrities living in Worcestershire, other than the pop star Toyah Willcox, whose chart-topping hit 'It's A Mystery' I have always liked, and her husband, the musician Robert Fripp of King Crimson. They live in our local market town of Pershore. The TV interrogator Jeremy Paxman grew up in our village, Peopleton, and is still remembered in The Crown Inn.

'I hope you're successful in discovering the secret passage,' said a neighbour. We knew nothing of any secret passage. 'It was certainly still there during the war,' he went on. 'The Secret Army requisitioned the hall, and were planning on using it to run insurgency raids behind German lines, if they invaded.'

Beyond this one fact, there was no consensus about the location, purpose or direction of the fabled Wolverton underground passage. Some said it emerged two miles away in the village of White Ladies Aston. Others said it went to Peopleton, one mile away, and surfaced in the churchyard. Paul Jeavons, the gentleman farmer whose land surrounds our own, remembers entering the entrance of the tunnel as a child. A local historian suggested the tunnel was utilized by a pair of Dutch brothers, the Van Moppes, who stored industrial diamonds in it during the war, and may have been visited at Wolverton by Winston Churchill in 1940. Or there again, may not have been. Others insist the tunnel was built as an escape route for the Roman Catholic Acton family, during the years of papist persecution. Wolverton is in the heart of the Gunpowder Plot belt.

The film star Julian Sands* came to visit with his wife Evgenia† (my old friend who had once slipped out through the back window of an Italian trattoria to escape me), and made a thorough search for the passageway. Julian became convinced it lay behind the drawing-room chimney. He tapped on a section of wall and could hear a hollow echo, indicating a concealed chamber. In no time, he found a pickaxe and began bashing away in clouds of dust. We stood meekly watching, too mesmerized

---

* *The Killing Fields* (1984); *A Room with a View* (1985); *Arachnophobia* (1990).

† Author, *Ether* (2010); *The Shades* (2018).

to stop him. Soon, he was furiously removing bricks. There was a definite void in there. It would surely contain, at the very least, a pouch of gold sovereigns. Julian inserted his hand and wiggled it about. Suddenly we could see his fingers . . . inside the fireplace. He had punctured the flue, there was no secret room.

We have spent the past fifteen years searching. The children are disappointed I refuse to dig up the lawn with a JCB until we find it, if it ever existed.

Tommy, as a child, envisaged a perfectly preserved tunnel with flaming braziers, flagstone floor and, very likely, suits of armour. Several of our friends have tried dowsing to locate the passage, egged on by Georgia. Kit and Georgie Hunter Gordon received irrefutable twitches on their dowsing sticks, leading across the fields in the direction of Bredon Hill. Trelawny and Olivia Williams experienced ironclad signals, leading in the exact opposite direction. At the time of writing, the Secret of the Wolverton Passage remains unsolved.

Georgia mostly decorated our house in Chelsea, to which we had moved from Notting Hill, and I mostly did Wolverton. It helped that *House & Garden* shared my floor at Condé Nast; the decoration department is lined with shoe boxes of fabric swatches and wallpaper samples. You can ask, 'Any pink peony wallpaper?' or, 'I'm looking for curtain material that's a bit Islamic, predominantly blue but with a touch of red,' and minutes later it is produced. Georgia and I both like a lot of colour in our houses; we're never much good with beige, that whole Armani oatmeal-taupe-neutral-ecru palette leaves us cold.

My school friend Hugh St Clair helped design the kitchen; he has legendary good taste but is arguably vague. I showed Georgia his kitchen plan and she said, 'It looks great, but where's the fridge?'

'Hugh, where's the fridge?'

'Ah . . . a fridge. I suppose you do want a fridge? Sometimes a larder can be nicer.'

We needed plenty of new furniture, beds especially. So it was lucky when Sarah and Johnnie Standing gave us Robbie Williams' double bed – which had somehow come into their possession. Freddie was delighted to inherit the great rock star's cot. Not long afterwards, Victoria Mather rang us. She was helping clear out Lady Thatcher's house at 73 Chester Square, and Carol Thatcher wondered whether we might like Mrs T's bed. 'Not the one she died in,' Victoria said. 'She died at the Ritz.'

The top floor of Wolverton Hall was rapidly turning into a celebrity bed museum.

Unfortunately, the Thatcher bed offer was withdrawn by Sir Mark Thatcher at the last minute. He was concerned that, in years to come, it might fall into the wrong hands, and become the focus for a Momentum-inspired demonstration against his mother.

In contrast to Oxfordshire, we knew hardly anybody in Worcestershire. There is an almost Jane Austenish vibe, with the same restricted cast of characters cropping up again and again. Long before we moved there, we had two sets of friends living around Bredon Hill: Penelope and Bruce Bossom at Overbury, and Cressida* and Charles Hudson at Wick. They remain our closest friends in the county, and we have the nicest time at their houses.†

---

* Author, *My Former Heart* (2012); *After the Party* (2018).

† There are other neighbours, just about within driving distance: Lucy and James Hervey-Bathurst over the Herefordshire county border at Eastnor Castle, Lucy and Nick Morris over the Gloucestershire border at Cold Aston, Camilla and Ed Peake at Sezincote (the Mogul house, subject of NC's carelessly written Cambridge dissertation), the fashion stylist Jo Levin

The Bossoms inhabit the prettiest, best kept estate in Worcestershire. The moment you cross the boundary onto their land, the hedges are perfectly cut, every tree symmetrical, streams flow freely, wild flowers bloom, pea-fed sheep frolic. Bruce is tall, slim and elegant, perpetually alert to a double entendre; Penelope is a champion of the countryside, a broadband evangelist.

Charles and Cressida live in a remarkable faux-Tudor house, Wick Manor; you feel you are entering the world of Shakespeare's Globe Theatre, with its courtyard, beams and panelling, but the house was mostly built in 1923. There is a strong flavour of the Bloomsbury set about the place: Cressida is the novelist daughter of Cyril Connolly, with her huge eyes, fragile prettiness and thirties tea dresses.

About three times a year, we stir ourselves to fill the house with friends, and the children are allocated one weekend a year each to do likewise. The maximum we can sleep, including extra mattresses on floors, is twenty-eight. I very much enjoy the house being filled with our children's unfeasibly tall male friends, all of them at least six feet three inches, looming above us, and by the bright, pretty girls they bring home.

We are lucky that our children still like coming home for weekends. When Freddie was at Bristol University, he would ring at midday: 'Are you guys at Wolverton? I'll be there for lunch at five past one.' (The journey took sixty-five minutes.) Sophie and Tommy take the train down from Edinburgh to

---

and Charlie Hambro at Dumbleton, the Afghanistan adventurer Gilbert Greenall at Bromsberrow, the publisher and literary agent Anthony and Georgina Cheetham at Paxford, Millie and Nick Wentworth-Stanley at Broadway, Elizabeth Hurley near Ledbury. In the north of the county near Tenbury Wells, Annie and Patrick Holcroft, the Lord Lieutenant. And William and Laura Cash over the Shropshire border at Upton Cressett.

Worcester. Alexander, back from Brooklyn, comes too. The house has played a big part in keeping the family together. It is something I learnt from my parents: the importance of family bonding, of holidays, Christmas and weekends. In the end, everything else is off-stage noise, only family matters; it is one's only meaningful legacy.

We have a running family dispute about the etiquette of visitor's books, with me on one side of the argument, and Georgia on the other.

I like a visitor's book to be severely minimalist: a departing guest signs their name and the date of their stay. No home addresses, no comments or remarks. It is my intrusive habit to loom above the open book, policing it, in Basil Fawlty mode. 'Just your signature and the date, please. No need for anything else.'

From time to time, I'm outmanoeuvred, and someone will write 'What fun that was!' or 'Delicious strawberries'.

When Sophie was at Cheltenham Ladies' College, and her school friends used to come for sleepovers, they were serial offenders. They would scrawl 'OMG I had such an AMAZING TIME. The food was AMAZING. My room was AMAZING. The walk was AMAZING. The DVD was AMAZING. Love you ♥☺.'

There would be seven or eight of these accolades, filling at least a page.

Georgia is more accommodating. In fact, she actively encourages comments. She considers me control-freaky. She said recently, 'If David Hockney came to stay, and wanted to draw a sketch of the garden in the visitor's book, would you really prevent him?' Sadly we don't know David Hockney, so the moral dilemma will not arise.

Flicking back through the photograph albums at the dozens

of weekend gatherings, it is fun to be reminded of the friends who passed through, smiling out of the pages at one lunch in the garden or other.★

There is a point in life when you are supposed to become interested in trees. Generally it strikes at the age of fifty, when you are already too old to have much expectation of seeing any tree you plant grown to maturity.

No sooner did I hit fifty than, right on cue, I properly noticed trees for the first time.

★ Written with the punctuation of the late Mrs Betty Kenward of Jennifer's Diary (see Chapter 9) I am delighted to record the names of some of the guests welcomed for sleepovers: The Hon James Stourton and Miss Charity Charity, Mr and Mrs Edward Stourton, The Hon Mr and Hon Mrs Peter Pleydell-Bouverie; Mr and Mrs Nicholas Allan, Mr and Mrs Kit Hunter Gordon, Mr and Mrs Charles Joly, Miss Alexandra Shulman and Mr David Jenkins, Lady Romilly McAlpine; Mr and Mrs Will Bevan, Mr and Mrs Geordie Greig, the Marquess and Marchioness of Normanby; Mr Nicholas Haslam. Miss Rachel Johnson and Mr Ivo Dawnay, Miss Sarah Sands and Mr Kim Fletcher, Sir John and Lady Leon; Lord Black of Brentwood and Mr Mark Bolland; Mr and Mrs Stephen Quinn, Mr Loyd Grossman and Miss Melissa Knatchbull, Miss Bettina von Hase, the Hon Lizzie Norton, Mr Bruce Palling and Miss Lucinda Bredin, the Duchess of Rutland and her three social media-savvy Manners girls; Mr Simon Thurley and Miss Anna Keay, Mr and Mrs David Shaughnessy, Lord Rose of Monewden; Miss Kate Reardon, Mr and Mrs Charles Moore, Mr William Sieghart and Miss Molly Dineen, Mr and Mrs Neil Mendoza, Miss Harriet Sergeant, Miss Charlotte Metcalfe, Mr and Mrs William Dalrymple, the Hon Mr and Mrs Sebastian Grigg; Mr Ed and Mrs Carol Ryan Victor, Mr and Mrs Craig Brown, Mr Andrew Roberts and Miss Susan Gilchrist, Mr and Mrs Mark Rowan, Princess Rajni and Princess Reynu Malla of Kathmandu. Mr and Mrs James Seymour, Lady Balniel; Mr and Mrs Anthony Coleridge, Mr and Mrs Tim Coleridge, Mr and Mrs Christopher Coleridge, Mr and Mrs George Metcalfe, former Lord Mayor of Canterbury. Miss Becca Metcalfe, Miss Luisa Metcalfe, Mr and Mrs Daniel Metcalfe.

Our best tree is a giant holm oak (*Quercus ilex*), standing proud at the end of our lawn. And right next to our house stands a hundred-foot Wellingtonia (*Sequoiadendron giganteum*). It was planted in the early nineteenth century, far too close to the building; its roots periodically make an appearance up the U-bend of the downstairs loo. One day, the Wellingtonia will topple onto the house, crushing it flat. I hope we are out at the time.

We had arrived in Worcestershire almost by accident, but it was the happiest of happenchance. I hope never to have to leave.

26

I had been appointed President of Condé Nast International in 2011, the loftiest position in the company open to anyone not born with the lucky-gene Newhouse surname. In addition to the slight embarrassment of an American-style corporate job title, it principally meant a lot more business travel. The first half of my Condé Nast years had largely been London-focused, coping with the daily diva-action of Vogue House. The second half was spent at Heathrow Terminal 5, en route to review our different overseas businesses. Soon I was making twenty-five to thirty trips a year. Jonathan Newhouse, as Chairman, had first pick of the cities he wished to inspect, with a preference for China, Japan, Sao Paolo and Le Bristol hotel in Paris. My beat included most of the 'M's – Mumbai, Moscow and Munich.

We were arguably late into India. Our competitors had doled out licences for their magazines a decade or two earlier, so *Elle*, *L'Officiel*, *Cosmopolitan* and so forth were already well established. It was hard to tell how well they did, since there is no audited circulation in India, and most of the licences were held by super-rich Indian families who enjoyed publishing trophy magazines. Their fortunes derived from manufacturing, haulage, car dealerships and manganese quarries, but they ran a magazine division to please their wives, and if this were loss-making it was immaterial.

A recent change in the law meant that, in theory at least, Western publishers could now operate in India without local partners. This was good news. Local partners are generally a pain; they get in the way, hold opinions, under-invest, and are chiefly interested in swanking to their friends about owning *Vogue*. No overseas company had yet tested the new freedom to publish, and it took two years of lobbying in Delhi for us to secure the go-ahead. But first we needed to hire some staff.

It was fun to be back in India, this time with a purpose. Starting our India business was the most enjoyable of assignments, exposing me to aspects of the country I would never otherwise have seen. For a time, the Taj Palace hotel, opposite the Gateway to India, became a virtual third home; I soon knew every waiter and pool man by name, and could order from the room-service menu without bothering to open it.

With a Condé Nast friend, my deputy Albert Read, I flew to Mumbai and we embarked upon a search for a Managing Director. The monsoon was so heavy and relentless that year, it didn't let up for four solid days, it was like standing in a wet room in a boutique hotel; our plane made three attempts before landing on the flooded runway. India had that special monsoon smell of damp, drains, floor polish and dead dog. Driving through the waterlogged city, it seemed almost insane that we intended launching luxury magazines here. Through the fogged-up windscreen, I could spot neither potential readers nor advertisers. At traffic lights, small children tapped on the windows, clutching armfuls of *Elle*s and *India Today*s for sale. This, apparently, was the supply chain.

Albert and I interviewed twelve candidates, each one more hopeless than the one before. On the basis of this process, you would have thought there were only two flavours of Indian manager: very arrogant ones, who saw the role as sitting behind a vast, veneered desk, or else vapid, cringing creatures, who couldn't make eye contact. We were approaching despair, when Alex Kuruvilla strolled in. We liked him at once: he had run

Indian MTV, was witty and astute, and liked jazz and Pink Floyd. We had dinner that night at Indigo, a cool Italian in Colaba, and our search was over.

Day after day, beneath the poolside loggia at the Taj, we interviewed potential *Vogue* staff. Anna Harvey, the great British *Vogue* doyenne, flew in to help. When seeking a *Vogue* Editor, regardless of country, there are always two ways you can go. There are rich, social candidates, from rich, social families, who look great, talk the talk, already wear couture and long to sit front row. Or there are proper journalists who work hard. My vote always goes for the second kind, though a twist of the first in their DNA is welcome too. In Mumbai, we found Priya Tanna, who clinched the deal by saying she had read every issue of British *Vogue* for twenty years, and proved it by referring in forensic detail to particular articles, shoots and front covers.

A glamorous Creative Fashion Director, Anaita Shroff Adajania, who styled half of Bollywood's film stars, followed close behind. And then a Publisher, Arjun Mehra, who stated he consulted a guru on Juhu Chowpatty beach, and delivered offerings each time he sold an advertising page to Rolex. And a clever Parsee Marketing Director, Oona Dhabhar, completed the first trawl. By our fourth visit, we had snazzy offices on the Ballard Estate, near the naval port, and already employed a hundred staff. Condé Nast India was impatient to start.

Our permission to publish from the Ministry of Information and Broadcasting, however, had still not come through. Each week it was promised, but never happened. Our strict policy of not paying small bribes to functionaries in government offices (or to anyone else, for that matter) may have been a factor.

We were awaiting at least six more vital signatures, seals and stamps, and were stuck in treacle. Alex and I flew up to Delhi, and eventually got a meeting with the minister. We were led through room after vast room of civil servants, clerks in white shirts. The stairwells were stained red with gobbets of betel juice. Everywhere were towering in-trays of pending documents. One of these was ours.

The Minister of Information and Broadcasting was young and hip. He had recently graduated from an Ivy League university in the States. He listened attentively to our pleas. Then he said, 'My God, if my wife thought I'd stood in the way of *Vogue*, she'd be hopping mad at me. She worships *Vogue*.' He clapped his hands and barked orders in Hindi. The clerks in white shirts sprinted to and fro. Others wrung their hands and wobbled their heads.

'I think you will be receiving all the necessary tomorrow,' declared the minister. 'Some of these fellows have been regrettably lackadaisical and dilatory.'

Before any important launch, we always did reader research. This took the form of focus groups, at which forty or so potential readers sat on one side of a two-way mirror, and we sat on the other, spying on them and taking notes. A moderator conducted a conversation, from which we hoped to glean a feeling for the audience: their levels of sophistication, prior impressions of *Vogue*, interest in fashion, beauty, celebrities.

Alex Kuruvilla, Albert, Jean Faulkner (the clever British Marketing Chief) and I assembled at the Orchid airport hotel in Delhi's Aerocity (it is axiomatic that all focus groups be held in sad, soulless locations). It was immediately obvious that Indian readers are several times better educated than equivalent British ones. They referenced Jane Austen and Henry James's *Portrait of a Lady* as readily as British readers (experienced a fortnight earlier in Wembley) referenced Katie Price and Davina McCall.

Fascination with Western celebrities was low, fascination with Bollywood movie stars intense. Engagement with Western fashion designers was high ('Everyone adores Gucci and Chanel, but what about Dolce & Gabbana this season? Oh my God, right off the scale!'). And yet, at weddings and dinners ('and especially when you have to visit your parents, you know') it was still saris-first. *Vogue* India was going to be a balancing act.

I immersed myself in the local social scene, to get the feel. For a country with 1.4 billion citizens, it was odd how often you encountered the same tiny cast of characters. A social X-ray named Queenie Dhody was at every party. So was Prince Tikka Singh, Maharaja of Kapurthala, the brand ambassador for Louis Vuitton. And Tarun Tahiliani, the effervescent Delhi fashion designer.

Throughout our negotiations with the government, I had become accustomed to speaking of 'Mumbai'. But I was quickly put right by Dior's glamorous 'face', the socialite Kalyani Chawla.

'What is all this "Mumbai this, Mumbai that" rubbish talk, Nicholas? *Nobody* calls it Mumbai. Well, maybe some government goons, but seriously! I'm surprised at you, you of all people. Call the place Bombay, for God's sake.'

And she was right, virtually nobody in the city, from billionaire to cab driver, calls it anything but Bombay.

The photographer Patrick Demarchelier flew out to shoot the front cover. It starred the Australian model Gemma Ward with a gatefold of fabulous Bollywood stars and models: Priyanka Chopra, Bipasha Basu, Preity Zinta, Lakshmi Menon and Monikangana Dutta. The idea was an exciting *thali* of Indian and international talent, signalling global ambition. Meanwhile, a launch party with a guest list of thousands was being planned, to be held in Jodhpur at Bapji Jodhpur's Umaid Bhawan Palace. A plane was chartered to fly guests in.

Whenever I asked, 'Isn't three thousand guests rather a lot?' everyone looked surprised.

'Actually we are struggling to hold numbers down, the original invitations list had five thousand.'

Once, in the Condé Nast India offices, I was asked how many guests had come to Georgia's and my wedding, all those years earlier. I'd replied, 'It was about six hundred, I think.' They looked at me pitifully, thinking what a sad, furtive, cheapskate, hole-in-the-wall event that must have been. India respects big numbers.

The launch party was fabulous. As the saying goes, everyone was there: Bollywood royalty, Maharaja royalty, fashion royalty, politicians, Queenie Dhody, Prince Tikka Singh, Tarun Tahiliani. And the launch issue itself was a smash hit, leapfrogging the competition to become market leader from day one. Giant billboards toasting *Vogue* dominated the key cities. A shoot inside the issue by the Indian photographer Bharat Sikka, showcasing the model Lily Cole on Delhi trams, in sleazy Bombay nightclubs, at the Taj Mahal and Calcutta's Howrah Bridge, remains one of my favourite ever fashion shoots.

With *Vogue* off the blocks, we quickly launched Indian *GQ*, edited by Che Kurrien, followed by Indian *Condé Nast Traveller*, edited by the glamorous Divia Thani, and Indian *Architectural Digest*, edited first by Manju Rajan, then Greg Foster. In no time, we were nudging 300 staff. Indian Editors are imaginative and resourceful. Alex Kuruvilla had proved himself to be terrific, and the company was nicely profitable.

It was interesting to learn what works editorially in India and what doesn't. Indian travellers dislike beaches and sunshine – they like spa breaks to Dubai, Singapore, London and New York, and never step outdoors. Rich Indian families have two kitchens – a 'show' kitchen from a Western kitchen company like Poggenpohl or Häcker, for the family to eat in and make cappuccinos, and a second, working kitchen with clay ovens and woodsmoke for battalions of servants.

It became my fixed routine to catch the 10.05 British Airways flight out of Heathrow on Monday morning, returning on the 13.10 from Bombay on Thursday lunchtime, allowing two full days in the office. One November, however, three years in, I made a weekend of it and flew back home a day early on the Wednesday flight instead. It was a lucky decision. A few hours after I checked out of the Taj, the 26 November 2008 terrorist attack began, when ten members of the Islamic Lashkar-e-Taiba from Pakistan invaded through the poolside entrance. Within minutes, they had shot up the area around the pool, including the loggia where we conducted our hiring interviews, and murdered half my friends, the breakfast waiters. In a four-day rampage, they killed 168 people in the Taj, Oberoi, Chhatrapati railway station, the hippy-style Leopold's café where we often hung out, St Xavier's College and the hospital. Several friends were trapped in the hotel for forty-eight hours, hiding under beds or in wardrobes, including Nadia and Swami La Valle, from my Michael Roberts and San Lorenzo days. The General Manager of the hotel, Karambir Kang, lost his wife and two sons in the attack. Alex's daughter's schoolteachers were gunned down in the railway station, queuing to buy train tickets. Stories of the bravery of the Taj staff, saving the lives of hotel guests by throwing themselves into the line of fire, are something I shall never forget.

GQ Men of the Year was launched in Bombay. It followed the well-established British model, with a gala dinner and awards for Actor of the Year, Politician, Businessman, Entrepreneur and Best Dressed. Alex Kuruvilla told me proudly, 'We've got John Travolta coming to collect a Lifetime Achievement Award. He is piloting himself from Florida to Bombay in his personal Boeing 707.'

'Perhaps you'd better check we're not paying for his fuel?'

'Oh no, all we have to pay for is his toupée assistant, who flies separately with his collection of wigs as hand baggage.'

Travolta landed at Chhatrapati Airport at two in the morning. A crowd of 4,000 fans were waiting outside the terminal building to greet him. He is immense in India. *Saturday Night Fever* may be the closest Hollywood ever got to a Bollywood blockbuster, and India the last place on earth where you can still wear a white suit to a disco without embarrassment. The Indian GQ awards were awash with Bollywood celebrities: Aishwarya Rai, Deepika Padukone, Shah Rukh Khan, Kareena Kapoor Khan, Katrina Kaif . . . The Indian star system is like post-war Hollywood, with the studio system fully intact.

It was through Alex's wife, Namita, that I was introduced to another side of India. She took me to visit the six notorious cross-streets in Kamathipura, the red-light district of Bombay. It is an area of winding alleyways, grotesque leering pimps, random violence and dimly lit staircases up to chawls used as brothels. Six thousand prostitutes, some as young as ten, operate in these grimy, Dickensian lanes. The price for an encounter with a woman is ten rupees (10p), one fifteenth of the price of an issue of Indian *Vogue*. (Here is an interesting comparison: an hour with a London escort girl costs £200, British *Vogue* is £4.) When an Indian prostitute reaches the age of fifty, her price halves. Namita was supporting a hostel where prostitutes could leave their children while they were working, otherwise the children cower underneath their mother's bed. The children were the sweetest I have ever seen, their predicament quite heartbreaking. *Vogue* (and I) tried to help, but the challenge is overwhelming.

I know from immigration stamps that I have visited India eighty-five times. Flights land in Bombay in the early hours, and my practice is to bolt through Customs, race to the hotel, and try to catch a few hours' sleep before my day in the office. One time, I had turned off the bedroom light and was virtually asleep, when I heard gentle tapping at the door. I ignored it, the tapping became louder, then the doorbell rang. I groaned, pulled on a towelling robe and padded to open it.

Outside, in the marble corridor, was a large reception committee: the Assistant General Manager of the hotel, two marketing ladies in saris, two public relations ladies, one room butler, two waiters and a photographer, who immediately started taking flash photographs. A waiter was presenting me with a two-litre bottle of Whyte & Mackay whisky. The PR lady offered a garland.

'Congratulations, Mr Coleridge, on your thirtieth stay at Taj Palace.' There were heartfelt handshakes and more photographs.

I am glad never to have seen the pictures of a tousled guest in a bathrobe, garlanded, and brandishing the giant whisky bottle. I wonder what became of them?

Another trip, I flew out on the same flight as Andrew Mitchell MP, former Secretary of the Ashdown House Stamp Club, now Secretary of State for International Development. We were both staying at the Taj.

This time, I was actually asleep when the bedside telephone rang.

An Indian voice said, 'Hello? Hello? Is that Mr Nicholas? Hello? This is Mr Magoo speaking, from Concierge Desk.'

'Er, yes?'

'Yes, sir. I have two young ladies here with me downstairs, very beautiful, very clean. They are available to entertain you in your suite, if you so wish.'

'What, *now*? It's two thirty in the morning, you realize? I'm asleep. And, anyway, no.'

There was an explosion of laughter. It was Mitchell. His impression had been faultless. 'Don't worry,' he said. 'If you'd said yes, your secret would have been safe with me.'

Other evenings, I would visit Roddy Sale, a delightfully eccentric expat, whose flat near Kemps Corner is decorated with Indian miniatures, hunting prints and items of Eton memorabilia, tapestry floreat cushions and house photographs. He gave dinners for eclectic groups: you could expect maharajas, fashionable designers, the photographer Derry Moore,★ the artist Julian Barrow,† backpacking posh English girls who'd been given his address. The menus were derived from the Queen Mother's Castle of Mey cookbook: Mint Sauce Soup, Oeufs Drumkilbo (lobster and hard-boiled eggs in aspic) and Eton Mess. Roddy's flat should be preserved in perpetuity by the National Trust of India. So, come to that, should Roddy himself.

After the sweltering heat of Bombay, it was refreshing to land in sub-zero Moscow. For a period of seven years, I visited Moscow six times a year, it became a favourite gig.

Shortly before my first visit, the Estée Lauder heir, William Lauder, cautioned, 'I hope the Newhouses are providing you with bodyguards? You can't visit Moscow without personal security.'

'They're not, actually. I'm not planning on having any.'

'Then you're crazy,' he replied. 'Tell Si I said so. You need to watch your back in Russia. Always.'

On every visit, I walked to the Condé Nast offices, unarmed,

★ Earl of Drogheda, photographer, *Architectural Digest, Harpers & Queen, Town & Country*. Indophile.
† Gentlemanly British artist (1939–2013) of Indian landscapes and English country houses.

unchaperoned and (I think) unshadowed. It felt spookily safe. Out of the hotel with its under-pavement heating, past the Tsum department store, past Cartier, up Tretyakovsky Proyezd, past Prada and Nobu, underneath the arch to the Condé Nast offices. They occupy a tall, pink, converted fur depository with Tsarist entablature on the facade. Several of the floors, being former cold rooms for storing mink and wolf pelts, are windowless, and now occupied by the IT department.

Condé Nast had entered Russia in the early nineties, at the worst possible time. In the week *Vogue* launched, the oil price crashed and the rouble went into freefall. There were mile-long queues of depositors outside the banks, withdrawing their cash, and the brief post-glasnost boom was predicted to be over. But it recovered, and the Condé Nast Russian business exploded. Soon we had 8 glossy magazines, 400 staff, a 37 per cent profit margin, and every international fashion and beauty company was piling into the market. The GUM department store on Red Square, which I had first visited with John Scott and Trelawny Williams during our gap year adventure, to be faced with near-empty shelves, was now the blingiest department store in the world, with giant Dior, Vuitton and Chanel concessions at every turn, and an oligarch-enticing watch department selling million-dollar timepieces. The enigmatic Bernd Runge, the Stasi informer, had overseen the Condé Nast business for us, but now it had come my way.

I took to Moscow at once. I like the city, the massed tower blocks on the Domodedovo Airport expressway, the silver birch forests, the Stalinist skyscrapers, the golden domes of the churches, and the vaguely menacing walls of the Kremlin. From my window at the Ararat Park Hyatt, I could see the illuminated red stars of the Kremlin rooftops, and sometimes the Putin helicopter coming in to land, with two further helicopters hovering as decoys. Our Russian company was run by two remarkable, strong women, Karina Dobrotvorskaya and Anita Gigovskaya. I liked them both: clever, cultured and mildly ruthless. If they were horrified by the arrival of an over-polite Old Etonian in their midst, they got over it. Both became friends.

If I had to choose where to be poor, between Bombay and Moscow, I'd choose Bombay by a mile. But if I could choose where to be rich, I'd go for Moscow. The Company started a restaurant in Moscow, *Vogue* Café, run by the Marco Pierre White of Russia, Arkady Novikov, filled each night by the wives of oligarchs, so chic, so dazzling, dripping in Chopard and Bulgari jewellery, and drinking iced vodka. We had a *Tatler* Club in a Stalinist tower on Kutuzovsky Avenue, always full, where members were invited to leave their handguns in the cloakroom before entering. I fear it may have been a magnet for escort girls. We staged an annual *Tatler* Debutante Ball, an almost unimaginable event, held in the Leninist House of the Unions on Bolshaya Dmitrovka, at which seventeen-year-old daughters of billionaire oligarchs and legacy Communist apparatchiks waltzed in white dresses with male leads from the Bolshoi Ballet. As you surveyed the dance floor, you saw the daughter of Putin's Press Secretary, Dmitry Peskov, the granddaughter of Shostakovich, the daughter of Energy Minister Novak and ex-Foreign Minister Shevardnadze, all whirling about with their partners in the old Council of Trade Unions building, used for the lying-in-state of Lenin, Stalin, Brezhnev and Andropov after their deaths.

Jonathan Newhouse said his older Newhouse relations would have been horrified at the thought of doing business in Communist Russia, though the profits would have helped them get over it.

My children sometimes asked, 'What do you actually do on

these trips, Dad? Apart from go to parties?' The answer was: we held long, long meetings, at which we reviewed advertising numbers by brand. (Prada down 6 per cent, why? What can we do to reverse that? Can the Milan office intervene? Tag Heuer is up 12 per cent. Fendi up 22 per cent. Good.) Armani has an issue with their advertising positioning, they demand to run ahead of the Chanel ads. Chanel has a problem with positioning, they insist on being ahead of Dior. Gucci Group has a problem, they can't understand why they're behind Dior, and are also unhappy about the positioning for Bottega Veneta and Alexander McQueen. Dior has a problem – and this goes right to the top. Bernard Arnault, owner of LVMH, is furious; he cannot accept that Loewe is running behind Armani.

We reviewed circulation, we reviewed profitability on events. We reviewed margins. We reviewed staff issues, FTEs [Full Time Equivalent staff numbers], we reviewed the oil price. Moscow is the only Condé Nast market where the oil price is always Slide One in any presentation. Then I would visit the various Editors in their offices, review upcoming issues, front covers and exchange gossip. Then we all went out for lunch.

The Russian magazines are intriguing. Russian *Vogue* was full of fur, a bold, graphic edition. Russian *Tatler* was filled with interviews with oligarchs' wives, and reviews of the English boarding schools where they sent their children. It made more profit than the British edition of *Tatler*. Russian *GQ* was challenging, since Putin's anti-gay laws included a ban on fashion photographs with homoerotic overtones. It was goodbye to *Brokeback Mountain* cowboy fashion shoots.

Our Russian Editors were remarkable. Earlier in this chapter, I lauded the Indian Editors and so it was with the Muscovites. Victoria Davydova of *Vogue*, Ksenia Solovieva of *Tatler*, Masha Fedorova of *Glamour*, Eugenia Mikulina of *AD* . . . I could go on. They were appealingly well read. At Russian schools, they study Somerset Maugham and Conan Doyle as part of the English syllabus. Does any British school still do this?

One morning, as temperatures dropped to polar levels, I strolled off as usual to the office. I was wearing a suit, overcoat, no hat. The streets were filled with Russian women in fur coats and fur hats.

At the halfway mark, my head turned blue with cold, not as a turn of phrase, but literally blue from the neck up, then a migraine erupted. It was −30°. My lips grew icicles, I could no longer think. I was blabbering to myself. Somehow, I staggered into the office. I bought a fur hat at lunchtime in GUM. Whenever the *Daily Mail* announces 'the Beast from the East' is arriving in Kent, I say, 'Pah!' The Beast from Siberia . . . now you're talking.

We were in a review meeting when the building began to shake. At first I thought it was just me, but then everyone bolted for the staircase. Russia's worst earthquake in years had hit the capital. Seven thousand kilometres away, under the Sea of Okhotsk, a volcano had erupted, and Moscow was in full tremor. It was like exercising on a vibration plate in the gym. As we filed outside the Condé Nast building, tiles crashed down from the rooftops of adjacent buildings.

That evening, I returned to the hotel, but the pavement was barred by policemen. 'You cannot enter.' Inside, through revolving doors, I could see yellow police exclusion tape. A security guy shrugged, 'Murder. There has been a murder.'

And so there had been. A checking-in guest had been approached from behind by two gunmen and shot in the head. He died instantly. The gunmen scarpered. Both hotel and police were commendably efficient. In less than twenty minutes, the yellow tape was gone, normal life carrying on.

I asked the concierge, 'What happened?'

He rolled his eyes. 'Nothing happened. This is Moscow.'

With the lovely Anita, I went to the ballet, to parties, we chose new Publishers and Editors. We had dinners with advertisers, often with the owner or executives from Mercury, which controls half the luxury brands in Russia, as well as the Barvikha Luxury Village, the super-bling shopping hamlet near the Odintsovsky District where Vladimir Putin and his cronies have homes in a gated community. Or we went to visit the Tretyakov Museum, or Dasha Zhukova and Roman Abramovich's gallery in Gorky Park, named Garage.

One day, there was alarming news. The Russian government, in response to one round of Western sanctions or other, was introducing a new law, the Foreign Media Ownership Law, designed to prevent foreign publishers from owning Russian titles. The general idea was that we should sell them off to Putin's mates at knock-down prices. The Politburo, frequently paranoid, was concerned that American and German publishers might drip-feed anti-regime propaganda into their media, fanning sedition and undermining Putin's Russia.

For a year, we invented different ways of complying with the letter of the law, while somehow ensuring Condé Nast retained control, and the Newhouse family retained the profits. My sacred task was to ensure the Newhouses never suffered. We held meetings in the Kremlin with Press Secretary Peskov, and were amused by the piles of free postcards in the waiting room of a macho, shirtless President riding a Siberian horse. Peskov was disarmingly charming, declaring he read *Vogue* and *Tatler* every issue.

We had meetings with Nikolay Nikiforov, Minister of Communications and Mass Media, who enquired about Kate Moss. We had a showdown meeting back at the Kremlin with Alexander

Zharov, when Anita and I and our lawyer sat on one side of a vast conference table, and two dozen Russian officials faced us on the other, beneath Russian Federation flags. For two hours, we communicated through interpreters, presenting our ingenious new corporate structure. Nobody cracked a smile. There was an impressive socialist realist relief decorating the room, with sculptures of factory workers holding spanners and peasants holding rakes.

At the very end of the meeting, Mr Zharov, who I had assumed spoke not a word of English, said, 'I am perfectly satisfied with this new structure. I understand that editorial responsibility and accountability rests with Russian citizens, but the profits will flow to the Americans. That is acceptable. The Russian Federation is not concerned with these profits.'

Visiting Munich, after Moscow and Mumbai, felt like being chauffeured in a top-of-the-range Mercedes, comfortably within the speed limit, following rides in sports cars and autorickshaws. Munich is an under-appreciated city: courteous, bourgeois, unexpectedly beautiful with its skyline of Bavarian churches, the neo-Gothic Neue Rathaus and an almost unworldly sense of order and calm. And so it was at Condé Nast Verlag. If a Condé Nast staff member ever resigned, they gave a year's notice and worked to the last day. Our magazines were engineered with the precision of a BMW, smooth and perfectly tooled, and built to last.

German Condé Nast occupied a preposterously grand headquarters building in Karlstrasse. It felt like the headquarters of Lehman Brothers before the crash: monolithic, overwhelming, with giant atriums and vistas of empty space. It was the final legacy of Bernd Runge, who had created for himself a vast duplex office, large enough to later house the entire staff of *Architectural Digest*.

By the time I arrived on the scene, the joint was run by Moritz von Laffert, a dashing young Bavarian aristocrat whose family owned forests in old East Germany. He was smart, likeable, a professional publisher. At weekends, he hunted boar, and the basement of his suburban Munich home contained a butchery room where he skinned and prepared them himself. During Oktoberfest, he wore the family lederhosen. For dinner, we ate in venison restaurants.

For decades, the predictability and correctness of the German people had made the company rich. German readers were more loyal to the magazines they read than in any other market. If you took *Vogue*, you took *Vogue* every issue, without fail, probably purchasing it at the same railway kiosk. If you were a *Glamour* reader, that is what you bought: *Glamour*. German readers showed none of the promiscuity of the British, who play the field like Tinder users.

German advertising clients and media agencies were similarly reliable. They booked their pages year after year, seldom quibbling over price. In London, a brand like Chanel would spin out an advertising negotiation for months, chiselling a few hundred pounds from a million-pound contract. In Germany, the price was the price.

I had to be careful what I said in Munich, since, unlike anywhere else, staff had a tendency to take up suggestions. If I told a British Editor that their typeface was too small and hard to read, or they should add more beauty pages, nothing happened. They would think about it, discuss it with their teams, and have several compelling reasons not to do it at all.

In Germany, it was instant action. 'Herr Coleridge says the type is too small. Change it overnight! Action stations – alter all pages at the printers . . .'

The German titles are more inflexible in design and more

orderly than other editions. When German *GQ* published an article about cufflinks, it showcased sixteen pairs, all of equal size: four rows of four. When British *GQ* ran a similar piece, one or two cufflinks would be blown up big, dominating the page, with other pairs diminutive. In German men's magazines, the concept of the 'Gentleman' – all but extinct elsewhere – still thrived: the Gentleman's collection of prestige watches, the Gentleman's closet of shiny brogues and loafers, the Gentleman's briefcase.

Sometimes I felt that the historic, cultural lineage of Condé Nast – the line of descent that runs from Iva Patcevitch and Alexander Liberman to the present day – was more intact in Munich than anywhere. The Editor of German *Vogue*, Christiane Arp, had the most rigid idea of what was, and what wasn't, *Vogue*. Black and white fashion images, Helmut Newton, Karl Lagerfeld, contemporary sculpture, a certain elegance: all this was her *Vogue*. She was horrified when hip-hop stars and celebrities started appearing on *Vogue* front covers elsewhere, in American *Vogue* especially. 'But it isn't *Vogue*.'

'Shouldn't we have more celebrities in the German magazines?' I would propose from time to time, like a Vandal at the Gates of Rome.

'You forget,' I would be told, 'we *have no celebrities* here in Germany. We aren't a yellow press publishing house [derogatory term for gossip publisher]. We are Condé Nast Verlag.'

Of all the Condé Nast companies, the French was the chicest. Probably the Italians came close. But the combination of a headquarters on the Faubourg Saint-Honoré, next to the Élysée Palace, the habitual air of hauteur of its staff, and the fact that French *Vogue* is correctly named *Paris Vogue* (thus signalling itself as more sophisticated than any other edition) gave it the edge. And it lay at the very epicentre of the fashion industry. If you draw up a list of the fashion brands that really count, those with pedigree, the top ten are almost all French, headquartered within a short walk of our offices.

For half a dozen years, I visited the Paris office for business reviews six times a year. First Carine Roitfeld, then Emmanuelle Alt were *Vogue* Editors-in-Chief, Central Casting fashion mavens. It was a world of Le Smoking, of low-level squabbles with Nicolas Ghesquière of Balenciaga (now Louis Vuitton), of film noir, of models puffing on Gitanes in fashion shoots. The French issues were gloriously disdainful, never pandering to the readers. If our editorial version is too chic for you, if it's too intellectual, well, ·shrugs·, read something else. Alexandra Shulman's British *Vogue* sold three times as many copies as *Paris Vogue*, and made four times the profit, but this was of no consequence to the keepers of the sacred flame.

The French Company was run by an elegant boulevardier, Xavier Romatet, who in another life could have been a movie actor. By disposition a pessimist, he was paradoxically a risk-taker who brought *Vanity Fair* to France.

During this decade of executive travel, I lived by two rules: never permit yourself to appear tired or jet-lagged during a country visit, and never yawn, regardless of how many presentations a market throws at you. Sometimes there were a dozen, running sequentially, and it became a matter of pride to be alert till the end. Irrespective of what business you're in, the routine of a senior executive visiting a reporting market is the same. The long flight sitting towards the front of the plane, luggage carousels, cars, hotel receptions, agendas, presentations, lunches, dinners, reviews, reports, long flight home.

Whoever runs the business day-to-day is intent upon you seeing only the bits they want you to see, and hearing what they want you to hear. Your visit is as often an intrusion as a benefit. But in magazines I felt lucky, because the people I worked with were witty and civilized, and enhanced my life.

I organized my travel so that, wherever I'd been that week, and however far away, I always landed back at Heathrow as close to 6 p.m. on Friday evening as possible. Brian drove me to Wolverton while I slumped in the back of the car.

As long as I could wake up on Saturday morning in our own bed, with the light streaming through our own curtains, I could survive.

27

In the thirty years since I'd written my university dissertation in the National Art Library at the Victoria and Albert Museum, the V&A had been the museum I visited most regularly. Several of the areas I collect, including Indian miniature painting and fashion photography, have their national collections there, and it has always felt like a museum with the widest scope: from Medieval and Renaissance to contemporary, with deep collections of South Asian treasures, British paintings, Mick Jagger and Adam Ant's stage costumes, the Victorian Cast Courts, and a rapid-response unit collecting iPods and Amazon drones.

Furthermore, I love the South Kensington building with its Aston Webb facade (the architect who also designed the principal facade of Buckingham Palace, the Queen Victoria Memorial and Admiralty Arch) and seven miles of galleries and Stygian passageways, impossible to navigate. There are multiple unexpected courtyards and staircases. All this had always intrigued me.

Photographed from the sky, the museum looks impossibly large and sprawling, a whole village, occupying six blocks between the Natural History Museum and the Brompton Oratory.

I heard there was a Trustee vacancy on the museum board, and applied. It was the first time I'd gone for a government appointment since the Royal College of Art; in fact, the first time I'd applied for anything in decades. I thought it would be stimulating to see how another organization works, having worked for so long inside Condé Nast, and the subject matter appealed.

The Chairman of the V&A was the hedge fund tycoon Sir Paul Ruddock, and it was he who interviewed me. He sat on one side of a table, flanked by his deputy, Samir Shah, and two alert women from the Public Appointments Office. The questions were simple enough, and I felt it had gone okay. Nothing then happened for weeks and weeks, until a letter arrived signed by the Prime Minister, David Cameron, saying I was in.

I found the V&A intriguing. I recognized many parallels with Condé Nast: the Keepers and Senior Curators felt like Editors-in-Chief, presiding over their own large departments, knowledgeable, siloed, chiefly preoccupied by their own fiefdoms. The Development Department was like a Condé Nast advertising team, intent on raising exhibition sponsorships from many of the same clients, but also rattling the begging bowl at a muster of philanthropists and donors. In the magazine world, we fretted about circulation: that was an important measure of our success. In museums, it is visitor numbers. Footfall is monitored daily, not only in absolute numbers but by demography: foreign visitors versus domestic, London visitors versus regional, old versus young, ethnic groups by sub-category. The demography of the V&A struck me as a cultural superblend of all the Condé Nast magazine segments at once: smart Knightsbridge ladies, Fine Arts and Applied Arts students, scholars, LGBTQIA supporters (the museum runs gender and sexual identity tours), BAME artists and designers, tech geeks, Guildford day-trippers, fashionistas, jewellers: all passing through the Cromwell Road revolving doors.

But there were differences: the V&A belonged to the British government, ultimately to the nation, rather than the Newhouse family, and was run by a board populated by alpha-males and alpha-females, almost all accustomed to having the last word in their day jobs. We met six times a year for board meetings, and triple that for committees, in a boardroom above the Secretariat arch. A bust of our founder, Prince Albert, stands on an exuberant Renaissance-style fireplace by James Gamble for Minton, Hollins & Co. Above the fireplace hangs a portrait of Queen Victoria by Heinrich von Angeli, on loan from Prince Michael of Kent.

To my mind, it is rather a gloomy boardroom, not helped by black wallpaper. I had no idea how much of my life was destined to be spent inside it, at meetings and dinners.

The Director of the V&A was Dr Martin Roth, an East German professor, broad-shouldered and distinguished, with a thick head of grey hair. He had arrived a couple of years earlier from the Staatliche Kunstsammlungen Dresden – the fifteen museums which comprise Dresden's art collection. He had an international reputation as a museum visionary and philosopher. By the time I joined the board, many of his qualities were already being re-evaluated and marked down, and there was a prevailing air of anxiety. It didn't help that his English was imperfect. A man of unexpected flashes of warmth, and sudden imparted confidences (he would pour out his feelings in the back of a car), he found day-to-day decision making at the museum onerous, and his relations with several of the curators was bumpy. It was cultural disconnect. Accustomed to the sleek obedience of the German curatorial tradition, Martin was confounded by the dusty, serpentine, diva-like wilfulness of British scholarship, which was how he saw it.

The museum Martin directed was entering a golden period. Many of the building projects initiated under the directorship of Sir Mark Jones – the Medieval Renaissance Galleries, the European Galleries, the half-built Exhibition Road Quarter – were already open or shortly would be, and visitor numbers spiralled. A succession of hit exhibitions about David Bowie and

Alexander McQueen were drawing huge crowds. In the days of Sir Roy Strong, the V&A had 1 million visitors a year, now it was 3.5 million.

What does the Board of Trustees of a national museum actually do? We heard reports from the Director, reports from the Chairman, reviewed exhibition plans, debated whether or not to build new V&A museums in Scotland and China, we tried not to go bust. We discussed governance issues and education issues, we deliberated on whether or not to repair the roof of the Porter Gallery or to renovate the Chinese Galleries. We debated whether to accept sponsorship money from tobacco companies (no) or donations from borderline-dodgy individuals (possibly no, possibly yes, depending). We received reports from Keepers about sculpture and ceramics, and whether we could afford to acquire this treasure or that for the collection.

I enjoyed the contrasting board styles of my fellow Trustees: Mark Damazer (Master of St Peter's College, Oxford, former Controller of BBC Radio 4 – forensically brainy, you could see the muscle of his intellect moving inside his egghead), Sir John Sorrell (designer and creative industries guru – softly spoken, instinctively right), Andrew Hochhauser QC (commercial barrister – passionate, trenchant), Dame Theresa Sackler (civilized, sincere, only speaking when she had something worth saying), Edmund de Waal (ceramicist, author – clever, thoughtful), Paul Thompson (RCA Rector – ex officio, experienced). And, in the Chair, Paul Ruddock: a Tom Wolfe Master of the Universe, hedge fund rich, brisk, urgent, but also a collector of Medieval reliquaries and Ethiopian Coptic icons. There was something of Cardinal Wolsey about Paul, striving, connected, acquisitive, that I admired. There were others on the board too, but those are the ones I summon up most clearly from those early days.

It was rewarding to get to know the Keepers and executives of the museum: Julius Bryant of Word and Image, Anna Jackson of the Asian Department, Jane Lawson the Development Chief, with whom I reviewed lists of impossibly rich people we hoped might help us. Antonia Bostrom joined as Keeper of Sculpture, Metalwork, Ceramics and Glass from the Nelson-Atkins Museum in Kansas City, and I sent her rather a formal note of welcome. She replied, 'You have obviously forgotten we know each other already, we used to go to the same parties in Rupert Forbes Adam's bedroom in Mulberry Walk.' It was a whole new world, but an oddly familiar one. And I relished it.

A scheme was being floated to build a new cultural district in East London, on the banks of the River Lea on the Olympic Park. It was a Boris Johnson brainwave. He was Mayor of London, and had a vision for universities and museums filling the vast, empty margins of Queen Elizabeth Park, where the Olympic Games had recently been held. It would be a gargantuan regeneration project, putting Stratford on the cultural map and providing a cultural focus for expanding East London. Boris already had a catchy name for his vision – Olympicopolis – and he wanted the Victoria and Albert Museum to be part of it. So did George Osborne. It was their joint legacy project. So Boris approached Martin Roth, who liked the idea, and soon Paul and the board had committed to be part of it. We would build a brand-new museum from scratch – V&A East – next to a brand-new Smithsonian Institute from Washington, a brand-new Sadler's Wells theatre, a brand-new University of the Arts, London College of Fashion . . . it was gloriously ambitious. We could not possibly have predicted the months and years of planning, plotting, anguish and elation that lay ahead.

★

Paul was approaching the end of his second term as Chairman, and the search for his replacement would shortly begin. The process by which Chairs are appointed to national museums and galleries is complicated and protracted, involving an external search company, an appointments committee of the great and the good, longlists, shortlists and interviews. Ultimately it is a Prime Ministerial appointment, and the PM retains a right of veto and the right to select the winner from a shortlist. But the interviews are conducted by a five-person panel, chaired by a grandee from the Cabinet Office.

For two months I pondered on whether or not to go for it. I had been told there would be at least seventy candidates (anyone can apply, it's an open contest), so the odds weren't great. And the prospect of going for something, and then not getting it, never appeals. I prefer pushing at an open door. Ever since my teenage party days in Hampshire, I have a fear of being rebuffed, or of appearing presumptuous.

I did not share my tortuous inner turmoil with Georgia. Her default position is always to encourage me to take on less, not more. But I had fallen in love with the Victoria and Albert Museum, and it played on my mind.

We spent Christmas with the children in Goa. Each day, we swam in the rough sea off Fort Aguada. I was always thinking, 'Dare I go for it?'

I was haunted by a track by the Norwegian singer Ane Brun, 'The Opening'. I was listening to it all day on an iPod. The lyrics felt prescient: 'Do you wanna rediscover, or do you want it all to be over? / Do you want to see the meaning of the circling? / It's up to you . . . / It's not too late to find an opening.'

I filled in the application forms and sent them off, then disappeared on a Condé Nast tour of Mumbai, Moscow, Munich and the Geneva Watch Fair. The Geneva Watch Fair and the Basel

Watch Fair had become annual gigs, filled with our luxury advertisers. My role was to attend twenty-minute encounters with the
CEOs of forty Swiss watchmakers, one after another, and express
rapt admiration for their million-dollar timepieces, each with
more diamonds and 'complications' than the one before. The
luxury watch industry is the only place where a 'complication' –
such as some special mechanism to track the ocean's tides, or the
orbit of the planets – is seen as a positive. Most of these watches
were destined to be sold to Chinese and Nigerian customers who
paid in cash.

A message arrived to say I had made the V&A longlist, then
the shortlist. Then another to say I was required for interview.
Would I be available for ninety minutes at the Treasury, where
they were to be conducted?

Shortly before the interviews, I received a telephone call
from a minister. 'So . . . you're in the last six, Nick. Want to
know who else is on it?'

'Am I allowed to know?'

'Of course not! That's why I'm ringing you from outside on
the pavement on Parliament Street. I shouldn't give you names,
but by my assessment you're in the final four. But you have a
serious problem.'

'I do?'

'You're not a woman. There are two credible female candidates.'

'Not much I can do about that, is there, at short notice?'

'No. But the other man in the final four probably won't get
it, just a hunch.'

'Well, thank you for the intel.'

The minister rang off.

The big day arrived. The interview was like a scene from a
film: vast Edwardian conference room with frescoed ceiling,

vast mahogany table, the panel of five, a dozen civil servants seated behind them, taking notes. The Chair of the Appointment Panel was a man in a wheelchair from the Cabinet Office, who looked serious and impervious to charm. It was reassuring to see friendlier faces in Mark Damazer and the Carphone Warehouse co-founder, David Ross.

I replied to the questions as best I could. Although being an existing Trustee is not seen as an advantage to appointment, I think it was helpful to know the lie of the land. The grilling seemed to be going okay.

The Chair suddenly said, 'Mr Coleridge, I must now ask you a *very serious and important question*. Please give proper consideration before replying to it. Is there anything you have done in your life – *anything at all, at any time* – that, were it to come out later, might cause embarrassment to the Prime Minister, to the Secretary of State for Culture, Media and Sport, and to the institution you seek to chair?'

Until that moment, I had responded to every question gravely and with utmost seriousness, but now I felt levity rising up, at exactly the wrong moment.

'Well, the whole of my Cambridge student days have just flashed before my eyes. I'm rather relieved this committee wasn't there to witness all that.'

The appointments panel chuckled away.

Except one.

'That was a *serious question*, Mr Coleridge.'

I felt chided.

'Finally, Mr Coleridge,' he went on, 'I am sure you are fully conversant with Lord Nolan's Seven Principles of Public Life. Tell us, which of his Seven Principles do you hold to be the most important?'

There is an episode in Tom Wolfe's novel *A Man in Full* when

the Atlanta real estate developer Charlie Croker is being threatened with foreclosure by a group of activist investors. Under
the onslaught, he develops saddlebags of sweat under his arm-
pits. I was now experiencing my own Charlie Croker moment.
I had read the Seven Principles, but not for a few years. Could I
remember one?

'I'm going to say "Integrity",' I replied eventually, as though
carefully deliberating between the entire list of seven, 'since
everything else flows from that.'

'Thank you, Mr Coleridge,' said the Chair. 'We have no further questions. You are dismissed.'

Outside on Horse Guards, I googled the Seven Nolan Principles. There *is* a God: integrity is one of the seven.

As is the nature of these things, nothing whatever was heard
for several weeks, then urgent action. A call from the Cabinet
Appointments Office: 'The Prime Minister is minded to appoint
you Chair of the V&A. Can you confirm you are still able to do
it? We need to announce the appointment tomorrow morning,
because Parliament is going into pre-election purdah at midday.'

A letter of confirmation from 10 Downing Street was cour-
iered later that same day.

28

On my first official morning as Chairman of the Victoria and Albert Museum, I padded downstairs to collect the newspapers off the doormat. It is my routine to read them in the bath with a cup of coffee. The headline of the *Daily Telegraph* leapt out. It said: 'V&A rejects Lady Thatcher's gift of her clothes to the nation.'

There followed the startling information that the museum had 'dissed' Thatcher's legacy, and several Tory MPs were quoted saying how appalled and outraged they were. It was the first I'd heard of it. Nobody had mentioned any snub to Mrs T. On the Radio 4 *Today* programme, Norman Tebbit was already at full throttle on the subject. He wasn't the least bit surprised: the V&A is a notorious nest of lefties, he asserted. Boris Johnson was next man up: the museum had made a cataclysmic, ideological blunder.

I rang Martin Roth, but the Director was at a conference in Venice. He was frequently at conferences somewhere or other, often Rwanda. His office knew nothing about any Thatcher clothes. Paul Ruddock didn't either. It was disconcerting. Meanwhile, every news organization in the world was piling in on the story. The *Guardian* and *Independent* were congratulating the V&A on their principled stand. The *Daily Mail* was fanning the outrage. The *New York Times* was 'going big with it', *BBC News at One* was rounding up further incensed MPs and wanted to film them sounding off inside the museum.

The Secretary of State for Culture, Media and Sport was requesting an urgent briefing on our decision, as was Number

Ten. After three hours, I still couldn't find a soul at the museum who knew anything about it. I rang Charles Moore, *Daily Telegraph* columnist and Thatcher biographer, for any lowdown. He made swift enquiries.

It seemed that, five or six years earlier, at a big dinner held at the British Museum, Lady Thatcher's executor, Sir Julian Seymour,★ had floated the possibility of the V&A one day taking some of her dresses for the archive. He had been chatting over coffee to one of the museum team. She hadn't mentioned the overture to the Director. That was it. The museum had never rejected the bequest, nor even considered it, because they hadn't known about it.

Carol Thatcher rang me from a ski resort. 'Cripes, Nick,' she said, 'what's all this codswallop about Mummy's old clothes? You haven't been offered any.'

But the story was too good to die, it was unstoppable. It ran and ran. To this day, we are variously applauded or condemned for spurning the Thatcher power suits, depending on who's talking. Shortly afterwards, Julian Seymour and the Thatcher children kindly organized a gift of several of Lady T's best outfits and some handbags, and these now live at the V&A, for anyone to inspect.

I found myself spending multiple hours a week on museum business, drawn deeper and deeper into the South Kensington vortex. Astoundingly, we were now working on five major building projects; headed by the half-completed Exhibition Road project, designed by the architect Amanda Levete,† still a

★ Director of Lady Thatcher's private office. Communications executive.
† Stirling Prize-winning British architect. The Museum of Art, Architecture and Technology, Lisbon.

deep hole in the ground when I became Chairman. It was the most ambitious and expensive intervention in the museum's history, a £54 million miracle of engineering, with a vast new underground Sainsbury Gallery inserted between two Grade I buildings, the new porcelain-tiled Sackler Courtyard above, and at the time, a yet-to-be-named and yet-to-be-paid-for new entrance hall. I stared down into the muddy abyss, four storeys deep, and wondered what would happen if the Aston Webb facade and the Henry Cole building toppled over into the excavations; it seemed all too possible.

Meanwhile, the V&A galleries in Shekou, in the Chinese city of Shenzhen, were rising above the Pearl River Delta. The new V&A in Dundee, a miraculous design like a ship in full sail by the Japanese architect Kengo Kuma, was rising over the Tay. (The locals were already calling it the V&Tay.) And, out on the Olympic Park, some initial (rather dreary) designs were being imagined for V&A East. Martin Roth and I made multiple visits to Stratford in East London, along with the Deputy Director, Tim Reeve, who was leading the charge. If you added together the cost of all these projects, they exceeded £300 million. It was mildly alarming.

I was summoned by Boris Johnson, still Mayor of London, to City Hall. He held strong opinions on what the new V&A East should look like, and wanted to make sure I was fully on side. His vision was a million miles from the brief already issued by his team to the architects, and he was in classic, barnstorming, Boris form.

'We don't want some stunted, Eastern Bloc, Communist state, post-Corbusian monstrosity. What we want is a cross between the British Museum and the V&A in South Kensington, something *magnificent* rising above the Olympic Park. We want Corinthian columns. We want Ionic pillars. We want the

Babylonian Palace of Tiglath-Pileser! That's what we're after, Nick. That's the vision. I hope you're with me on this.'

Sitting behind the Mayor, the representatives of the London Legacy Development Corporation looked increasingly anxious, and began muttering about budgets and the 'public realm'. They communicated with the Mayor as though he was the slightly wilful eight-year-old child of a maharaja, who needed humouring. There was much appeasing laughter.

Boris replied, 'Budgets, budgets . . . we're all in favour of budgets. If we need more money, we'll find it. Remind me to call Michael Bloomberg★ and Lakshmi Mittal.† In fact, get me Lakshmi on the phone now. No, I'll call him myself, he's on this mobile somewhere.' Boris began punching numbers on the speed dial. 'Hello? Hello? Lakshmi? Is that you? Boris here. Where are you, I hear music? *Ibiza?* Yikes, Lakshmi, are you in a disco, you old swinger? Now, look here, Lakshmi, I'm going to need your help . . .'

I was getting to know Martin Roth better, and liked him a lot. He was tentative and diffuse, his mind veering off in several directions at once, but clever and international in temperament. He and his wife, Harriet, came to stay at Wolverton, and we saw a more relaxed side to him. We had breakfast together once a month in a hotel, to chew over the museum.

One summer morning he came to visit me in Vogue House. He spoke for an hour about this and that, but I sensed there was something he wasn't yet saying; he was working up to it. At last, he blurted, 'I want to quit the museum.'

★ American businessman. Founder and owner, Bloomberg L.P. Mayor of New York City (2001–13).
† Indian steel magnate. Three houses on Kensington Palace Gardens collectively valued at £500 million.

'Why on earth?'

He waved his hand in the air. All sorts of reasons, family reasons, their children lived far away in Berlin and Vancouver. 'My job here is done.' Harriet was lonely in London. Other projects . . . It was a long list.

Martin was flying to Canada the next day on holiday, I was flying with my family to Iran. I tried to persuade him not to resign, to think about it. 'If you did leave, do you have a date in mind?'

'Two weeks?' said Martin.

'That's insane. You have a six-month rolling contract.'

We agreed to keep it quiet until after our respective holidays, but discussed a tentative announcement for the autumn. I informed the Board.

On the eve of our announcement, it leaked in the *Sunday Times*. 'V&A's German Director resigns in protest over Brexit.'

Martin rang me at dawn. 'It has nothing to do with Brexit. I honestly don't know where that came from.'

But, as the week unfolded, Martin rather warmed to the Brexit narrative, and the positive reaction it was getting in the arts community, and was soon running with it. He gave interviews about a growing xenophobia across Europe and the perils of nationalism, and soon the Brexit referendum result became the only reason for his resignation. He departed the V&A in glory, the museum having just been named Museum of the Year. Tragically, he died of cancer within months, though he only became aware of the illness after he left the museum.

There are multiple strands to a national museum's mission, each prioritized by different clusters.

For many curators, the care and acquisition of the collections is the overriding purpose; scholarship and study. The impulse to add more objects to their department's archive, to plug gaps, to accrue more treasures, can be a craving close to kleptomania. They pore over catalogues from auction houses, butter-up collectors, thrilling to the chase. Every couple of months, a new piece will be identified – a rare print, a precious scroll, a Qing Dynasty bowl – and declared 'a once-in-a-generation opportunity to acquire'. Then the Development team cranks into action, seeking a willing philanthropist to fund the purchase.

But other groups see the museum's primary mission as educational, galvanizing schoolchildren with our treasures. Or industrial, inspiring the next generation of manufacturers and designers. The government tends to evaluate the success of museums and galleries by visitor figures, as tangible evidence of taxpayers' money hitting the spot, so crowd-pleasing exhibitions are always front of mind.

I quickly came to love the intrigues which incubate around museums, the politics and courtships to secure this treasure or that, frequently in direct competition with other suitors; sagas played out in multiple acts.

The saga of Clive of India's flask – the gold, jade, emerald and ruby carafe presented to Robert Clive after the Battle of Plassey – and the threat of its export from the V&A to Qatar and the Doha Museum of Islamic Art, was a gold-plated saga, involving whispery meetings with sheikhs and princes from Paris to Hyderabad.

One sheikh was so concerned that the hotel butlers serving tea might be eavesdropping on our conversation that we whispered to each other behind a hedge beyond his private swimming pool, plotting and planning.

There was the successful intrigue over Queen Victoria's sapphire and diamond coronet, designed as an engagement present to his wife by Prince Albert, saved from export to Singapore and now in pride of place in the Bollinger jewellery gallery.

The V&A jewellery curator, Richard Edgcumbe, played a decisive role.

There was the episode surrounding the Fabergé gift from the Snowman family of Wartski, and the episode of the Harewood House Chippendale tables and pier glass mirrors. All these unfolding goings-on fed my affection for the museum. And, every day, newer acquisitions were arriving: rare copies of the *Oz* 'Schoolkids' issue; Grayson Perry's Brexit vases; a vast brutalist chunk of Robin Hood Gardens, the demolished housing estate in Poplar, East London; Beyoncé's 'Papillon' ring; Tommy Cooper's 'gag file' of jokes; Hoefnagel's 1568 watercolour of Henry VIII's Nonsuch Palace; Prince the rock star's black satin shoes . . .

We embarked on a process to find a new Director, working with the search firm Saxton Bamfylde. In Britain, anyone can apply to be Director of a national museum and, as the applications rolled in, it became clear that almost everyone had. Hearing there was a vacancy at the top of the V&A, random people all over the world had eureka moments, thinking, 'I could be the new Director. Why not me?'

Antiques dealers, curators, National Trust tour guides, museum Directors from Holland to Houston, all gave it a whirl. I took the complete set of files of applicants home to read over the weekend. The top one in the pile was from a cinema usher at a Vue cinema in the West Midlands; he had no experience at all, beyond guiding people to their seats with his torch. He didn't see this as a problem, he would be bringing 'fresh eyes'. Another applicant said she worked in a crab shack near Polzeath, but 'fancied a change of scenery'. Other candidates were more plausible.

In the end, there were 22 credibles, 10 strong and 6 very strong, including wild cards. Our appointments committee comprised three Trustees (Mark Damazer, the academic Professor Margot Finn, McKinsey's Nick Hoffman), me and Dame Sue Owen,

Permanent Secretary at the Department of Culture, Media and Sport, whom I hadn't met properly before, but liked on sight. Compact, dynamic, with a Twiggy-style bob, she packs a punch. Six candidates became three, three became two. Curatorial skills versus management experience, reliability versus risk, corduroy trousers versus metrosexual suit, communication skills, people skills, academic credentials, x-factor, all were weighed. All weekend, the debate raged on, but it was stalemate. One colleague argued against falling into the trap 'of being seduced by a candidate's charisma, charm and verbal skills'.

I called an extraordinary meeting of the whole V&A board, and both finalists had an hour to project their vision, followed by questions. Both performed strongly. I asked Trustees to go home and sleep on it, and send me their preferences by 4 p.m. the following day, a Saturday.

From 10 a.m., votes began to trickle in, then came in a rush. By teatime, we had chosen Dr Tristram Hunt, Labour MP for Stoke on Trent Central, as the new Director. He had been Shadow Secretary of State for Education, and he resigned to Jeremy Corbyn a couple of days later, after his appointment at the museum had been ratified by the Prime Minister, Theresa May.

Tristram's appointment was big news, front page of the broadsheets. It was a miracle there had been no leak, there could so easily have been: the DCMS, Downing Street, sixteen Trustees, several others who'd been canvassed for opinions and due diligence, were all in the know. By this point, I had met Tristram a total of four times, and each time been more impressed. His backlist of history books, including several on subjects of clear relevance to the V&A, his lectures at Queen Mary's College, London University, his role in helping save the Wedgwood Museum in Barlaston (now owned by the V&A), his presence and speaking skills, all boded well. And he struck me as realistic and pragmatic, and a listener, and a doer, and someone likely to click with the Keepers and curators, but also with philanthropists. All these things turned out, over time, to be true.

Boris Johnson had left City Hall for the Foreign and Commonwealth Office, and his successor as Mayor, Sadiq Khan, took a while to embrace the Olympic Park cultural project, partly on the grounds that it was Boris's big idea. We spent months conniving with Sadiq's Deputy Mayor for Culture, Justine Simons, to keep the project alive. Three times it came within a whisker of collapse, and three times it rose again from the dead. Everything that could possibly go wrong, went wrong: funding crises, aesthetic crises, political crises over provision for affordable housing. But eventually, miraculously, it all fell into place. Boris's suggested name for the district – 'Olympicopolis' – was quietly dropped as too elitist, and replaced by East Bank, which certainly isn't, and the project rolled on.

V&A East's architects, O'Donnell + Tuomey, came up with a new, innovative museum design, ostensibly inspired by a Balenciaga couture dress in the V&A fashion collection, but reminding me of Darth Vader's helmet. There wasn't a trace of a Corinthian column or Babylonian frieze in the whole scheme, but it has impact. In our competitive way, we wanted V&A East to be the standout building on the cultural strip, the one that gets chosen to illustrate every article about East Bank, the landmark elevation. And then, if things weren't complicated enough already, we embarked on a scheme to move the V&A's entire reserve collection of two million treasures from Blythe House in Olympia to new super-sleek, open-access storage in Stratford, close to V&A East. The New York High Line architects, Diller Scofidio + Renfro, were chosen to design a glorious new edifice, a glass-floored Tutankhamun's tomb.

There is an informal network of museum Chairs, and I was grateful to be included, because it enabled me to pick up all sorts of nuances I wouldn't otherwise have grasped. Sir Richard Lambert, whom I had known when he was editor of the *Financial Times*, was Chairman of the British Museum; a tall, friendly figure of distinction, who always correctly predicted the outcome of the next governmental spending review. Dame Mary Archer, Chair of the Science Museum, was impeccably turned out and organized; deceptively stern, but actually warm. We had a custom of visiting each other's exhibitions as they opened – a Chairs' tour with curator – and swapped intel about ministers between exhibits. Or else we met, in wider conclave, at regular Chairs' breakfasts hosted by Sir Nicholas Serota at the Arts Council in Bloomsbury.

I accompanied Mary and Jeffrey Archer around the V&A Opera exhibition with a curator, and Jeffrey was in prime form. Spotting a small canvas by Degas on display of the interior of an opera box, he declared, 'I don't know why you didn't ask to borrow my Degas of an opera scene? Nobody asked me.' Then, turning to me, he said, 'You probably know this already, young man, but one should always hang one's best pictures on the walls of the lavatory. That's what I do. My Degas and a Picasso, both in the loo. When friends visit us, I ask, "Did you like the Degas and the Picasso in the loo?" and, do you know, half the time they haven't even noticed them. They've been right there in front of them, but they never noticed them.'

Hannah Rothschild, Chair of the National Gallery, became an ally. She had been friends for years with half the people I like, but I'd never really known her properly. We had hilarious breakfasts to discuss tricky philanthropists and tricky trustees; we share the same high-low interests in culture, writing and gossip. Rupert Gavin, Chair of Historic Royal Palaces, became another world of heritage friend.

I wanted to see every last square inch of the museum. With a map, I walked the seven miles of public corridors and found every gallery, then the offices, conservation studios, delivery bays and stores. A tour of the roof was arranged, along perilous metal walkways, offering sudden unexpected views of court-yards and glimpses through skylights of galleries far below. And then, clambering rusty iron ladders to the Aston Webb dome, tier upon tier, like scaling a wedding cake, you arrived at a des-erted loggia with the best views across the rooftops of South Kensington. All that was up there were two empty cider cans and a Golden Wonder crisp packet drifting in the breeze.

I suppose I must have walked through the Cromwell Road entrance of the V&A more than a thousand times now, but you need to stop and properly look to fully appreciate it. Surely no public building will ever again be designed and built with this level of decoration and sculptural ornament? I love the sequence of thirty-two figures of British luminaries, each in niches: painters, sculptors, craftsmen and architects. Constable, Millais, Turner, William Morris, Chippendale, Wren, Wedgwood and G. F. Watts are just some of them. And the statue of Queen Vic-toria, flanked by St George and St Michael, high above the recessed entrance, and the statue of Prince Albert below, and the statues of Edward VII and Queen Alexandra. And, carved into the arch, the great quotation from Sir Joshua Reynolds which acts as a museum mission statement: *The excellence of every art must consist in the complete accomplishment of its purpose.*

New Trustees joined the board, having somehow negotiated the tortuous process to appointment. Ben Elliot, the boss of Quintessentially, was a fearless fund-raiser and much else. Ste-ven Murphy, the former CEO of Christie's, became our point-man on Chinese philanthropists, Nigel Webb of British

Land a vital expert on commercial property. Lynda Nead, the
Pevsner Professor of Art History at Birkbeck, was another good
academic hire. Caroline Silver, Mark Sebba and Nick Hoffman
kept us on the financial straight and narrow, and usefully curbed
our buccaneering tendencies without smothering them. A slick
Amex executive, Robert Glick, chaired the Commercial Development Committee.

Having been raised in the Condé Nast school of spontaneous
decision making, where everything was done on instinct, and
no Audit Committee held you to account for rotten decisions, I
was struck by the precision, process and 'terms of reference' of
a national institution. The Chairman's role, I felt, was to mod-
erate between the risk-adverse and the too risky lobbies, while
ensuring we were highly ambitious. In the end, a Board of
Trustees is judged by what it achieves, not by what it suppresses.
The parable of the servant who buries his master's talents in the
earth for safekeeping has relevance here (Matthew 25: 14–30).

You had to keep your wits constantly about you, chairing
the museum board. As Mark Damazer explained it, there is a
danger on high-powered boards of over-intervention, with
everyone pushing their particular hobby horses, returning to
them like dogs with bones. Half of our board were corporates,
half were mavericks; the corporates prioritized process, but had
a keener respect for collective responsibility and moving on
after a decision is taken. And there were individuals who wanted
to railroad the board, affronted if their opinion didn't prevail,
and reopening issues long after they were already decided. As
the saying goes: when your horse is dead, dismount.

Fund-raising was constant. The V&A has more than thirty
people engaged in it, in one guise or another, and no gallery can
be renewed, no new wing erected, no curatorial post endowed,
without a campaign. British cultural institutions have been

dependent upon a handful of mega-donors for decades – the Sainsburys, Gettys, Sacklers and Westons – plus a network of perhaps forty secondary ones, who are serial contributors. We spent months preparing pitches to foundations and to the Heritage Lottery Fund, which has been a saviour of us all.

It requires practice and courage to ask individuals for big money. The line 'What we are looking for is five million pounds' has a way of getting stuck in the throat. But I learnt: no billionaire minds being asked for money, if you ask nicely. They can say no, and usually do. But it isn't unflattering to be asked; the implication – that you can afford it – being quietly satisfying. When Sir Len Blavatnik named and funded the new Exhibition Road entrance – the Blavatnik Hall – I felt I'd earned my spurs.

We stalked new donors, tricky to identify, and trickier still to engage. Ben Elliot kick-started an International Council of younger, well-networked supporters, which brought a fresh angle to our efforts.

Tristram and I visited Hong Kong and Shanghai with Steven Murphy on a tour of philanthropists. It was like Groundhog Day, pitching to sixteen Chinese billionaires over four days, all in 100-storey office blocks. It was gold prospecting, and when a nugget hit the sieve, we were elated.

Ben Elliot made me laugh before our pitches to tycoons. Brimming with determination, he'd say, 'For fuck's sake, this guy is a billionaire twenty times over. I'm asking him for ten million. It's peanuts to him. It's like you and me giving fifty quid.'

With Jane Lawson, I visited Palm Beach and we worked our way down the length of South Ocean Boulevard, where the V&A has multiple supporters. Every Palladian-style mansion and Spanish-style hacienda is worth at least $100 million, filled to the gunnels with Caravaggios and Picassos. Our donors were very gracious, with their chilled gazpacho chowder and linen-jacketed butlers. It is a fact that elderly, rich Americans are exceptionally hospitable. Our job was to keep the museum front of mind, in the hope of triggering a donation. It's a mating dance.

Tristram has the great advantage of being liked and organized. He carries a small notebook at all times to record ideas. We riffed forthcoming exhibitions a lot, which are a challenge for museums, being unpredictable. A major show takes three years in the planning, even four years when it involves multiple loans from galleries across the world, and from private owners needing convincing. If you own a major painting – say a Canaletto or a Matisse, hanging from chains in your Shropshire stately home or Park Avenue apartment – it's a pain to have a big gap and empty hooks on the wall for months and months. Against that, you have the kudos of saying, 'I'm sorry it looks so bare without the Canaletto, but we felt we had to lend it to the V&A when they asked.'

But, after so much curatorial effort, there is no guarantee which exhibitions will draw big crowds, and which won't. The discussions reminded me of our anguished Condé Nast debates over magazine front covers – trying to predict public appetite and taste. Here are eight V&A shows, six of which were smash hits and two which did fine but nothing special.

- Maharaja: The Splendour of India's Royal Courts
- Art Deco
- Alexander McQueen: Savage Beauty
- Plywood
- Frida Kahlo: Making Her Self Up
- Balenciaga
- Opera: Passion, Power and Politics
- Ocean Liners: Speed and Style

It was the first six that were big successes in visitor numbers. But there are other considerations too – museum reputation, the balance between academic and popular shows, what's on elsewhere. Sometimes, with exhibitions like Frida Kahlo, Dior and Pink Floyd, you know you have a sure-fire banker on your hands long before they open; but, all too often, it can go either way.

It was refreshing to spend time with a new cast of characters, and the cast at the V&A is broad. There are twenty-year-old student volunteers, elderly donors, scholars of every area of art and design, shopkeepers, guides, and a revolving cast of politicians overseeing the cultural sector, some out of passion, others as a temporary berth on the way up (or down). Old acquaintances I hadn't seen for decades reappeared in my life, through the museum. It also gave me common cause with my uncle, Anthony Coleridge, who had been a Director of Christie's for forty years and wrote the definitive book on Thomas Chippendale, and who visits the museum several times a month. And we revved up the annual V&A Summer Party, filling the courtyard with a thousand guests from the creative industries, fashion designers and film producers, interior designers, potters and prime ministers, young royals, old queens, 'It girls' and IT tech girls, plus celebrities from Kylie Minogue to Kate Moss.

The Duchess of Cambridge became Royal Patron of the museum (there hadn't been one since Queen Victoria), having officially opened the Sainsbury Gallery, Sackler Courtyard and Blavatnik Hall a few months earlier. She had been a hit opening the new wing, smiley and unexpectedly tall in a Gucci suit; towering above us as she drew back the little curtain to reveal the plaque commemorating her visit. She was a neat fit as museum Patron, with her love of photography and the applied arts. Shortly afterwards, the Duchess opened our new suite of photography galleries, and it was a boost when Sir Elton John and David Furnish, and one of our new Shanghai supporters, the Chinese publisher Thomas Shao, as well as the Bern

Schwartz family of San Francisco, came through and named galleries.

By the end of 2017, visitors to the main Victoria and Albert site in South Kensington reached a record 4 million for the first time, and our new museum partnerships were spreading the V&A message across the world. I felt intensely lucky to be involved during such a period of expansion and fun. I was re-appointed for a second four-year term as V&A Chairman by Prime Minister Theresa May, at the height of the Brexit meltdown. It was surprising she found the time really, all things considered.

29

It was the Centenary Celebration year of *Vogue* (launched 1917), and we planned a huge dinner and jamboree in a marquee in Hyde Park. Very few magazines last for a hundred years, and those that do are generally limping and stumbling to the finish. But *Vogue* was storming ahead, and we wanted to make the most of the Centenary with a bonanza *Vogue* Festival, specially decorated shop windows across the nation, a Centenary issue with a royal front cover, and a Centenary *Vogue* dinner rammed with fashion designers, celebrities and friends of the magazine.

It is remarkable that British *Vogue* had been launched at all in the middle of the First World War, while the Battle of the Somme was raging. There was paper rationing and clothes rationing, and I would like to have listened in on the business case discussion: 'Gentlemen, we have no paper to print it on, and no clothes to photograph, but this is the perfect moment to start a luxury fashion magazine. We must strike while the iron is hot . . .' Nobody could have predicted the extraordinary magazine *Vogue* would turn out to be, showcasing every important photographer, decade after decade, from Cecil Beaton to Norman Parkinson to David Bailey, and all the way to Nick Knight, Alasdair McLellan, and Mert and Marcus.

Alexandra Shulman persuaded the Duchess of Cambridge to do her first official magazine shoot. She was styled-down in an Amish-style wide-brimmed hat, and looked funky: a cross between Boy George and the singer-songwriter James Bay. The Centenary dinner was fabulous, entered down a tunnel of a thousand *Vogue* covers, awash with supermodels, politicians, designers, photographers and alumni. I made a speech, and Alex made a speech, and it was unexpectedly emotional. I had a lump in my throat. Perhaps it was hay fever?

Was I alone in detecting a faint fin de siècle mood in the air? Alex had edited *Vogue* for a quarter of a century, and the Centenary felt like a celebration and culmination of her tenure. She hadn't yet disclosed her plan to step down, but it didn't really surprise me when she did.

The question I get asked most often is, 'Will magazines survive?' To which my answer is, 'Yes, definitely, and the strong ones will survive in print form too, well beyond our lifetimes.' But the weaker ones, the hazier propositions, the number threes and number fours in each category, were already suffering. You could see the change when travelling on trains and on the underground. Only a decade earlier, when you walked through the carriages, you saw dozens of young women, faces buried in a *Cosmopolitan*, *Marie Claire* or *Glamour*. Now they were staring, mesmerized, Moonie-like, at smartphones, waiting for a message or a Like, or an emoji, to drop onto their screens. The circulations of middle-market titles were falling like stones into a well. Even *Glamour*, our shooting star, wasn't immune, with a new digital-first business model, and only a couple of print editions a year. But the upmarket British titles – the hard-core glossies – were defying gravity and holding on tight. So far, nobody has invented a digital way to replicate the gloss and sheen of a printed glossy, or the way that ink shimmers on the page, like moonlight on the surface of a lake.

Nevertheless, you couldn't escape the uneasy feeling that the best of the Glossy Years lay behind us rather than ahead: the unprecedented thirty-year run of supercharged growth and glory. Suddenly no major publishing company was launching new print titles, perhaps never will again. The job now was to manage the portfolio, in expectation of future decline, without precipitating that decline by inadvertently provoking it, by cutting budgets and reducing staff numbers so much that it showed on the pages.

Our International Board Meetings, once devoted to discussions about expansion and editorial quality, now seldom included those topics at all. Instead, we devoted ourselves to agreeing corporate positioning papers on morals and ethics, and commissioning teams of consultants to conduct studies into ten-year prospects. For years, the only sin for which a Condé Nast Managing Director could be fired was failure to launch enough new magazines quickly enough; now this principle was reversed. Our digital efforts redoubled, with hordes of recruits specializing in user satisfaction, content management and best practice. All of it felt absolutely logical and sensible, but less to do with journalism.

To clear my brain, I had developed a taste for holidays in dangerous places, or anyway in places which sounded dangerous but turned out not to be. With Alexander, Freddie and Tommy I embarked on a 'boys' adventure' in a jeep across Eastern Turkey, along the borders with Syria, Iran and former Soviet Georgia. It was exciting to drive along the dusty, deserted, mountainous roads from Diyarbakir to Mardin and then further south to Dara, where the tracks run parallel to the razor-wire frontier with Syria. And to revisit, for the first time in decades, the scarcely changed archaeological sites at Nemrut Daği and Ani, and the Noah's Ark Museum at Mount Ararat (surely the crummiest museum in the world). Eastern Turkey remains one of the least developed parts of Asia, and it was refreshing to stay in authentically scuzzy dives; the Southern Anatolians lead the field in flea-infested mattresses. I have a theory that, if you stay only in grand hotels, and never stay anywhere grotty, you lose all sense of perspective, and become crabby and dissatisfied, and end up shouting at housekeeping for failing to replenish the nuts or the bath salts. It was good for the soul to stay in the last available hotel room in Van, all four of us piled in. The alternative was sleeping in the jeep.

After a fortnight on the road, we flew to the other side of Turkey to live it up a bit. The Maçakızı in Bodrum may be the coolest hotel on earth. Most of the guests are models or fashion designers, many the same ones who'd been at our Centenary *Vogue* dinner.

It took an hour or two, after the dosshouses of the East, to acclimatize to the pulsing beat and overpowering glamour of the Maçakızı.

We were having dinner on the terrace, when Kate Moss and Naomi Campbell rolled up at the next table.

Kate came over. 'Oy, Nick, oy've got a bown to pick wiv yow . . .'

As she started, it all came flooding back. A few months earlier, it had been reported in the newspapers that Kate had bought Samuel Taylor Coleridge's former home in Highgate. The opium-smoking poet had only, in fact, lived there for a few years, and the house had changed hands many times in between.

But the *Evening Standard*, spotting an angle, had rung me about it. 'What do the Coleridge family feel about Kate Moss buying your old ancestral home?'

I had replied, 'We're delighted. It means the house will never again be associated with drug abuse.'

Londoner's Diary went big with it, illustrating the item with headshots of Kate, STC and me.

Kate said, 'About forty of me mates rang me about it. They found it very funny. Which I s'pose it woz, really.'

The boys were thrilled by the arrival of Kate Moss at our table, and her public grumble.

I have a recurring daydream. In this dream, I buy a red Routemaster London bus, customize it, and drive it overland to India. Or, more precisely, someone else does the driving, while I inhabit the upper deck, decorated to the highest spec.

The London bus daydream kicks in most nights. The front quarter of the top deck has been shorn off and opened up, to create an outdoor area with banquette seating, with steps to a sundeck on the roof. There is a large bed, floor-length curtains, lined and interlined, in a Robert Kime or Bennison fabric. Carpets, rugs, a small sofa, and paintings secured to the walls complete the scene. With the curtains drawn, you might think you were in an English country house bedroom.

The bus is sometimes parked on a plateau overlooking Chittorgarh fort in Rajasthan. I am sitting with friends on the balcony, drinking cold beers, and enjoying the view from our high, safe vantage point.

How would a psychotherapist interpret the dream? Probably they would seize on the juxtaposition of rugged, adventurous locations and the hermetic sanctuary of the upper deck, immune from intrusion.

As a child, I loved the original 1964 *Jonny Quest* TV series, an action-meets-sci-fi cartoon. In the closing credits, you saw Jonny sprinting towards his spacecraft across a hostile African savannah, pursued by native tribesmen. He reached the spaceship just in time, the door slid shut, and was immediately embossed by a dozen shuddering spears. Inside, Jonny was perfectly safe. Perhaps here lay the origin of my fantasy?

I have a taste for bare, craggy landscapes over verdant ones: Eastern Turkey, Iran, large tracts of India, in which the occasional tree clings to sun-baked terrain. Georgia is the exact opposite. She favours lush green fields, untrimmed hedgerows, unmanaged woods. And gently overcast skies. To me, a day without sunshine is a wasted day.

Georgia and I took Sophie and Tommy to Iran, with Nick and Sarah Allan. And later the same year we went as a family to Ethiopia, to trek in the Tigray mountains and to visit the rock churches at Lalibela, and camp amidst the yellow and lime-green sulphur pools and salt flats of the Danakil Depression, near the Eritrean border. There was some remote danger of Eritrean militia swarming over the frontier and kidnapping us for ransom, so we were obliged to hire four bodyguards with Kalashnikovs, who posed for selfies all day in the blazing sunshine.

One evening, our guide proposed an outing to Lalibela's only nightclub, Torpedoes. We set off in a convoy of white Land Cruisers, feeling like Richard Onslow Roper and the cast of John le Carré's *The Night Manager*. As we approached the club, the drivers pulled over to the grassy kerb.

Unfortunately, the driver taking Georgia and I misjudged the distance, and suddenly the jeep was balancing over the edge of a deep ravine. Then it tipped and fell over the side, rolling and rolling, turning over, upside down, upright again, then over, while we were thrown about inside. From the cliff edge, our children could hear the vehicle crashing into the gorge, but could see nothing in the darkness. We hit a stone shepherd's hut and the jeep came to rest.

Miraculously, we crawled out unhurt, only bruised, and clambered back up the ravine. The jeep was a write-off.

Torpedoes is the best, indeed only, nightclub in Lalibela, with its blood-red walls and vintage photographs of Emperor Haile Selassie. We drank a lot of gin to recover. The *Mail on Sunday* gossip column, which somehow heard the news, headlined

'*Vogue* chief in miracle escape after cliff plunge', which was over-egging it slightly.

Shortly afterwards, in celebration of being alive, I commissioned a folly for the walled garden at Wolverton. It is a tower, an octa-gon, forty-two feet in height, in a Tudor-meets-early-Georgian style with a nod to the folly at Long Melford Hall in Suffolk. The architect is the great Quinlan Terry,* whom I have long admired. The piano nobile will be my study, with views towards Bredon Hill, and there is a viewing platform on the roof with just about space for four people to sit and have drinks. It is a place to escape to in my retirement, and generally stew.

I had become an Ambassador for the Landmark Trust, a delight-ful sinecure mostly, but fun to support its Director, the gorgeous historian Anna Keay,† and Chairman, Neil Mendoza,‡ on such a noble, heritage cause. I also became a Patron of the Elephant Family, Mark Shand's environmental charity to save the Asian elephant, run by the charismatic Ruth Powys. The Elephant Family is an easy venture to support, being glamorous, energetic and authentic all at the same time. With Georgia and Sophie, I travelled across Rajasthan with a hundred other elephant support-ers on tuk-tuks, motorcycles and chagdas (highly decorated Indian wedding vehicles), sleeping in Rajput tents at night and partying on remote sand dunes. Funds raised are spent on protect-ing the elephants' migratory routes through the jungle.

---

* British architect working in Palladian and Georgian styles. Favourite architect of the Prince of Wales.
† Director, Landmark Trust (2012–). Married to Simon Thurley, Chief Executive, English Heritage (2002–15).
‡ Publisher; Provost Oriel College, Oxford; Chair, Landmark Trust; non-executive board member, DCMS.

Our children were growing up fast, children no more. Alexander was twenty-seven and tall, a thinker and strategy wonk, recently returned from a long stint in New York and an apartment in Brooklyn, following four years at Trinity College, Dublin. Now a charming and resourceful start-up entrepreneur, and engaged to be married to his girlfriend Davina Collas.

Freddie is even taller at six feet five, with a corporate job at Amazon in Shoreditch. Funny, social, a communicator, he has a gift for impressions and accents. His impressions of me, though grossly exaggerated and over-posh, are disconcertingly recognizable.

Sophie has just finished her Art History degree at Edinburgh and is starting her first job as a headhunter. Pretty, a creative dresser, organized, impulsive, serious in her studies, she has inherited her parent's FOMO and will drive any distance in her red Mini to a party.

Tommy is our most laid-back, arguably most artistic child, studying Architecture at Edinburgh. For years, being the youngest, the family errand boy: 'Tommy, go and fetch some crisps. Tommy, we need ice. Tommy, get some beers.' But latterly on strike. Once faintly resembling Harry Potter in his glasses, now cultivating a cooler, metropolitan architect look.

We are lucky that our children, despite periodic explosions of inter-sibling fury, mostly get along together very well and, furthermore, tolerate their parents. They remain available for all-expenses-paid summer holidays, and visit us regularly in London and Worcestershire, bringing their friends for weekends, and come and go as they please. In the end, nothing matters quite so much as a functioning family and the belief that, for decades to come, even after you are gone, your children might continue to see each other, and like one another, and watch each other's backs where they can.

Georgia, meanwhile, has expanded her healing practice and written important books about sacral chakras and the power of spiritual energy, published to acclaim.

I had idly begun reading a book named *Coal Baron*, a semi-fictionalized history of my mother's maternal ancestors, the Joicey family of Northumberland. As mentioned near the start of these memoirs, my grandmother had often spoken about her childhood at Ford Castle, and the lucky discovery in the mid-nineteenth century of deep seams of coal beneath their estate. The coal mines, conveniently situated some distance from the castle, were never discussed in detail.

Coal Baron overturned this version of family history, in its entirety. Far from discovering coal under the estate, my ancestors had been actual coal miners, working underground with pickaxes down the pits in the 1820s, near Chester-le-Street in County Durham. Rising to foreman, the first James Joicey was able to buy the pit, then a dozen more. His nephew, the 1st Lord Joicey, bought all Lord Lambton's coal mines, then more and more pits across the North-East, until he was the largest coal owner in the world at the time. The Ford and Etal estates followed later, along with the peerage, paintings and the rest.

My previously undisclosed working-class coalmining roots were rather an enticing surprise, perhaps explaining my work ethic, and also, perhaps, my dislike of dark and confined spaces.

In his early eighties, my father started to become forgetful, which accelerated noticeably over three or four years into dementia, then Alzheimer's. Sensibly, my parents sold the house in Sussex just in time and consolidated their lives in London, at their tall white house in Egerton Terrace. For my mother, full-time life in Egerton Terrace meant she had moved precisely 100 yards in eighty years from her childhood home in Egerton Place.

Each time we went round for a drink or for dinner, the

deterioration in my father's brain was more evident, it was as though whole sections of his memory were shutting down, room by room, beginning in the present and working backwards. If you asked him, 'Did you enjoy going to lunch at Daphne's [a favourite neighbourhood restaurant] yesterday, Dad?' he wouldn't remember anything about it. But, for a while at least, he could talk about his early days working at Lloyd's, and going racing in Windsor with friends from school, and rowing on the Thames to Queen's Eyot and Boveney Lock.

He sat in his favourite armchair at the window, overlooking the front garden, holding the *Daily Telegraph*, though no longer able to decode the words on the pages. A tumbler of well-watered J&B whisky sat beside him on a table. My mother, and various carers, kept him conspicuously smart, always dressed in a jacket, shirt and tie, cardigan. Until you spoke to him, you would have imagined he was perfectly fit and well, handsome and well presented, hair neatly brushed. As time went by, he slept more, and went upstairs to bed earlier and earlier, impatient of conversation. We would visit him for a drink in my parents' bedroom, where he was propped up on a pillow, in pink New & Lingwood pyjamas and a navy-blue silk dressing gown. My parents' wedding photographs, taken more than sixty years earlier, when they were still practically teenagers, by Antony Armstrong-Jones, later Lord Snowdon, stood on a chest of drawers, as they had in every bedroom they ever inhabited; the linen and eiderdown were always perfectly laundered, the whole room smelling faintly of my mother's scent.

It is said that, as your life closes in, and especially when Alzheimer's takes hold, your conversation narrows until eventually you become the pure essence of yourself, your vocabulary increasingly a matter of instinct and habit. So it was with my father. When our children went round to visit, he would say, 'Now, Tommy, have you started at Eton yet?' and then ask the same question again ten minutes later, 'Have you started at Eton?' and then again. Or he would ask Freddie, who was already twenty-four, 'Now, remind me, which house at Eton are you in?' Or he would amble around the drawing room, holding a bottle of wine, courteously enquiring, 'Would you like a glass of wine? Or would you prefer a gin and tonic?' Eton and the family ritual of pre-lunch and pre-dinner drinks; it all boiled down to that.

Many people with dementia become furious with frustration against the world, but my father seldom did. Instead, he drifted away in benign contentment, gradually speaking less, until he fell almost silent, fading gently from the stage.

I have several particular pictures of my father in my photograph albums, taken before the Alzheimer years at the end, which is how I remember him: taking Alexander and Freddie racing at Goodwood as schoolboys, the three of them standing side by side in panama hats, the azaleas behind in full bloom; circulating at some Lloyd's of London drinks party in a navy-blue suit, confident and charismatic, the big dog; sitting with my mother on a garden bench at their fiftieth wedding anniversary lunch, the epitome of relaxed happiness.

I stepped back from my big roles at Condé Nast, and became Chairman of the British group for a few wind-down years. My old job was divided between three excellent successors: I was glad my loyal deputy of ten years, Albert Read, became Managing Director of the British company; James Woolhouse became COO of International, and took on most of my gruelling overseas company visits; a bright German digital expert, Wolfgang Blau, took on the rest of my Presidential duties. All of them seemed perfect appointments.

Quite a number of my colleagues took the cue, over the ensuing months, to call it a day at Condé Nast; there was a sense of an unusually tight team, successfully intact for twenty-five years or more, disbanding, and new faces refreshing the party. Edward Enninful came to *Vogue* as Editor-in-Chief in a blaze of publicity, Richard Dennen inherited *Tatler* from Kate Reardon, Jo Elvin moved to the *Mail on Sunday*'s *You* magazine, Nicky Eaton to Christie's, Graydon Carter departed *Vanity Fair*, Si Newhouse died in Manhattan, and Stephen Quinn, Annie Holcroft and Trisha Stevenson all retired. But the magazines continued to appear, right on cue, and I still feel an excited buzz of anticipation, opening them up, when a new issue lands on my desk.

The years after I downsized at Condé Nast, and felt the decades of responsibility melt away like a man on a massage table, were amongst the happiest of my working life. The perpetual low-level anxieties which had coloured my days, and which I had worked so hard to conceal, fell away along with a 50 per cent decline in the number of emails, and the long-haul business travel. I no longer worried incessantly about circulation, profitability or margins. Some people suffer intense withdrawal symptoms from any reduction in responsibility, but I felt none. I felt like someone who had swum a thousand miles through raging seas and reached, at last, a calm lagoon, and crawled up onto warm white sands. The fact that the Victoria and Albert Museum was booming was a bonus; visitor numbers continued to rise, and our new satellite museums in Shenzhen and Dundee were opening at dizzying speed. Furthermore, the new V&A East on the Olympic Park was all systems go.

I kept an office in Vogue House, and my relationship with the company transformed into one of an affectionate godfather, delighted by their successes, benignly spectating, but no longer engaged in the minute-by-minute struggle for supremacy and survival. I shuttled between Hanover Square and South Kensington, often several times a day, back and forth, back and forth, and it was a sweet period.

People habitually underestimate the importance of luck, and the importance of timing, in life and in any career. Had I not written that first article for *Harpers & Queen*, and had Ann Barr not read my handwritten submission and bothered to type it out, I might never have become a journalist at all. Had I not come up with the punning headline 'Saturday Night Belvoir' in my interview with Tina Brown, I might never have worked for her or for *Tatler*. Had I not sat next to Louis Kirby at Richard Compton-Miller's dinner in Fulham, I might never have been given my *Evening Standard* column. Had my mother not been at the hairdresser in Walton Street, and read about my incarceration in Welikada Prison in Sri Lanka, I might still be there now.

Had Georgia not done work experience at *Harpers & Queen*, and had I not come into the office on that particular day, we might never have met. Had the Newhouse family not owned Condé Nast . . . had Mark Boxer not died young . . . had Daniel Salem not read *The Fashion Conspiracy* on holiday in Lucca . . . had Prince Albert not founded the Victoria and Albert Museum . . . I could have lived an entirely different life.

Had Charles Moore not advised me to get into Trinity College, Cambridge, the easy way by reading Theology, I would have gone somewhere completely different and made entirely different friends. Had I not travelled across India on the Bombay–Madras Express during my Around the World adventure, I might never have fallen in love with that wonderful country, and never have returned more than eighty times. And, had I not already loved India so much, I might not have followed Georgia out to Rajasthan, married my soulmate and had our four children.

I think it is lucky if you know what it is you like doing from an early age, and then find you can get paid for doing it, and turn it into a whole enjoyable career.

In the end, almost everything is about luck, and whether or not it finds you, and whether you find it. And having found it, whether you fix it with a glittering eye and hold on tight while the going is good.

> He holds him with his glittering eye –
> the Wedding-Guest stood still,
> And listens like a three years' child:
> The Mariner hath his will.

The Rime of the Ancient Mariner, Samuel Taylor Coleridge (1797)

Acknowledgements

I would like to thank my Editor, Juliet Annan, of Penguin Fig Tree, and the team at Penguin Random House for their work in publishing this book, including John Hamilton, Natalie Wall, Sara Granger and Olivia Mead. Shân Morley Jones did an excellent job line editing the manuscript.

I would like to thank my agent, Jonathan Lloyd at Curtis Brown, and my previous agent, Ed Victor of Ed Victor Ltd – the sale of this memoir was Ed's final deal before his sad death.

I would like to thank the several friends who read early drafts of the manuscript, including Nicholas Allan and Geordie Greig, and my brother Christopher Coleridge, who made countless valuable suggestions. Emma Brown in my office made sharp-eyed corrections and clarifications, and Georgina Middleton typed the handwritten draft.

My wife, Georgia, and our children read the manuscript on holiday in Datça, Turkey, and were restrained enough to censor very little of it, and to chuckle away encouragingly on their sunbeds.

Zdeněk and Michaela Schaffer have looked after our house in Worcestershire for fourteen years, where the majority of this book was written in inspiring surroundings, thanks largely to them.

I would like to pay tribute to the eight magazine and newspaper honchos who played vital roles in my life and journalistic career: Ann Barr, Tina Brown, Louis Kirby, Willie Landels, Terry Mansfield, Daniel Salem, Si Newhouse and, in particular, Jonathan Newhouse. I am eternally grateful to them all.

Credits and Permissions

Thanks are due to the following photographers and agencies for permission to reproduce the pictures used in this memoir: Snowdon, Terry O'Neill, Clive Arrowsmith, David Montgomery, Mary McCartney, Jonathan Becker, Hugo Burnand, David Ellis, Perry Ogden, Richard Young, Nicholas Harvey, Alan Davidson, Dave Benett, Victor Watts, Anthony Osmond-Evans and Antoinette Eugster, as well as Getty Images, Rex Features and Iconic Images. The remainder of the photographs were mostly taken by Nicholas Coleridge, or whoever was holding his camera at the time.

Music copyright from Headstomp Productions, EMI, Sony/ATV Music Publishing, Domino Publishing Company, Peermusic Publishing and Warner/Chappell Music, Inc. 'Feel': Words and music by Robbie Williams and Guy Chambers. Copyright 2001 Farrell Music Limited & BMG Rights Management (UK) Limited, a BMG company. Used by permission of Hal Leonard Europe Limited.

Index